CAMPA
ADDRE

OF

GOVERNOR
ALFRED E. SMITH

DEMOCRATIC CANDIDATE
FOR PRESIDENT

1928

ISSUED BY
THE DEMOCRATIC NATIONAL COMMITTEE
WASHINGTON, D. C.

PRINTED IN THE UNITED STATES BY
J. B. LYON COMPANY, ALBANY, N. Y.

Foreword

IN the following pages will be found the principal addresses which I made in the campaign for the Presidency in the fall of nineteen hundred and twenty-eight.

These addresses set forth my views on the principal subjects of discussion before the people. It must be kept in mind that, like all similar addresses, they were limited as to time and based upon the conditions which normally prevail in a political discussion.

They appear here substantially as they were delivered, and represent the convictions which I entertained during the campaign, and which I still cherish. They are reprinted in this volume for the benefit of the Democratic National Committee, as my contribution to establish the party as an active and militant force in the life of the nation.

Alfred E. Smith.

January 1929

CONTENTS

ILLUSTRATIONS

CAMPAIGN ADDRESSES

I

ADDRESS OF ACCEPTANCE

State Capitol, Albany, New York, August 22, 1928

UPON the steps of this Capitol, where twenty-five years ago I first came into the service of the State, I receive my party's summons to lead it in the nation. Within this building, I learned the principles, the purposes and the functions of government and to know that the greatest privilege that can come to any man is to give himself to a nation which has reared him and raised him from obscurity to be a contender for the highest office in the gift of its people.

Here I confirmed my faith in the principles of the Democratic Party so eloquently defined by Woodrow Wilson: " First, the people as the source and their interests and desires as the text of laws and institutions. Second, individual liberty as the objective of all law." With a gratitude too strong for words and with humble reliance upon the aid of Divine Providence, I accept your summons to the wider field of action.

Government should be constructive, not destructive; progressive, not reactionary. I am entirely unwilling to accept the old order of things as the best unless and until I become convinced that it cannot be made better.

It is our new world theory that government exists for the people as against the old world conception that the people exist for the government. A sharp line separates those who believe that an elect class should be the special object of the government's concern and those who believe that the government is the agent and servant of the people who create it. Dominant in the Republican Party today is the element which proclaims and executes the political theories against which the party liberals like Roosevelt and La Follette and their party insurgents have rebelled. This reactionary element seeks to vindicate the theory of benevolent oligarchy. It assumes that a material prosperity, the very existence of which is challenged, is an excuse for political inequality. It makes the concern of the government, not people, but material things.

I have fought this spirit in my own State. I have had to fight it and to beat it, in order to place upon the statute books every one of the progressive, humane laws for whose enactment I assumed responsibility in my legislative and executive career. I shall know how to fight it in the nation.

It is a fallacy that there is inconsistency between progressive measures protecting the rights of the people, including the poor and the weak, and a just regard for the rights of legitimate business, great or small. Therefore, while I emphasize my belief that legitimate business promotes the national welfare, let me warn the forces of corruption and favoritism, that Democratic victory means that they will be relegated to the rear and the front seats will be occupied by the friends of equal opportunity.

Likewise, government policy should spring from the deliberate action of an informed electorate. Of all men, I have reason to believe that the people can and do grasp the problems of the government. Against the opposition of the self-seeker and the partisan, again and again, I have seen legislation won by the pressure of popular demand, exerted after the people had had an honest, frank and complete explanation of the issues. Great questions of finance, the issuance of millions of dollars of bonds for public projects, the complete reconstruction of the machinery of the State government, the institution of an executive budget, these are but a few of the complicated questions which I, myself, have taken to the electorate. Every citizen has thus learned the nature of the business in hand and appreciated that the State's business is his business.

That direct contact with the people I propose to continue in this campaign and, if I am elected, in the conduct of the nation's affairs. I shall thereby strive to make the nation's policy the true reflection of the nation's ideals. Because I believe in the idealism of the party of Jefferson, Cleveland, and Wilson, my administration will be rooted in liberty under the law; liberty that means freedom to the individual to follow his own will so long as he does not harm his neighbor; the same high moral purpose in our conduct as a nation that actuates the conduct of the God-fearing man and woman; that equality of opportunity which lays the foundation for wholesome family life and opens up the outlook for the betterment of the lives of our children.

In the rugged honesty of Grover Cleveland there originated one of our party's greatest principles: " Public office is a public trust." That principle now takes on new meaning. Political parties are the vehicle for carrying out the popular will. We place responsibility upon the party. The Republican Party today stands responsible for the widespread dishonesty that has honeycombed its administration.

During the last presidential campaign the Republican managers were partially successful in leading the American people to believe that these sins should be charged against the individual rather than against the party. The question of personal guilt has now been thoroughly disposed of and in its place, challenging the wisdom and good judgment of the American people, is the unquestioned evidence of party guilt.

The Democratic Party asks the electorate to withdraw their confidence from the Republican Party and repose it with the Democratic Party pledged to continue those standards of unblemished integrity which characterized every act of the administration of Woodrow Wilson.

But I would not rest our claim for the confidence of the American people alone upon the misdeeds of the opposite party. Ours must be a constructive campaign.

The Republican Party builds its case upon a myth. We are told that only under the benevolent administration of that party can the country enjoy prosperity. When four million men, desirous to work and support their families, are unable to secure employment there is very little in the picture of prosperity to attract them and the millions dependent upon them.

In the year 1926, the latest figures available show that one-twentieth of one per cent. of the 430,000 corporations in this country earned 40 per cent. of their profits; 40 per cent. of the corporations actually lost money; one-fourth of 1 per cent. of these corporations earned two-thirds of the profits of all of them. Specific industries are wholly prostrate and there is widespread business difficulty and discontent among the individual business men of the country.

Prosperity to the extent that we have it is unduly concentrated and has not equitably touched the lives of the farmer, the wage-earner and the individual business man. The claim of governmental economy is as baseless as the claims that general business prosperity exists and that it can exist only under Republican administration.

When the Republican Party came into power in 1921 it definitely promised reorganization of the machinery of government, and abolition or consolidation of unnecessary and overlapping agencies. A Committee was appointed. A representative of the President acted as Chairman. It prepared a plan of reorganization. The plan was filed in the archives. It still remains there. After seven years of Republican control the structure of government is worse than it was in 1921. It is fully as bad as the system which existed in New York State before we secured by constitutional amendment the legislation which consolidated more than one hundred offices, commissions and boards into eighteen coordinated departments, each responsible to the Governor. In contrast with this, the Republican Party in control at Washington when faced with the alternative of loss of patronage for faithful or more efficient and economical management of the government permitted the old order to continue for the benefit of the patronage seekers.

The appropriations for independent bureaus and offices not responsible to any cabinet officer increased from $3,400,000 in 1914 to $163,000,000 in 1921, and to $556,000,000 in 1928. No wonder that a cabinet officer of the Republican President of 1921 said "if you could visualize the government as a business or administrative unit, you would see something like one of those grotesque spectacles of a big oyster shell to which in the course of years, big and irregular masses of barnacles have attached themselves without symmetry or relevancy." And the Chamber of Commerce of the United States said in its annual report this year: "No progress has been made on the plan of reorganization of the government's departments as advocated by the Chamber." The administration spokesman answers only: "We have given an economical administration," and that has been repeated so often that some people begin to believe it without the slightest proof. I assert that there is no proof.

The appropriation bills signed by the President of the United States for the last year are just one-half a billion dollars more than they were for the first year of his administration. The appropriations for the Executive Department itself (The President and Vice-President) have increased more than 10 per cent. under President Coolidge.

The figures for expenditure as distinguished from appropriations tell the same story. Aside from interest on the public debt which has been reduced by retirement of bonds or by refinancing at lower interest rate, the actual expenditures for governmental activities during the fiscal year ending in 1928 were just $346,000,000 more than in President Coolidge's first year.

If the defenders of the administration answer that taxes have been reduced, they find themselves in a similar dilemma. The total taxes collected are $24,000,000 more than in the first year of the Coolidge administration. While tax rates have been reduced and some war-time taxes abandoned, the government actually took from the people in income taxes $383,000,000 more during the last fiscal year than during the first year of the Coolidge administration. And even these reductions in tax rates have been brought about primarily because the administration has committed the government to appropriations authorized but not made, amounting approximately to one billion dollars, which is an obligation that is being passed on to succeeding administrations. I wish to focus the public attention on these fundamental facts and figures when it is fed with picturesque trifles about petty economies, such as eliminating stripes from mail bags and extinguishing electric lights in the offices at night.

With this has gone a governmental policy of refusal to make necessary expenditures for purposes which would have effected a real economy. The Postmaster-General states that there was a large annual waste in the handling of mail, resulting from lack of modern facilities and equipment. Scarcely a large city in the country has adequate quarters for the transaction of Federal business. The government pays rent in the city of Washington alone of more than one million dollars annually. It is estimated that the government is paying rentals of twenty million dollars in the nation. True economy would be effected by the erection of Federal buildings, especially in the numerous instances where sites acquired many years ago have been left vacant because the administration did not desire to have these expenditures appear in the budget. It is not economy to refuse to spend money and to have our soldiers living in barracks which the Chief of Staff of the Army recently stated were indecent and below the standard for the meanest type of housing permitted anywhere. And the wise, properly timed construction of needed public improvements would substantially tend to lessen the evils of unemployment.

If the people commission me to do it, I shall with the aid of the Congress effect a real reorganization and consolidation of governmental activities upon a business basis and institute the real economy which comes from prudent expenditure. I shall aid programs for the relief of unemployment, recognizing its deep, human and social significance and shall strive to accomplish a national well-being resting upon the prosperity of the individual men and women who constitute the nation.

Acting upon the principle of "Equal opportunity for all, special privileges for none," I shall ask Congress to carry out the tariff declaration of our platform. To be sure the Republican Party will attempt in the campaign to misrepresent Democratic attitude to the tariff. The Democratic Party does not and under my leadership will not advocate any sudden or drastic revolution in our economic system which would cause business unheaval and popular distress. This principle was recognized as far back as the passage of the Underwood Tariff Bill. Our platform restates it in unmistakable language. The Democratic Party stands squarely for the maintenance of legitimate business and high standard of wages for American labor. Both can be maintained and at the same time the tariff can be taken out of the realm of politics and treated on a strictly business basis.

A leading Republican writing in criticism of the present tariff law, said: "It stands as one of the most ill drawn pieces of legislation in recent political history. It is probably near the actual truth to say that taking for granted some principle of protection of American business and industry, the country has prospered due to post-war conditions abroad and in spite of, rather than on account of, the Fordney-McCumber tariff."

CAMPAIGN ADDRESS

What I have just quoted is no part of a campaign document. It was written a few months ago by Professor William Starr Myers of Princeton University, writing the history of his own party.

Against the practice of legislative log-rolling, Woodrow Wilson pointed the way to a remedy. It provided for the creation and maintenance of a non-political, quasi-judicial, fact-finding commission which could investigate and advise the President and Congress as to the tariff duties really required to protect American industry and safeguard the high standard of American wages. In an administration anxious to meet political obligations, the Commission has ceased to function and it has been publicly stated by former members of it that the work of the Commission has been turned over to the advocates of special interests. To bring this about, it is a matter of record that the President demanded the undated resignation of one of its members before he signed his appointment.

I shall restore this Commission to the high level upon which President Wilson placed it, in order that, properly manned, it may produce the facts that will enable us to ascertain how we may increase the purchasing power of everybody's income or wages by the adjustment of those schedules which are now the result of log-rolling and which upon their face are extortionate and unnecessary.

Pay no attention to the Republican propaganda and accept my assurance as the leader of our Party that Democratic tariff legislation will be honest. It will play no favorites. It will do justice to every element in the Nation.

The Constitution provides that treaties with foreign powers must be ratified by a vote of two-thirds of the Senate. This is a legal recognition of the truth that in our foreign relations we must rise above party politics and act as a united nation. Any foreign policy must have its roots deep in the approval of a very large majority of our people. Therefore, no greater service was ever rendered by any President than by Woodrow Wilson when he struck at the methods of secret diplomacy. Today we have close relations, vital to our commercial and world standing, with every other nation. I regard it, therefore, as a paramount duty to keep alive the interest of our people in these questions, and to advise the electorate as to facts and policies.

Through a long line of distinguished Secretaries of State, Republican and Democratic alike, this country had assumed a position of world leadership in the endeavor to outlaw war and substitute reason for force. At the end of President Wilson's administration we enjoyed not only the friendship but the respectful admiration of the peoples of the world. Today we see unmistakable evidences of a widespread distrust of us and unfriendliness to us, particularly among our Latin American neighbors.

I especially stress the necessity for the restoration of cordial relations with Latin America and I take my text from a great Republican Secretary of State, Elihu Root, who said: "We consider that the independence and equal rights of the smallest and weakest member of the family of nations deserve as much respect as those of the great empires. We pretend to no right, privilege or power that we do not freely concede to each one of the American Republics."

The present administration has been false to that declaration of one of its greatest party leaders. The situation in Nicaragua fairly exemplifies our departure from this high standard. The administration has intervened in an election dispute between two conflicting factions, sent our troops into Nicaragua, maintained them there for years, and this without the consent of Congress. To settle this internal dispute, our marines have died and hundreds of Nicaraguans in turn have been killed by our marines. Without consultation with Congress, the administration entered on this long continued occupation of the territory of a supposedly friendly nation by our armed troops.

To no declaration of our platform do I more heartily commit myself than the one for the abolition of the practice of the President of entering into agreements for the settlement of internal disputes in Latin American countries, unless the agreements have been consented to by the Senate as provided for in the Constitution of the United States. I personally declare what the platform declares: "Interference in the purely internal affairs of Latin American countries must cease" and I specifically pledge myself to follow this declaration with regard to Mexico as well as the other Latin American countries.

The Monroe Doctrine must be maintained but not as a pretext for meddling with the purely local concerns of countries which even though they be small are sovereign and entitled to demand and receive respect for their sovereignty. And I shall certainly do all that lies in my power to bring about the fullest concerted action between this country and all the Latin American countries with respect to any step which it may ever be necessary to take to discharge such responsibilities to civilization as may be placed upon us by the Monroe Doctrine.

The evil effect of the administration's policy with respect to Latin America has extended to our relations with the rest of the world. I am not one of those who contend that everything Republican is bad and everything Democratic is good. I approve the effort to renew and extend the arbitration treaties negotiated under the administration of President Wilson. But the usefulness of those treaties as deterrents of war is materially impaired by the reservations asserted by various nations of the right to wage defensive wars as those reservations are interpreted in the light of President Coolidge's record. Defending his policies he announced on April 25, 1927, the doctrine that the person and property of a citizen are a part of the national domain, even when abroad. I do not think the American people would approve a doctrine which would give to Germany, or France, or England, or any other country, the right to regard a citizen of that country or the property of a citizen of that country situated within the borders of the United States a part of the national domain of the foreign country. Our unwarranted intervention in internal affairs in Latin America and this specious reason for it constitute the basis upon which other countries may seek to justify imperialistic policies which threaten world peace and materially lessen the effectiveness which might otherwise lie in the multilateral treaties.

The real outlawry of war must come from a more substantial endeavor to remove the causes of war and in this endeavor the Republican administration has signally failed. I am neither militarist nor jingo. I believe that the people of this country wish to live in peace and amity with the world. Freedom from entangling alliances is a fixed American policy. It does not mean, however, that great nations should not behave to one another with the same decent friendliness and fair play that self-respecting men and women show to one another.

In 1921 there was negotiated a treaty for the limitation of the construction of battleships and battle cruisers of over ten thousand tons. It was approved without party dispute as a start of the process of removing from the backs of the toiling masses of the world the staggering burden of the hundreds of millions of dollars that are wrung from them every year for wasteful transformation into engines of destruction. For seven years the Republican administration has followed it with nothing effective. No limitation has been placed upon land armaments, submarines, vessels of war of under ten thousand tons displacement, poisonous gases or any of the other machinery devised by man for the destruction of human life. In this respect our diplomacy has been futile.

I believe the American people desire to assume their fair

share of responsibility for the administration of a world of which they are a part, without political alliance with any foreign nation. I pledge myself to a resumption of a real endeavor to make the outlawry of war effective by removing its causes and to substitute the methods of conciliation, conference, arbitration and judicial determination.

The President of the United States has two constitutional duties with respect to prohibition. The first is embodied in his oath of office. If, with one hand on the Bible and the other hand reaching up to Heaven, I promise the people of this country that "I will faithfully execute the office of President of the United States and to the best of my ability preserve, protect and defend the Constitution of the United States," you may be sure that I shall live up to that oath to the last degree. I shall to the very limit execute the pledge of our platform "to make an honest endeavor to enforce the 18th Amendment and all other provisions of the Federal Constitution and all laws enacted pursuant thereto."

The President does not make the laws. He does his best to execute them whether he likes them or not. The corruption in enforcement activities which caused a former Republican Prohibition Administrator to state that three-fourths of the dry agents were political ward heelers named by politicians without regard to Civil Service laws and that prohibition is the "new political pork barrel," I will ruthlessly stamp out. Such conditions can not and will not exist under any administration presided over by me.

The second constitutional duty imposed upon the President is "To recommend to the Congress such measures as he shall judge necessary and expedient." Opinion upon prohibition cuts squarely across the two great political parties. There are thousands of so-called "wets" and "drys" in each. The platform of my party is silent upon any question of change in the law. I personally believe that there should be change and I shall advise the Congress in accordance with my constitutional duty of whatever changes I deem "necessary or expedient." It will then be for the people and the representatives in the national and State legislatures to determine whether these changes shall be made.

I will state the reasons for my belief. In a book "Law and its Origin," recently called to my notice, James C. Carter, one of the leaders of the bar of this country, wrote of the conditions which exist "when a law is made declaring conduct widely practiced and widely regarded as innocent to be a crime." He points out that in the enforcement of such a law "trials become scenes of perjury and subornation of perjury; juries find abundant excuses for rendering acquittal or persisting in disagreement contrary to their oaths" and he concludes "Perhaps worst of all is that general regard and reverence for law are impaired, a consequence the mischief of which can scarcely be estimated." These words written years before the 18th Amendment or the Volstead Act were prophetic of our situation today.

I believe in temperance. We have not achieved temperance under the present system. The mothers and fathers of young men and women throughout this land know the anxiety and worry which has been brought to them by their children's use of liquor in a way which was unknown before prohibition. I believe in reverence for law. Today disregard of the prohibition laws is insidiously sapping respect for all law. I raise, therefore, what I profoundly believe to be a great moral issue involving the righteousness of our national conduct and the protection of our children's morals.

The remedy, as I have stated, is the fearless application of Jeffersonian principles. Jefferson and his followers foresaw the complex activities of this great, widespread country. They knew that in rural, sparsely settled districts people would develop different desires and customs from those in densely populated sections and that if we were to be a nation united on truly national matters, there had to be a differentiation in local laws to allow for different local habits. It was for this reason that the Democratic platform in 1884 announced "We oppose sumptuary laws which vex the citizens and interfere with individual liberty," and it was for this reason that Woodrow Wilson vetoed the Volstead Act.

In accordance with this Democratic principle, some immediate relief would come from an amendment to the Volstead Law giving a scientific definition of the alcoholic content of an intoxicating beverage. The present definition is admittedly inaccurate and unscientific. Each State would then be allowed to fix its own standard of alcoholic content, subject always to the proviso that that standard could not exceed the maximum fixed by the Congress.

I believe moreover that there should be submitted to the people the question of some change in the provisions of the 18th Amendment. Certainly, no one foresaw when the amendment was ratified the conditions which exist today of bootlegging, corruption and open violation of the law in all parts of the country. The people themselves should after this eight years of trial, be permitted to say whether existing conditions should be rectified. I personally believe in an amendment in the 18th Amendment which would give to each individual State itself only after approval by a referendum popular vote of its people the right wholly within its borders to import, manufacture or cause to be manufactured and sell alcoholic beverages, the sale to be made only by the State itself and not for consumption in any public place. We may well learn from the experience of other nations. Our Canadian neighbors have gone far in this manner to solve this problem by the method of sale made by the state itself and not by private individuals.

There is no question here of the return of the saloon. When I stated that the saloon "is and ought to be a defunct institution in this country" I meant it. I mean it today. I will never advocate nor approve any law which directly or indirectly permits the return of the saloon.

Such a change would preserve for the dry states the benefit of a national law that would continue to make interstate shipment of intoxicating beverages a crime. It would preserve for the dry states Federal enforcement of prohibition within their own borders. It would permit to citizens of other states a carefully limited and controlled method of effectuating the popular will wholly within the borders of those states without the old evil of the saloon.

Such a method would re-establish respect for law and terminate the agitation which has injected discord into the ranks of the great political parties which should be standing for the accomplishment of fundamental programs for the nation. I may fairly say even to those who disagree with me that the solution I offer is one based upon the historic policy of the Democratic Party, to assure to each State its complete right of local self-government. I believe it is a solution which would today be offered by Jefferson, or Jackson or Cleveland or Wilson, if those great leaders were with us.

Publicity agents of the Republican administration have written so many articles on our general prosperity, that they have prevented the average man from having a proper appreciation of the degree of distress existing today among farmers and stockraisers. From 1910 to the present time the farm debt has increased by the striking sum of ten billions of dollars, or from four billion to fourteen billion dollars. The value of farm property between 1920 and 1925 decreased by twenty billions of dollars. This depression made itself felt in an enormous increase of bank failures in the agricultural districts. In 1927 there were 830 bank failures, with total liabilities of over 270 millions of dollars, almost entirely in the agricultural sections, as against 49 such failures during the last year of President Wilson's administration.

The report of November 17, 1927, of a Special Committee

of the Association of Land Grant Colleges and Universities states: "Incomes from farming since 1920 have not been sufficient to pay a fair return on the current value of capital used and a fair wage for the farmer's labor, or to permit farm people to maintain a standard of living comparable with other groups of like ability." The Business Men's Commission on Agriculture said in November, 1927, "Since the war, the prices of farm products have persisted in an uneconomic and unfavorable adjustment to the general scale of prices of other goods and services;" and "the disparity between urban and farm incomes has emphasized the disparity in standards of living in the rural and urban populations." "The value of farm land and farm property decreased heavily in the postwar deflation " and " large numbers of farmers have lost all their property in this process."

We have not merely a problem of helping the farmer. While agriculture is one of the most individualized and independent of enterprises, still as the report of the Business Men's Commission points out, "Agriculture is essentially a public function, affected with a clear and unquestionable public interest." The country is an economic whole. If the buying power of agriculture is impaired, the farmer makes fewer trips to Main street. The shop owner suffers because he has lost a large part of this trade. The manufacturer who supplies him likewise suffers as does the wage earner, because the manufacturer is compelled to curtail his production. And the banker cannot collect his debts or safely extend further credit. This country cannot be a healthy, strong economic body if one of its members, so fundamentally important as agriculture, is sick almost to the point of economic death.

The normal market among the farmers of this country for the products of industry is ten billions of dollars. Our export market according to latest available figures is, exclusive of agricultural products, approximately one billion, six hundred millions of dollars. These large figures furnish striking indication of the serious blow to national prosperity as a whole which is struck when the buying power of the farmer is paralyzed.

When, therefore, I say that I am in accord with our platform declaration that the solution of this problem must be a prime and immediate concern of the Democratic administration, I make no class appeal. I am stating a proposition as vital to the welfare of business as of agriculture.

With the exception of the administrations of Cleveland and Wilson, the government of this country has been in Republican hands for half a century. For nearly eight years the President and Congress have been Republican. What has been done to solve this problem? Many promises were made which have never been fulfilled. Certainly the promise of relief by tariff has not been fulfilled.

The tariff is ineffective on commodities of which there is exportable surplus without controlled sale of the surplus. Our platform points the way to make the tariff effective for crops of which we produce a surplus. There has been government interference with laws of supply and demand to benefit industry, commerce and finance. It has been one-sided because business, industry and finance would have been helped more if proper attention had been given to the condition of agriculture. Nothing of substance has been done to bring this basic part of our national life into conformity with the economic system that has been set up by law. Government should interfere as little as possible with business. But if it does interfere with one phase of economic life, be it by tariff, by assistance to merchant marine, by control of the flow of money and capital through the banking system, it is bad logic, bad economics and an abandonment of government responsibility to say that as to agriculture alone, the government should not aid.

Twice a Republican Congress has passed legislation only to have it vetoed by a President of their own party, and whether the veto of that specific measure was right or wrong, it is undisputed that no adequate substitute was ever recommended to the Congress by the President and that no constructive plan of relief was ever formulated by any leader of the Republican Party in place of the plan which its Congress passed and its President vetoed. Only caustic criticism and bitter denunciation were provoked in the minds of the Republican leaders in answer to the nation-wide appeal for a sane endeavor to meet this crisis.

Cooperative, coordinated marketing and warehousing of surplus farm products is essential just as coordinated, cooperative control of the flow of capital was found necessary to the regulation of our country's finances. To accomplish financial stability, the Federal Reserve System was called into being by a Democratic administration. The question for agriculture is complex. Any plan devised must also be coordinated with the other phases of our business institutions. Our platform declares for the development of cooperative marketing and an earnest endeavor to solve the problem of the distribution of the cost of dealing with crop surpluses over the marketed unit of the crop whose producers are benefited by such assistance. Only the mechanics remain to be devised. I propose to substitute action for inaction and friendliness for hostility. In my administration of the government of my State, whenever I was confronted with a problem of this character, I called into conference those best equipped on the particular subject in hand. I shall follow that course with regard to agriculture. Farmers and farm leaders with such constructive aid as will come from sound economists and fair minded leaders of finance and business must work out the detail. There are varying plans for the attainment of the end which is to be accomplished. Such plans should be subjected at once to searching, able and fair minded analysis, because the interests of all require that the solution shall be economically sound.

ADDRESS OF ACCEPTANCE

If I am elected, I shall immediately after election ask leaders of the type I have named irrespective of party to enter upon this task. I shall join with them in the discharge of their duties during the coming winter and present to Congress immediately upon its convening, the solution recommended by the body of men best fitted to render this signal service to the nation. I shall support the activities of this body until a satisfactory law is placed upon the statute books.

Adequate distribution is necessary to bring a proper return to production. Increased efficiency of railroad transportation and terminal handling means lowering of cost which in turn reflects itself in the form of increased purchasing power through reduction in the cost of every-day necessities of life.

Nor do railroads exhaust means of transportation. I believe in encouraging the construction and use of modern highways to carry the short haul of small bulk commodities and to aid in effective marketing of farm products.

Of great importance and still in a highly undeveloped state are our transportation routes by waterways. Commodities of great bulk, where the freight cost is a large part of the cost to the ultimate consumer, are among the least profitable to railroads to carry and lend themselves most readily to water transportation.

Certain areas of our country are deeply interested in opening up a direct route from the middle west to the sea by way of the Great Lakes and adjacent waterways. Controversy has arisen over the relative merits of the St. Lawrence route or the All-American route. As Governor of New York, I have heretofore expressed a preference for the All-American route, basing my view on engineers' reports made to me. The correctness of these reports and also of those favoring the St. Lawrence route has been challenged. As President of the United States, therefore, it would be my clear duty to restudy this question impartially upon engineers' reports the accuracy of which must be above question. When the results of such a study are given to Congress, I am entirely willing to abide by the decision of Congress.

With the development of inland waterways goes the control of floods thereon. The Mississippi flood of last year brought home to the nation the imperative need for a national policy of flood control. The last two administrations waited for this calamity and for universal demand that something be done instead of taking leadership in this important work. Forethought, courage, and leadership and knowledge of what real ultimate economy means would have done much to prevent this calamity with its ensuing waste and misery. An ounce of prevention is worth a pound of first aid and relief. In the last Congress the Reid-Jones Bill laid down sound lines for the solution of this great problem. The policy thus initiated for the Mississippi must be carried through. The money actually appropriated for flood relief is too small to make even a start. Too much time has been spent in squabbling over who shall pay the bill.

The Mississippi river and its tributaries constitute a great network of waterways flowing through a large number of States. Much more than flood control is involved. Fullest development of the Mississippi river and its tributaries as arteries of commerce should be the goal.

Wide possibilities for public good are latent in what remains of our natural resources. I pledge myself to a progressive liberal conservation policy based upon the same principles to which I have given my support in the State of New York, and to fight against selfish aggression in this field wherever it appears and irrespective of whom it may involve. No nation in history has been more careless about the conservation of natural resources than has ours. We have denuded our forests. We have been slow to reclaim lands for development and have allowed to run to waste or have given to private exploitation our public waters with their great potential power for the development of electrical energy.

ADDRESS OF ACCEPTANCE

The value of this heritage can best be measured when we consider the recent disclosures of the methods employed by private monopolies to wrest our remaining water powers from public control.

No more dishonest or unpatriotic propaganda has ever been seen in this country than that disclosed by the investigation into the methods of certain utility corporations. Private corporations to gain control of public resources have procured the writing of textbooks for the public schools; have subsidized lecturers pretending to give to the country their own honest and unbiased advice; have employed as their agents former public officials and have endeavored to mislead public opinion by the retention of the services of leaders of the community in various parts of the country. Highly paid lobbyists, penetrated into every State and into the legislative halls of the nation itself.

As against propaganda, it is the duty of the Democratic Party to set up truth. The ownership of some of these great water powers is in the nation, of others in the several states. These sources of water power must remain forever under public ownership and control. Where they are owned by the Federal Government, they should remain under Federal control. Where they are owned by an individual State, they should be under the control of that State, or where they are owned by States jointly, they should be under the control of those States.

Wherever the development, the government agency, State or Federal as the case may be, must retain through contractual agreement with the distributing companies the right to provide fair and reasonable rates to the ultimate consumer and the similar right to insist upon fair and equal distribution of the power. This can be secured only by the absolute retention by the people of the ownership of the power by owning and controlling the site and plant at the place of generation. The government — Federal, State or the authority representing joint States — must control the switch that turns on or off the power so greedily sought by certain private groups without the least regard for the public good.

I shall carry into Federal administration the same policy which I have maintained against heavy odds in my own State. Under no circumstances should private monopoly be permitted to capitalize for rate-making purposes water power sites that are the property of the people themselves. It is to me unthinkable that the government of the United States or any State thereof will permit either direct or indirect alienation of water power sites.

Electrical energy generated from water power as an incident to the regulation of the flow of the Colorado river is the common heritage of all the States through which the river flows. The benefits growing from such development should be equitably distributed among the States having right of ownership. The duty of the Federal Government is confined to navigation. I am of the opinion that the best results would flow from the setting up of a Colorado River Authority, representative equally of all the States concerned. The development should be by the States through the agency of this authority by treaty ratified by Congress.

It will be the policy of my administration while retaining government ownership and control, to develop a method of operation for Muscle Shoals which will reclaim for the government some fair revenue from the enormous expenditure already made for its development and which is now a complete waste. In this way the original peace-time purpose of the construction of this plant will be achieved. The nation will be reimbursed, agriculture will be benefited by the cheap production of nitrates for fertilizer and the surplus power will be distributed to the people.

The remaining public natural resources now under control of the Federal Government must be administered in the interests of all of the people.

Likewise a complete survey and study of the remaining undeveloped public resources of land, coal, oil and other minerals is greatly needed and should be undertaken.

The United States because its people use more wood than any other or earth is therefore more dependent on the forest than any other great nation. At the same time we are the most wasteful of all people in the destruction of our forest resources.

The use of our national forests for recreation should be greatly extended. I also pledge myself to give the same continuing interest and support to a national park, reforestation and recreation program as have brought about the establishment of a great Conservation and State Park System in the State of New York.

It was Grover Cleveland who first made our national forest and conservation policy into a great public question. Theodore Roosevelt followed in his footsteps. What these two men began must be continued and carried forward.

The American people constitute a structure of many component parts. One of its foundations is labor. The reasonable contentment of those who toil with the conditions under which they live and work is an essential basis of the nation's well-being. The welfare of our country therefore demands governmental concern for the legitimate interest of labor.

The Democratic Party has always recognized this fact and under the administration of Woodrow Wilson, a large body of progressive legislation for the protection of those laboring in industry, was enacted. Our platform continues that tradition of the party. We declare for the principle of collective bargaining which alone can put the laborer upon a basis of fair equality with the employer; for the human principle that labor is not a commodity; for fair treatment to government and Federal employees; and for specific and immediate attention to the serious problems of unemployment.

From these premises it was inevitable that our platform should further recognize grave abuses in the issuance of injunctions in labor disputes which threaten the very principle of collective bargaining. Chief Justice Taft in 1919 stated that government of the relations between capital and labor by injunction was an absurdity. Justice Holmes and Justice Brandeis of the United States Supreme Court unite in an opinion which describes the restraints on labor imposed by a Federal injunction as a reminder of involuntary servitude.

Dissatisfaction and social unrest have grown from these abuses and undoubtedly legislation must be framed to meet just causes for complaint in regard to the unwarranted issuance of injunctions.

The Judiciary Committee of the United States Senate has already in progress a careful study of this situation. I promise full cooperation to the end that a definite remedy by law be brought forth to end the existing evils and preserve the constitutional guarantees of individual liberty, free assemblage and speech and the rights of peaceful persuasion.

I shall continue my sympathetic interest in the advancement of progressive legislation for the protection and advancement of working men and women. Promotion of proper care of maternity, infancy and childhood and the encouragement of those scientific activities of the National Government which advance the safeguards of public health, are so fundamental as to need no expression from me other than my record as legislator and as Governor.

None can question my respect for and cooperation with the Civil Service nor my interest in proper compensation for government service. I believe in that true equality of women that opens to them without restriction all avenues of opportunity for which they can qualify in business, in government service and in politics.

ADDRESS OF ACCEPTANCE

I have a full appreciation of what this country owes to our veteran soldiers. I know that when the country called, the veteran came promptly. When the veteran in distress calls to the country, the country should be equally prompt. Red tape and technicalities and autocratic bureaucracy should be brushed aside when the time comes for a grateful American people to recognize its debt to the men who offered themselves in our hour of need.

During all of our national life the freedom of entry to the country has been extended to the millions who desired to take advantage of the freedom and the opportunities offered by America. The rugged qualities of our immigrants have helped to develop our country and their children have taken their places high in the annals of American history.

Every race has made its contribution to the betterment of America. While I stand squarely on our platform declaration that the laws which limit immigration must be preserved in full force and effect, I am heartily in favor of removing from the immigration law the harsh provision which separates families, and I am opposed to the principle of restriction based upon the figures of immigrant population contained in a census thirty-eight years old. I believe this is designed to discriminate against certain nationalities, and is an unwise policy. It is in no way essential to a continuance of the restriction advocated in our platform.

While this is a government of laws and not of men, laws do not execute themselves. We must have people of character and outstanding ability to serve the nation. To me one of the greatest elements of satisfaction in my nomination is the fact that I owe it to no one man or set of men. I can with complete honesty make the statement that my nomination was brought about by no promise given or implied by me or any one in my behalf. I will not be influenced in appointments by the question of a person's wet or dry attitude, by whether he is rich or poor, whether he comes from the north, south, east or west, or by what church he attends in the worship of God. The sole standard of my appointments will be the same as they have been in my governorship — integrity of the man or woman and his or her ability to give me the greatest possible aid in devoted service to the people.

In this spirit I enter upon the campaign. During its progress I shall talk at length on many of the issues to which I have referred in this acceptance address, as well as other important questions. I shall endeavor to conduct this campaign on the high plane that befits the intelligence of our citizens.

Victory, simply for the sake of achieving it, is empty. I am entirely satisfied of our success in November because I am sure we are right and therefore sure that our victory means progress for our nation. I am convinced of the wisdom of our platform. I pledge a complete devotion to the welfare of our country and our people. I place that welfare above every other consideration and I am satisfied that our party is in a position to promote it. To that end I here and now declare to my fellow countrymen from one end of the United States to the other, that I will dedicate myself with all the power and energy that I possess to the service of our great Republic.

II

ADDRESS AT OMAHA

Omaha, Nebraska, September 18, 1928

THIS is my first speech of the campaign. It is, however, not a new experience to me. In the State of New York I led the Democratic Party in five State campaigns.

New York, for the major part of the time in the past thirty years, was a strong Republican State. That in four of those campaigns I led to victory is in no small part due to the fact that I talked frankly to the people of that State in very plain and understandable language. Beginning here to-night and continuing throughout the national campaign I propose to continue that policy.

The function of a political party is to ascertain the popular will on the subjects pressing the country for solution. It is the expression of that popular will, as it is understood by the parties, which brings about the adoption of a platform which, aside from defining fundamental issues, is a promise that, if entrusted with power, the party will attempt the solution of these problems along the lines laid down in the declaration.

If we accept that as true, and as a sound doctine, then this battle for the presidency of the United States demands consideration of the issues set forth in the platforms of the two great parties.

In the discussion of these issues it is fair to look back over the years and compare performance with promise, to the end that the people may have before them the record and be able to appraise the sincerity of the platform and the party in its true light.

CAMPAIGN ADDRESS

The Republican candidate for President in his speech of acceptance, referring to the Republican administration, said: " The record of these seven and one-half years constitutes a period of rare courage and leadership and constructive action. Never has a political party been able to look back upon a similar period with more satisfaction."

Here in Omaha tonight, in the center of one of the great farming regions of this country, I propose to discuss that Republican record of over seven years and a half on the important question of farm relief.

I challenge the statement that there has been courage or leadership or constructive action on farm relief. I assert that there is not the slightest basis upon which the Republican Party can indulge in any degree of self-satisfaction, in looking back over its record of seven and a half years, on the question of agriculture. On the contrary, I charge that they violated their platform promises, that they deceived the farmer, that they did nothing whatever to contribute in the slightest degree to relieve the distress or promote the welfare of the farmers of this country. Posing for decades as the friends of the farmer, the Republican leaders have, by their betrayal of the confidence which the farmers imposed in them, forfeited every right to the allegiance or support of the agriculturalists of this country. They have sown the wind and should reap the whirlwind.

In the 1920 platform, aside from some general statements known to the children in all public schools, no definite promise was made to the agricultural interests of the country; but immediately following the advent of the Republican administration the farm problem became acute and was recognized in the Republican platform of 1924, which said: " We recognize that agricultural activities are still struggling with adverse conditions that have brought deep distress. We pledge the party to take whatever steps are necessary to bring back a balanced condition between agriculture, industry and labor."

By the language of the 1924 platform, the Republican Party recognized the deep distress of the agricultural interests of the country. They further recognized the necessity of bringing back a balanced condition between agriculture and industry, and made a definite pledge as follows: " The Republican Party pledges itself to the development and enactment of measures which will place the agricultural interests of America on a basis of economic equality with other industry to insure its prosperity and success."

So that if today we have in this country a farm problem and a continuance of that distress it cannot be said, after a reading of the 1924 platform that the Republican Party and the Republican administration at Washington were without knowledge of the actual conditions.

After seven and a half years of promise and no performance, it is significant to note the Republican platform of 1928, which reads: " The general depression in a great basic industry inevitably reacts upon the conditions in the country as a whole and cannot be ignored."

Here we have definitely, at least, after all these years the confession that there is a general depression in the great basic industry and that it reacts upon conditions in the country as a whole and that it cannot be ignored, although that is the treatment, according to the record, it has received in the last four years.

Later on I shall deal with what their 1928 platform specifically recommends, but at this point it would be interesting to read the last paragraph of the plank devoted to agriculture: " The Republican Party pledges itself to the development and enactment of measures which will place the agricultural interests of America on a basis of economic equality with other industries to assure its prosperity and success."

I call your attention to the fact that this is identical with the language of the 1924 platform. What became of that promise in the 1924 platform if it had to be repeated word for word in 1928? What attention should be paid to the 1928 promise if nothing was done under the 1924 promise?

I can imagine myself in the Executive Session of the Republican Committee on platform at the recent convention in Kansas City, and I can picture for myself one delegate asking what has been done in the last four years to make good the platform of 1924. Meeting as he must with the reply that the previous platform's pledges remain unredeemed, he suggests that they be repeated, undoubtedly upon the theory that the Republican Party has handed the empty plate to the farmer so often they can probably take a chance and pass it once more. That this must be so can readily be seen by various expressions of opinion from members of their own party. Suffice it for the time being to sum it all up in the words of the distinguished Senator from your own State. Senator Norris said:

"The action of the Republicans at Kansas City, both as to platform and candidate for President, will be a sad disappointment to every progressive citizen of the United States.

"A direct slap is administered to the farmers of the country. Their plea, admitted by everybody to be well founded, is cast aside with the usual promise of a glittering generality. The party has been in power for eight years and during all that time it has been making promises to the farmer.

"Its leaders, the men who dominated this convention, both in the Senate and outside, have fought practically every proposition of a remedial nature for agriculture and, with the assistance of Presidential vetoes, have succeeded in frustrating all efforts at farm relief.

"Never have these so-called alleged leaders presented a farm relief measure of their own, but have contented themselves with opposing every comprehensive measure of farm relief presented by others; and now, after eight years of promise, they insult the intelligent farmers of America by making another promise."

This is the statement of an authority on farm conditions, who was Chairman of the Senate Committee on Agriculture. It clearly indicates that the condition has been known to the party for at least four years and that no adequate remedy is suggested even at this time, nor has one been forthcoming during the whole period of the last two Republican administrations.

The President himself recognizes it. In his message to the Congress in 1926, on the subject of agriculture, he said:

" The whole question of agriculture needs most careful consideration. In the past few years the government has given this subject more attention than any other and has held more consultations in relation to it than on any other subject. While the government is not to be blamed for failure to perform the impossible, the agricultural regions are entitled to know that they have its constant solicitude and sympathy."

This on its face appears to be a confession on the part of the Republican President that the problem cannot be solved by his party. Why else does he use the language that the government should not be blamed for not performing the impossible? After eight years of promise, coupled with failure to perform, it must be encouraging indeed to the farmers of the country to know that they have at least the constant solicitude and the sympathy of the Republican Party.

The farmer at this time might well recall the words of the one-time popular song: "All I Got Was Sympathy, But That Didn't Mean a Thing to Me."

As far as the President himself is concerned, Senator Norris sums it all up in a few words: " He stood against Congress in the measures that they offered but made no constructive suggestion himself, even after the exhaustive study he claims the Administration gave to the subject."

CAMPAIGN ADDRESS

He might well have added that Mr. Hoover, as the chief adviser of the last two administrations upon the subject of agriculture assumed a direct responsibility for the hostility and inaction of the administration and continues to assume that responsibility by his fulsome indorsement of the record of Coolidge policies.

It must be a great comfort to the farmers of this country to know that the policy which gave them the sympathy and solicitude of the Republican administration and gave them nothing else, would be continued in the event of Mr. Hoover's election. Particularly must this be a comfort to them when they recall that the result of the eight years of sympathy and solicitude by the Republican Party is thus summed up by Mr. Hoover in his acceptance speech: "The most urgent economic problem in our nation today is in agriculture."

If the promises made by the Republican Party in 1920 and 1924 had been fulfilled it would not be necessary for him to say today that in agriculture is the most urgent economic problem in our nation, and the occasion for the solicitude and sympathy for the plight of the farmers on the part of the Republican leaders would have ceased to exist.

What brought about all these promises of the Republican Party? If there was no critical condition in agricultural circles, why the promises of relief? Why the admissions in the platforms, and what led Governor McMullen of your own State, according to newspaper reports, to threaten the Republican National Convention that he would lead an army of men to knock at the doors of that assemblage demanding at the hands of the Republican Party a specific and definite solution of the farm problem? It could be nothing else except the very apparent distress of the farmers of the country who raise 60 per cent. of the country's crops.

In my speech of acceptance I took account of the suffering of agriculture. I there stated some facts and figures, not one of which has since been challenged or contradicted:

From 1910 to the present time the farm debt has increased by the striking sum of ten billions of dollars. The value of farm property between 1920 and 1925 decreased by twenty billions of dollars.

It would be unreasonable to expect that this great decrease in value would make itself felt only in agricultural circles. It was compelled, from the very nature of things, to have an influence on other lines of business. In 1927 there were 830 bank failures, with total liabilities of over $270,000,000, almost entirely in the agricultural sections, as against 49 such failures in the last year of the last Democratic administration. In the period since 1920 there have been almost 4,000 such failures.

The Business Men's Commission on Agriculture in November of last year said: " Since the war, the prices of farm products have persisted in an uneconomic and unfavorable adjustment to the general scale of prices of other goods and services. The value of farm land and farm property decreased heavily in the post-war deflation, and large numbers of families have lost all their property in the process."

I repeat that the figures herein given by me as far back as the 22d of last August have neither been contradicted nor challenged.

According to the figures, there is abundant reason for the recognition of this crisis in American agricultural life.

Viewing it from another angle, the reports of the United States Department of Agriculture show that during this period of depression, ten million people were driven from the farms with a net decrease, after deducting all who returned, of four million in the farm population of the nation. That means that four million American citizens were compelled to give up their chosen vocation. It meant suffering and distress in millions of families, and drove the tillers of the soil into competition with the workers in the cities.

CAMPAIGN ADDRESS

It requires no very great power of imagination or understanding of the problem to be able to realize the disastrous effect on our whole social and economic fabric that must grow from a situation such as that.

There are definite causes and reasons for this catastrophe which, to the ordinary person, are easy of understanding:

Twenty-five years ago wheat sold at approximately the same price that it brings today.

Twenty-five years ago the farmer paid $45 for a mower; today it costs him $75.

He paid $120 for a binder; he pays over $200 for the same implement today.

Statistics indicate that there has been a decline in the purchasing power of farm products of 20 per cent., as compared with the pre-war period. What other line of business in the United States could stand that? Suppose, for an instant, that the manufacturer of shoes was compelled to meet the wage scale of today, the increased cost of machinery, the increased cost along the whole line of plant operation, and then was compelled to offer the product of his factory at the price that it brought twenty-five years ago — how long could he remain in business? And what would become of an economic structure so designed?

The great fundamental trouble with the farm situation today lies in the undisputed fact that the farmer buys in a protected market, from the hat on his head to the shoes on his feet. For everything needed around the farm not produced by himself he makes his contribution to the tariff system for protection of American industries, and when he produces the crop he is compelled to sell it in an unprotected market. In the basic cash crops the American farmer raises more than the whole domestic market can absorb. He is, therefore, compelled to offer his whole crop at the price of the surplus that is exported. Putting it in other words:

The exportable surplus is offered first in the domestic market and drags down the price of the whole crop.

It has been abundantly demonstrated that the tariff, standing alone, with respect to crops of which we have an exportable surplus, does not function. The presence of the exportable surplus in the domestic market prevents the farmer from getting the benefit of the tariff. As to these commodities the tariff is like an engine running with no belting to connect it with the machine it is designed to move.

Under the protective system of this country we have interfered with the laws of supply and demand for the protection of industry and labor. No part of that protection has been given to the farmer on his major cash crops; and when we talk about putting agriculture on an equality with industry, we are talking primarily about the problem of making the tariff function for agriculture in the way that it functions for industry.

The leaders of the Republican Party know this. Prominent members of their own party have made it perfectly clear to the leaders. President Coolidge must know it, and he must also have known that an increase in the tariff on wheat was an empty gesture. Yet the Republican candidate for President says in his acceptance speech: "An adequate tariff is the foundation of farm relief."

But he makes no suggestion whatever as to how the adequate tariff is to be made to function and become effective with respect to the major cash crops. He refers to the tariff as though it really worked for the farmer. The solution has two parts: First, an adequate tariff; and, second, a method of making it function. Mr. Hoover refers to the first part and ignores the second.

Every student of the problem in the United States today is unanimous in the declaration that standing by itself the tariff is not the solution, so far as crops are concerned of which there is an exportable surplus. If the tariff alone is the foundation of farm relief, why not raise it some more? The solution is not as simple as that.

The trouble during all these years lies in the fact that the Republican Party has not been entirely frank with the farmer. I could go further and say they have not been honest with him. Had they been honest and frank with him, instead of extending sympathy and promising relief through tariff and promising economic equality, they would have frankly said to the farmer that the solution lies in providing a mechanism for the control of the exportable surplus with the cost of that control imposed on the crop benefited as the only way to make the tariff function. As to that important principle the Republican presidential candidate discloses obvious hostility.

On that subject the Republican platform says nothing.

But its convention repudiated the minority report seeking recognition of this principle. What that means is best shown by Governor Lowden's comment: " I have urged, however, that it is the duty of the Republican Party to find some way to rescue agriculture from the ruins that threaten it. That, in my judgment, the Convention by its platform just adopted has failed to do, and I therefore authorize the withdrawal of my name from before the Convention."

It would be interesting at this time to ask the question: Did the Republican candidate for President ever speak about this question of surplus crops? He did.

In 1924 he wrote as follows: " That (referring to the surplus) can only be corrected by prices low enough to make production unprofitable."

What does he mean by that? I can spell only one thing out of that. He wants to drive enough farmers out of business to pull down the surplus crops.

The way he wants to relieve the farmer is to destroy him.

Again in 1925 he said: " The fundamental need is a balancing of agricultural production to our home demand."

AT OMAHA

Is that the solution of the farm problem, to starve the farmer to death? To drive his prices down so low that he can have no production for his energy? Is the sweat of his brow to go for nothing and is he to be eventually driven out of agricultural pursuits?

As to the balancing of the agricultural production to our home demand, that would not be a good thing to my way of thinking, even if you could do it. But that it cannot be done is best shown by a report from the Bureau of Agricultural Economics, which says: "During the last twenty years, 95 per cent. of the changes in spring wheat production were due to differences in yields. As a whole perhaps three-quarters of the natural variation in crop production is due to yield variances and lies beyond human control through acreage adjustments."

That is in effect to say the solution of disposing of the surplus, advanced by Mr. Hoover, is impossible and is beyond the power of human control.

If the students of the agricultural problem understand their business, we have put our finger on the sore spot; we have discovered the primary cause of the illness in the agricultural industry. And it is now for the doctor to prescribe the remedy.

What does Mr. Hoover offer? First, the tariff. Everybody knows, and he knows himself, that the tariff is not effective as to the basic cash crops, without a supplemental device to make it work.

He offers inland waterways. Very good. The Democratic Party is in favor of inland waterways, just as strongly as the Republican Party, but I think it is only fair to say that nobody would offer that as an immediate remedy. The present condition needs a remedy at once, and not at a time far distant, when the improvement of the inland waterways could be an accomplished fact. At best, were they with us today, they would not exert sufficient influence to solve the problem.

He offers stabilization corporations. Stabilization corporations made up of voluntary associations of producers can no more stabilize agriculture than the banks of the country were able voluntarily to stabilize our financial system without the intervention of government in forming the Federal Reserve System.

He suggests aid to cooperatives. I strongly believe in cooperative marketing. It is clearly all right — as far as it goes. I have encouraged it in my own State. In New York today we have over one thousand cooperative marketing associations. With our major cash crops and with a device for taking care of the surplus at the cost of the commodity benefited, cooperatives would be given a great opportunity for development. Their field is limited, however, without such a device, for the reason that when the membership alone is compelled to pay the whole cost of the attempt at stabilization, those outside the membership receive the benefits of the increased prices without bearing any of the burdens incident thereto. And the attempt at stabilization is in large measure impaired by the activities of the non-members.

The fundamental fact is that none of these methods can function with respect to the major cash crops unless they are coupled with the control of the exportable surplus with the cost of lifting it out of the domestic market assessed back on the crop benefited.

Various people have attempted to misrepresent and confuse my attitude with respect to the McNary-Haugen Bill. I do not propose to leave the slightest doubt in anybody's mind on that subject.

As I read the McNary-Haugen Bill, its fundamental purpose is to establish an effective control of the sale of exportable surplus with the cost imposed upon the commodity benefited. For that principle the Democratic platform squarely stands, and for that principle I squarely stand. Mr. Hoover stands squarely opposed to this principle by which the farmer could get the benefit of the tariff. What remains of the McNary-Haugen Bill is a mere matter of method, and I do not limit myself to the exact mechanics and method embodied in that bill.

Here is a clean-cut issue, then, which the farmers and the voters of this country must decide. It remains but to work out the details by which this principle shall be put into effect, and I have pledged myself to name a non-partisan commission of farm leaders and students of the problem to work out these details. I shall make that appointment, if I am elected, not when I take the oath of office as President, but immediately after election; and I pledge to the farmers and to the people of this country that no stone will be left unturned to give immediate and adequate farm relief, by legislation carrying into practice this definite principle for which my party and I stand. This course alone gives promise of rescuing the farmers of this country from the complete ruin which threatens them today.

When I arrived in Omaha today my attention was called to a series of questions published in some of the newspapers. Some interested citizens of Omaha desired to ask me some questions, and they are so kind about it, starting with " Dear Governor," I thought I would endeavor to accommodate them. Entirely aside from my desire to be neighborly and kind to them on my visit to Omaha, I said in the beginning of this speech tonight that I believe in talking out frankly, plainly and openly. So that if this was intended as any embarrassment to me, it does not hit that way.

Question No. 1: " What specific Federal legislation do you propose for farm relief? "

If these gentlemen had read my speech of acceptance there would be no occasion for that question. I made that clear in Omaha tonight, that the legislation working out the principle of lifting the surplus is to be handed to a commission to be worked out during the winter. That is number one.

No. 2: "Do you believe the country will be more prosperous with liquor or without? Why?"

Well, I assume that this is an intelligent group of men that have an understanding of what is going on around the country. Nobody, no living person, no matter how wise, no matter how well informed, no matter how far-seeing, could make any answer to that question, because there has never been a time when there was no liquor in this country.

No. 3: "Do you believe that liquor is the great issue in this campaign?"

I certainly do not.

No. 4: "How can you square your support of Democratic candidates for Congress pledged against liquor with what you say you will do for liquor?"

Why, I don't know what idea these men must have of the debates, the platform and the speeches of acceptance. If they paid the slightest attention to any one they could not ask that kind of a question, because there is nothing that the President can do about liquor. All he can do is to recommend to the Congress, and he can assume the leadership of the American people in an effort to show them that his recommendation is right. That is what I propose to do. And let the American people make the decision, as they will have to do.

How can I support a Democratic candidate for Congress?

That question came up in the National Convention, and the National Convention deliberately, through the report of the Committee on Credentials, left every Democrat in the United States free to express his own individual opinion of what he thought on that subject.

Now, you have an admirable, scholarly gentleman running for United States Senator here, Mr. Metcalf. I understand that Nebraska is dry, but I would never ask Mr. Metcalf to turn his back on the people of his State until such time as he can come out here and convince them that they are not tackling the problem the right way.

No. 5: "How will your proposal for the sale of liquor in a few states meet your issue of personal liberty in the other states?"

The prevention of the sale of liquor is in the exercise of police power, and I have clearly shown that if a majority of the people of a given State voted for the exercise of that police power in that direction, they should get it to the limit. On the other hand, following the well-defined Jeffersonian principle of states' rights, the State that does not want the exercise of that police power ought to be in a position, through a majority of the people, to say so.

No. 6: "Are you still personally opposed to the St. Lawrence waterway?"

If the gentlemen had just looked at my speech of acceptance, they would have seen that I made as clear a declaration on that as any man could make. I frankly said to the American people that while I was the Governor of the State of New York, I favored the all-American route, because it went through that State, but inasmuch as the figures affecting the St. Lawrence canal, as well as the all-American route, are disputed by some eminent engineers, I am willing to leave it to Congress, after a study of the matter.

Now, No. 7 is something of a tricky question. It says: "You have stated that the Underwood Tariff Law fulfills the pledge of this year's Democratic platform."

My answer to these distinguished gentlemen is that I never said that, and I challenge them to find it in any public paper of mine.

The last one, No. 8, is this: "Are you in favor of higher food prices in the city or lower food prices on the farm?"

My answer to that is that the farmer can get the full benefit of the value of his crop without increasing the price in the city.

So much for that. But let me say this: Some gentlemen and myself were talking this afternoon over at the hotel, and this question of this "ad." came up. It was suggested by someone that the Republican National Committee paid for that "ad." I said, "I do not think so. I do not think ten upstanding citizens of Omaha would allow the campaign funds of the National Committee to be used with their names underneath it. They paid for it themselves."

Another man said: "Why, Governor, I would not answer that. That is to embarrass you." "Ah," I said, "wait; I do not believe that either. Hightoned gentlemen like these would not embarrass a visitor to the city of Omaha, a man who has come out here to be friendly with everybody he can meet, and to shake hands with them and talk to them. They would not do anything like that. I believe they were actuated by motives of patriotism. They were actuated by a desire to help the discussion in this campaign. They were actuated by a desire to get for the American people a sound, clear and sensible decision on the 6th of November." And he said, "Do you really think so?" I said, "I certainly do, and I further think that actuated by that same motive they ought to ask Mr. Hoover these same questions."

All during the campaign we will talk issues. We will fight this out in the open. We will have a good, clean, clear, open fight and the American people will decide it. But as I read the record I can see only one decision for the 6th of November, and that is an overwhelming Democratic victory.

III

ADDRESS AT OKLAHOMA CITY

Oklahoma City, Oklahoma, September 20, 1928

OUR country has achieved its great growth and become a model for the nations of the world under a system of party government. It would be difficult to predict what might be the evil consequences if that system were changed. If it is to survive, campaigns for the presidency must be fought out on issues really affecting the welfare and well-being and future growth of the country. In a presidential campaign there should be but two considerations before the electorate: The platform of the party, and the ability of the candidate to make it effective.

In this campaign an effort has been made to distract the attention of the electorate from these two considerations and to fasten it on malicious and un-American propaganda.

I shall tonight discuss and denounce that wicked attempt. I shall speak openly on the things about which people have been whispering to you.

A former Senator from your own State, a member of my own party, has deserted the party which honored him, upon the pretense, as he states it, that because I am a member of Tammany Hall I am not entitled to your support for the high office to which I have been nominated. Here tonight I challenge both the truth and the sincerity of that pretense. I brand it as false in fact. I denounce it as a subterfuge to cover treason to the fundamentals of Jeffersonian Democracy and of American liberty.

What Mr. Owen personally thinks is of no account in this campaign. He has, however, raised an issue with respect to my record with which I shall deal tonight without mincing words. I know what lies behind this pretense of Senator Owen and his kind and I shall take that up later.

What he says, however, has been seized upon by the enemies of the Democratic Party and the foes of progressive government. They have thus made my record an issue in this campaign. I do not hesitate to meet that issue. My record is one of which I am justly proud and it needs no defense. It is one upon which I am justified in asking your support.

For the present, let us examine the record upon which has beaten the light of pitiless publicity for a quarter of a century. I am willing to submit it to you and to the people of this country with complete confidence.

Twenty-five years ago I began my active public career. I was then elected to the Assembly, representing the neighborhood in New York City where I was born, where my wife was born, where my five children were born and where my father and mother were born. I represented that district continuously for twelve years, until 1915, when I was elected Sheriff of New York county.

. Two years later I was elected to the position of President of the Board of Aldermen, which is really that of Vice-Mayor of the City of New York.

In 1918 I was selected by the delegates to the State convention as the candidate of the Democratic Party for Governor and was elected.

Running for re-election in 1920, I was defeated in the Harding landslide. However, while Mr. Harding carried the State of New York by more than 1,100,000 plurality, I was defeated only by some 70,000 votes.

After this defeat I returned to private life, keeping up my interest in public affairs, and accepted appointment to an important State body at the hands of the man who had defeated me.

In 1922 the Democratic Convention, by unanimous vote, renominated me for the third time for Governor. I was elected by the record plurality of 387,000, and this in a State which had been normally Republican.

In 1924, at the earnest solicitation of the Democratic presidential candidate, I accepted renomination. The State of New York was carried by President Coolidge by close to 700,000 plurality, but I was elected Governor. On the morning after election I found myself the only Democrat elected on the State ticket, with both houses of the Legislature overwhelmingly Republican.

Renominated by the unanimous vote of the convention of 1926, I made my fifth State-wide run for the governorship and was again elected the Democratic Governor of a normally Republican State.

Consequently, I am in a position to come before you tonight as the Governor of New York finishing out his fourth term.

The record of accomplishment under my four administrations recommended me to the Democratic Party in the nation, and I was nominated for the presidency at the Houston convention on the first ballot.

To put the picture before you completely, it is necessary for me to refer briefly to this record of accomplishment:

In the face of bitter Republican opposition, I succeeded in bringing about a reorganization of the government of the State of New York, consolidating eighty or more scattered boards, bureaus and commissions into nineteen major departments and bringing about efficiency, economy and thoroughgoing coordination of all the State's activities.

Under it was set up for the first time the Cabinet of the Governor.

A drastic reform was secured in the manner and method of appropriating the public money, commonly referred to as the executive budget.

During my legislative career, as well as during my governorship, I sponsored and secured the enactment of the most forward-looking, progressive, humanitarian legislation in the interests of women and children ever passed in the history of the State. I appointed the first Commission on Child Welfare, while Speaker of the Assembly, as far back as 1913.

I had a large part in the enactment of the Workmen's Compensation Law and the rewriting of the factory code, which went as far as government possibly could to promote the welfare, the health and the comfort of the workers in the industrial establishment of our State.

I have stood behind the Department of Education with all the force and all the strength I could bring to my command.

The present Commissioner of Education is a Republican. Any one in Oklahoma, or in any other part of the United States, may write to Frank P. Graves, Department of Education, Albany, N. Y., and ask him the blunt question, " what Governor of that State rendered the greatest service to the cause of public education?" and I am confident he will write back a letter with my name in it.

Figures sometimes speak louder than words. In 1919, my first year in office, the State appropriated to the localities for the promotion of public education $11,500,000. Last year, for the same purpose, I signed bills totalling $86,000,000, an increase in appropriations for public education of $74,500,000 during the period of my governorship.

I have given of my time, my energy and my labor without stint to placing the Department of Public Health upon the highest level of efficiency and usefulness, to bettering the condition of the unfortunate wards of the State hospitals and institutions for the poor, the sick and the afflicted and to the development, over the opposition of a hostile Legislature, of a comprehensive, unified park system, having in mind not only present requirements but the needs and the welfare of the generations to come.

For ten years I battled against bitter Republican opposition to retain for the people of the State of New York the control of their water power, their greatest God-given resources, and have prevented their alienation and preserved them for our people and for our posterity.

I sponsored legislation which brought about reform of the ballot, on the passage of direct primary laws and provisions against corrupt practices in elections.

The first bill for a bonus by the State of New York to the World War veterans was signed during my administration.

Although a city man, I can say to you without fear of contradiction that I did more for agriculture and for its promotion in the State of New York than any Governor in recent history. Cooperative marketing was encouraged. New impetus was given to the construction of the State highways. State aid was furnished to towns and counties to bring the farm nearer to the city and, during my terms of office, there was appropriated in excess of $15,000,000 for the eradication of bovine tuberculosis.

The business of the State of New York was handled in a strictly business way. The number of public place holders was cut down. Appointments and promotions were made on a strictly merit basis. In consequence, there was effected a reduction in taxes to the farmer and the small home owner, from 1923 to 1928, of from two mills to one-half mill of the State's levy upon real property, together with a substantial reduction in the income tax.

Public improvements in the State, long neglected under Republican rule, are being carried out at a rate unprecedented in all its history.

Bear in mind that all this was accomplished without the cooperation of the Legislature, because during my entire career as Governor both branches of the Legislature have been Republican, except for a period of two years when one branch — the Senate — was Democratic. It was brought about because I took the issues to the people directly and brought the force of public opinion, regardless of party affiliation, to the support of these constructive measures.

During my governorship I have made appointment of scores of men to public office requiring the confirmation of the Senate, and while the Senate was in control of my party in only two out of the eight years I have been Governor, not a single appointment of mine was ever rejected.

The reason for this was that I made my appointments to public office in the State of New York without regard to politics, religion or any other consideration except the ability, the integrity and the fitness of the appointee and his capacity properly to serve the State.

Contrast this with the rejection of major appointments made by the President of the United States by a Senate of his own party.

I read in the press only recently that a Republican Congress passed four bills over the veto of the Republican President in one single day. During my entire eight years, the Legislature, hostile to me, never passed a single bill over my veto.

Has there been one flaw in my record, or one scandal of any kind connected with my administration that gives any meaning to this cry of Tammany rule, a cry which thousands of independent and Republican citizens of my own State treat with ridicule and contempt?

The Republican Party will leave no stone unturned to defeat me. I have reduced their organization in the State of New York to an empty shell. At the present time, $60,000,000 of public improvements are in progress in my State. If there was anything wrong or out of the way, does it not strike you, as men and women of common sense, that the Republican Party in New York would leave no stone unturned to bring it to light?

The fact is, they have searched, and searched in vain, for the slightest evidence of improper partisanship or conduct. They found no such thing; they could find no such thing; it did not exist. And in the face of this, Senator Owen and his kind have the nerve and the effrontery not to charge, but merely to insinuate, some evil which they are pleased to call Tammany rule.

One scandal connected with my administration would do more to help out the Republican National Committee in its campaign against me than all the millions of dollars now being spent by them in malicious propaganda. Unfortunately for them, they cannot find it, because the truth is it is not there. I challenge Senator Owen and all his kind to point to one single flaw upon which they can rest their case. But they won't find it. They won't try to find it, because I know what lies behind all this, and I will tell you before I sit down to-night.

I confess I take a just pride in this record. It represents years of earnest labor, conscientious effort and complete self-sacrifice to the public good in some endeavor to show my appreciation and gratitude to the people who have so signally honored me.

Don't you think that I am entitled to ask the people of this country to believe that I would carry into the service of the nation this same devotion and energy and sacrifice which I have given in service to the State? Don't you think that my party is entitled to make this argument to the American people, because it is not only the record itself that speaks in unmistakable language for me, it is the expressed approval of the leading fellow citizens of my State, who have never had the slightest affiliation with Tammany Hall, and many of whom have been its political opponents.

My election to the governorship four times has not been accomplished merely by Democratic votes, because New York is a normally Republican State. I have been elected by the votes of the Democrats, together with the votes of tens of thousands of patriotic, intelligent citizens of all forms of political belief who have placed the welfare of the State above party consideration.

Take the statement of a man who has not supported me for the governorship, Charles Evans Hughes; a statement not made for political purposes, but in presenting me to the Bar Association of New York City. He described me as " one who represents to us the expert in government and, I might say, a master in the science of politics."

He said of me, " the title that he holds is the proudest title that any American can hold, because it is a title to the esteem and affection of his fellow citizens."

Nicholas Murray Butler, President of Columbia University, in conferring upon me an honorary degree, stated that I was " alert, effective, public spirited and courageous, constantly speaking the true voice of the people."

The Very Rev. Howard Crobbins, Dean of the Episcopal Cathedral of St. John the Divine, stated that I had shown myself, " a singularly well-balanced, capable and forceful executive." He added: " He has been independent and fearless. He has had the interest of all the people of the State at heart and his sincerity and courage have won for him a nationwide recognition."

Robert Lansing, Secretary of State under President Wilson, said of me: " His public career is convincing proof that he possesses the true spirit of public service, and is eminently fitted to fill with distinction and ability any office for which he might be chosen candidate."

Virginia G. Gildersleeve, Dean of Barnard College, stated that I had " made an excellent Governor and shown a knowledge of State affairs which very few of our Governors have ever possessed."

A group of distinguished educators, headed by Prof. John Dewey of Columbia University, said of my record of public education: " His whole attitude on education has been one of foresight and progress."

I could tax your patience for the rest of this evening with similar expressions from men and women who are the leaders of thought and affairs in the State of New York, independents in politics, most of them never affiliated with any political organization.

Do Senator Owen and the forces behind him know more about my record than these distinguished men and women who have watched it and studied it? But Senator Owen and his kind are not sincere. They know that this Tammany cry is an attempt to drag a red herring across the trail.

I know what lies behind all this and I shall tell you. I specifically refer to the question of my religion. Ordinarily, that word should never be used in a political campaign. The necessity for using it is forced on me by Senator Owen and his kind, and I feel that at least once in this campaign, I, as the candidate of the Democratic Party, owe it to the people of this country to discuss frankly and openly with them this attempt of Senator Owen and the forces behind him to inject bigotry, hatred, intolerance and un-American sectarian division into a campaign which should be an intelligent debate of the important issues which confront the American people.

In New York I would not have to discuss it. The people know me. But in view of the vast amount of literature anonymously circulated throughout this country, the cost of which must run into huge sums of money, I owe it to my country and my party to bring it out into the open. There is a well-founded belief that the major portion of this publication, at least, is being financed through political channels.

A recent newspaper account in the City of New York told the story of a woman who called at the Republican National headquarters in Washington, seeking some literature to distribute. She made the request that it be of a nature other than political. Those in charge of the Republican Publicity Bureau provided the lady with an automobile and she was driven to the office of a publication notorious throughout the country for its senseless, stupid, foolish attacks upon the Catholic Church and upon Catholics generally.

I can think of no greater disaster to this country than to have the voters of it divide upon religious lines. It is contrary to the spirit, not only of the Declaration of Independence, but of the Constitution itself. During all of our national life we have prided ourselves throughout the world on the declaration of the fundamental American truth that all men are created equal.

Our forefathers, in their wisdom, seeing the danger to the country of a division on religious issues, wrote into the Constitution of the United States in no uncertain words the declaration that no religious test shall ever be applied for public office, and it is a sad thing in 1928, in view of the countless billions of dollars that we have poured into the cause of public education, to see some American citizens proclaiming themselves 100 per cent. American, and in the document that makes that proclamation suggesting that I be defeated for the presidency because of my religious belief.

The Grand Dragon of the Realm of Arkansas, writing to a citizen of that State, urges my defeat because I am a Catholic, and in the letter suggests to the man, who happened to be a delegate to the Democratic convention, that by voting against me he was upholding American ideals and institutions as established by our forefathers.

The Grand Dragon that thus advised a delegate to the national convention to vote against me because of my religion is a member of an order known as the Ku Klux Klan, who have the effrontery to refer to themselves as 100 per cent. Americans.

Yet totally ignorant of the history and tradition of this country and its institutions and, in the name of Americanism, they breathe into the hearts and souls of their members hatred of millions of their fellow countrymen because of their religious belief.

Nothing could be so out of line with the spirit of America. Nothing could be so foreign to the teachings of Jefferson. Nothing could be so contradictory of our whole history. Nothing could be so false to the teachings of our Divine Lord Himself. The world knows no greater mockery than the use of the blazing cross, the cross upon which Christ died, as a symbol to install into the hearts of men a hatred of their brethren, while Christ preached and died for the love and brotherhood of man.

I fully appreciate that here and there, in a great country like ours, there are to be found misguided people and, under ordinary circumstances, it might be well to be charitable and make full and due allowance for them. But this campaign, so far advanced, discloses such activity on their part as to constitute, in my opinion, a menace not alone to the party, but to the country itself.

I would have no objection to anybody finding fault with my public record circularizing the whole United States, provided he would tell the truth. But no decent, right-minded, upstanding American citizen can for a moment countenance the shower of lying statements, with no basis in fact, that have been reduced to printed matter and sent broadcast through the mails of this country.

One lie widely circulated, particularly through the southern part of the country, is that during my governorship I appointed practically nobody to office but members of my own church?

What are the facts? On investigation I find that in the cabinet of the Governor sit fourteen men. Three of the fourteen are Catholics, ten Protestants, and one of Jewish faith. In various bureaus and divisions of the Cabinet officers, the Governor appointed twenty-six people. Twelve of them are Catholics and fourteen of them are Protestants. Various other State officials, making up boards and commissions, and appointed by the Governor, make a total of 157 appointments, of which thirty-five were Catholics, 160 were Protestants, twelve were Jewish, and four I could not find out about.

I have appointed a large number of judges of all our courts, as well as a large number of county officers, for the purpose of filling vacancies. They total in number 177, of which sixty-four were Catholics, ninety were Protestants, eleven were Jewish, and twelve of the officials I was unable to find anything about so far as their religion was concerned.

This is a complete answer to the false, misleading and, if I may be permitted the use of the harsher word, lying statements that have found their way through a large part of this country in the form of printed matter.

If the American people are willing to sit silently by and see large amounts of money secretly pour into false and misleading propaganda for political purposes, I repeat that I see in this not only a danger to the party, but a danger to the country.

To such depths has this insidious manner of campaign sunk, that the little children in our public schools are being made the vehicles for the carrying of false and misleading propaganda. At Cedar Rapids, Iowa, the public prints tell us that a number of school girls asked their parents if it were true that there would be another war if Smith was elected. When questioned by their parents as to how they came to ask such questions, one of the girls said:

We were told at school that Wilson started the war in 1917, and if Governor Smith were elected he would start another war.

As contemptible as anything could possibly be is an article on the very front page of a publication devoted to the doings of a church wherein the gospel of Christ is preached. I refer to the Ashland Avenue Baptist, a publication coming from Lexington, Ky., in which a bitter and cruel attack is made upon me personally and is so ridiculous that ordinarily no attention should be paid to it. It speaks of my driving an automobile down Broadway at the rate of fifty miles an hour, and specially states I was driving the car myself while intoxicated.

Everybody who knows me knows full well I do not know how to drive an automobile, that I never tried it. As for the rest of the contemptible, lying statement, it is as false as this part.

On the inside of this paper, the morning worship on the following Sunday gives as the subject, "What think ye of Christ?" The man or set of men responsible for the publication of that wicked libel, in my opinion, do not believe in Christ. If they profess to, they at least do not follow His teachings. If I were in their place I would be deeply concerned about what Christ might think of me.

A similar personal slander against me was dragged out into the open about a week ago when a woman in the southern part of the country read what purported to be a letter from a woman in my own State. Fortunately, the names of both women were secured. One of my friends interviewed the woman in New York State, and she promptly denied having written such a letter. The woman in the southern part of the country refused to talk about it and refused to produce the letter.

I single out these few incidents as typical of hundreds. I well know that I am not the first public man who has been made the object of such baseless slander. It was poured forth on Grover Cleveland and upon Theodore Roosevelt, as well as upon myself. But as to me, the wicked motive of religious intolerance has driven bigots to attempt to inject these slanders into a political campaign. I here and now drag them into the open and I denounce them as a treasonable attack upon the very foundations of American liberty.

I have been told that politically it might be expedient for me to remain silent upon this subject, but so far as I am concerned no political expediency will keep me from speaking out in an endeavor to destroy these evil attacks.

There is abundant reason for believing that Republicans high in the councils of the party have countenanced a large part of this form of campaign, if they have not actually promoted it. A sin of omission is some times as grievous as a sin of commission. They may, through official spokesmen, disclaim as much as they please responsibility for dragging into a national campaign the question of religion, something that according to our Constitution, our history and our traditions has no part in any campaign for elective public office.

Giving them the benefit of all reasonable doubt, they at least remain silent on the exhibition that Mrs. Willebrandt made of herself before the Ohio Conference of the Methodist Episcopal Church when she said:

" There are two thousand pastors here. You have in your church more than 600,000 members of the Methodist Church in Ohio alone. That is enough to swing the election. The 600,000 have friends in other states. Write to them."

This is an extract from a speech made by her in favor of a resolution offered to the effect that the conference go on record as being unalterably opposed to the election of Governor Smith and to endorse the candidacy of Herbert Hoover, the Republican candidate.

Mrs. Willebrandt holds a place of prominence in the Republican administration in Washington; she is an Assistant Attorney-General of the United States. By silence, after such a speech, the only inference one can draw is that the administration approves such political tactics. Mrs. Willebrandt is not an irresponsible person. She was Chairman of the Committee on Credentials in the Republican National Convention at Kansas City.

What would the effect be upon these same people if a prominent official of the government of the State of New York under me suggested to a gathering of the pastors of my church that they do for me what Mrs. Willebrandt suggests be done for Hoover?

It needs no words of mine to impress that upon your minds. It is dishonest campaigning. It is un-American. It is out of line with the whole tradition and history of this government. And, to my way of thinking, is in itself sufficient to hold us up to the scorn of the thinking people of other nations.

One of the things, if not the meanest thing, in the campaign is a circular pretending to place someone of my faith in the position of seeking votes for me because of my Catholicism. Like everything of its kind, of course it is unsigned, and it would be impossible to trace its authorship. It reached me through a member of the Masonic order who, in turn, received it in the mail. It is false in its every line. It was designed on its very face to injure me with members of churches other than my own.

I here emphatically declare that I do not wish any member of my faith in any part of the United States to vote for me on any religious grounds. I want them to vote for me only when in their hearts and consciences they become convinced that my election will promote the best interests of our country.

By the same token, I cannot refrain from saying that any person who votes against me simply because of my religion is not, to my way of thinking, a good citizen.

Let me remind the Democrats of this country that we belong to the party of that Thomas Jefferson whose proudest boast was that he was the author of the Virginia statute for religious freedom. Let me remind the citizens of every political faith that that statute of religious freedom has become a part of the sacred heritage of our land.

The constitutional guaranty that there should be no religious test for public office is not a mere form of words. It represents the most vital principle that ever was given any people.

CAMPAIGN ADDRESS

I attack those who seek to undermine it, not only because I am a good Christian, but because I am a good American and a product of America and of American institutions. Everything I am, and everything I hope to be, I owe to those institutions.

The absolute separation of State and Church is part of the fundamental basis of our Constitution. I believe in that separation, and in all that it implies. That belief must be a part of the fundamental faith of every true American.

Let the people of this country decide this election upon the great and real issues of the campaign and upon nothing else.

For instance, you have all heard or read my Omaha speech on farm relief. Read the Democratic platform on farm relief, compare my speech and that platform plank with the platform plank of the Republican Party and the attitude of Mr. Hoover, so that you may decide for yourselves which of the two parties, or the two candidates, according to their spoken declarations, are best calculated to solve the problem that is pressing the people of this country for solution. By a study of that you will be conserving the interest of the cotton growers of this State and promoting its general prosperity.

Take my attitude on the development of our natural water power resources. Take the Democratic platform on that subject. Compare it with the Republican platform and with Mr. Hoover's attitude and record on the same subject, and find out from which of the two parties you can get and to which of the two candidates you can look forward with any degree of hope for the development of these resources under the control and ownership of the people themselves rather than their alienation for private profit and for private gain.

Compare the Democratic platform with the Republican platform and Mr. Hoover's attitude with mine on the all-important question of flood control and the conservation of our land and property in valley of the Mississippi. And then take the record and find out from which party you got the greatest comfort and hope for a determination of that question.

Take the subject of the reorganization of the government in the interest of economy and a greater efficiency. Compare the platforms. Compare the speeches of acceptance, and be sure to look into the record of the Republican failure to carry out its promises along these lines during the last seven and a half years.

I declare it to be in the interest of the government, for its betterment, for the betterment and welfare of the people, the duty of every citizen to study the platforms of the two parties, to study the records of the candidates and to make his choice for the Presidency of the United States solely on the ground of what best promotes interest and welfare of our great republic and all its citizens.

If the contest is fought on these lines, as I shall insist it must be, I am confident of the outcome in November.

IV

ADDRESS AT DENVER

Denver, Colorado, September 22, 1928

ONE of the very important issues of this campaign, to my way of thinking, is the policy of the government with respect to the development of water power. Following the custom I adopted in my various State campaigns, I propose to speak on this subject in the plain, everyday language which makes it understood by the rank and file of our people.

In the past I have stated that there is a lack of understanding of the whole subject by the people generally which makes it easy for public officials who do not hold very strong views on the necessity of conservation of natural resources to turn them over to private individuals for private profit and private gain.

Electrical energy is developed two ways, either through steam generated by coal or from falling water. Throughout the United States today there is sufficient water running to waste, to generate without the use of a single pound of coal, electrical energy sufficient to meet the needs of large sections of this country. Falling water has often been referred to as white coal. It is possible to exhaust the resources of a coal mine, but it is reasonable to suppose that water will flow on forever.

Let me give you some facts and figures that will bring strongly to your attention the possibilities of water power development. At Niagara Falls in the State of New York the Niagara Power Company in a three-story building covering a little more than an ordinary city block, with a minimum of expense for operation, generates 700,000 horsepower.

In order to get an idea of what 700,000 horsepower of electrical energy means, let us take the City of New York, with its many industries using electrical energy, its large number of department stores, residences and theatres. In fact, all of the electrical energy used on Manhattan Island south of 59th street and from the North to the East rivers is supplied by the New York Edison Company's Waterside Station at the foot of East 36th street. It is estimated by electrical engineers that on the 21st of December the peak load of electrical energy is carried. This generating station is an eight-story building, covering two full city blocks and on that day produces 375,000 horsepower. Bear in mind that the energy so produced requires the hauling of coal from the mines of Pennsylvania to tidewater and presents quite some problem in cost of maintenance and operation by contrast with the small plant where the wheels are turned by falling water and requires but the necessary number of men to oil the machinery. It must therefore be apparent that electrical energy generated from falling water should be sold to the ultimate consumer at a much cheaper rate than the same amount of energy generated from steam.

Throughout the United States there are great possible power sites. I view them as God-given resources of the country. I make the claim that the benefit of their development should accrue to the people themselves and that we should not permit them to fall into private hands for private development, which means private gain at the expense of all the users of the energy.

That private monopoly has its eyes upon these possible developments there can be no question. My own State of New York offers an example, and I am reasonably certain the same condition prevails throughout the country at every possible source of power development.

Private power companies drained Niagara Falls until the scenic beauty of that wonder of the world was threatened and as far back as 1905 the Federal Government entered into a treaty with the Dominion of Canada to limit the diversion of water from the Niagara river above the falls in order to prevent it from being despoiled by the private water power corporations of New York State.

Horace McFarland, President of the National Civic Federation, speaking of New York's record with regard to her water power, before my administrations, said that " The State itself had jobbed out all the sacred glories of Niagara for no return or recompense whatever to the people."

The great power combines, balked by the Burton Act in 1907, sought control of the possible power developments on the St. Lawrence river by the incorporation of a development company under special act of the Legislature. After practically giving away the great power resources at the St. Lawrence, the State in the same year adopted a policy of public development under public control and under public ownership. The story of the desire of private companies to gain control of the State's water resources is too long and too detailed for me to recite to you tonight. It suffices for me to say that today these power resources are the property of the State of New York, because of my insistent demand over a period of ten years that development be by the State itself under State ownership and State control. Development has been halted because of the insistent demand of the Republican Party in New York State that the water power resources of the State be leased to private individuals under long term leases.

In my speech of acceptance, I set up what, in my opinion, should be a definite policy for the future with regard to these water power resources. I claim that where they are owned by the Government they should remain under Federal control. Where they are owned by an individual State they should be under the control of that State, and where they are owned by states jointly they should be under the control of those states. By control I mean absolute retention of the ownership of the power itself, by owning and controlling the site and the plant at the place of generation. Only in this way can the Government agency, State or Federal, as the case may be, find itself in a position to provide fair and reasonable rates to the ultimate consumer, and insist upon a fair and equal distribution of the power through contractual agreements with the distributing companies.

The cost of electrical energy generated from water power is largely determined by the cost of the money used for the development. Private development involves a larger rate of interest on the underlying securities than does public development. And it is fair to assume that private companies will follow their practice of the past and give to the bondholders of prospective developments a stock bonus. That means an obligation on the ultimate consumer to pay a rate for electrical energy that will meet the cost not only of operation and maintenance of plant, with depreciation, but also the higher cost of the borrowed money.

For the State of New York,— and it would apply throughout the country — I suggested the creation of a quasi-public corporation, municipal in character and clothed with the authority to issue its bonds, exempt from taxation, to carry on the development.

Following the suggestions on farm relief that I made at Oklahoma City on Thursday night, I urge that the citizens of our country should study the platforms of both parties, as well as the speeches and statements of the candidates, in order that they may be able to make their decision on the 6th of November. I shall take up first the Republican platform in so far as it states anything relative to the water power development.

The platform reads:

"The Republican Party has been forehanded in assuring the development of water power in accordance with public interest."

I see no evidence of that. What does that mean? What plan has the Republican Party for assuring that development in accordance with public interest? What is their idea of public interest?

All that the platform does beyond that is to say that there has been assured a policy of permanent public retention for power sites on public land and power privileges on navigable streams and the public domain.

This part of the conservation plank of the Republican platform seems to me to be in line with the attitude of the Republican Party in the State of New York with regard to water powers that are the property of that State: They have always declared for public retention of power sites, but at the same time they prepare themselves to lease these same power sites for fifty years to private companies for private operation. To my way of thinking, a fifty-year lease is equivalent to the alienation of them.

On the question of ownership of the power plant for the purpose of control of rates to the ultimate consumer by contractual agreements it is silent, and all the benefit of cheap development through the use of public money is entirely lost sight of.

Let us pass from the platform for a minute to the speech of acceptance of the Republican candidate. It contains not one single word on the question of water power development.

The Republican candidate says that "nearly all of our greater drainages contain within themselves possibilities of cheapened transportation, irrigation, reclamation, domestic water supply, hydro-electric power, and frequently the necessities of flood control." That is his water power policy so far as he stated it in his speech of acceptance. He simply speaks about the possibilities of hydro-electric power, but how to develop it, how to control it, how to keep it in the hands of the people themselves that own it, he offers no program.

CAMPAIGN ADDRESS

By contrast let us look at the Democratic platform, which declares specifically that the sovereign title and control of water power must be preserved respectively in the State and Federal Governments, to the end that the people may be protected against exploitation of this great resource and that water powers may be expeditiously developed under such regulations as will insure to the people reasonable rates and equitable distribution.

Interpreting that platform plank in my speech of acceptance, I have declared for a guarantee of reasonable rates and equitable distribution, for the ownership by the Federal Government or the State, respectively of the power site and generating plant, and that the sovereign power must control the switch that turns on and off the power.

This does not mean that the Government — National or State — is required to engage in the business of distributing electrical energy, but it does mean that by virtue of this ownership, both of site and of plant, the Government shall have a contractual as well as a regulatory right to insist upon reasonable rates and equitable distribution.

Following the speech of acceptance by the Republican candidate, there was widespread disappointment expressed that this speech contained no reference to any plan with regard to the development of water power, and there was forthcoming a promise that it would be dealt with in a later speech. Consequently, at Los Angeles on the 17th of August, Secretary Hoover attempted to set forth his water power views. But he dealt with nothing but the Boulder Dam development, and all he said was that he would approve the highest dam that the engineers would recommend. He then spoke of the number of people who had come to live in Southern California. He spoke about the City of Los Angeles, its growth and its climate. He spoke about a water supply for California. He spoke about the great national asset of the Colorado river basin and predicted that in years to come it would be the scene of hundreds of thousands of new homes and voiced his hope for mutual cooperation in the development. He thanked the people for their gracious reception and their courtesy. This is the only water power policy that he has announced.

What is the difficulty standing in the way of public development? Inaction on the part of the Federal Government, the strange silence of the candidate and the meaningless plank of the Republican platform indicate, to say the least, a sympathy with the widespread propaganda against public ownership spread throughout this country by an organization known as the joint committee of the National Electric Light Associations.

Two recent steps taken by the Republican Party clearly show its attitude toward this important problem. The first is the appointment by the President of Mr. Roy O. West, of Chicago, as Secretary of the Interior, and the second is the election of H. Edmund Machold as Chairman of the New York State Republican Committee.

Mr. West for almost a quarter of a century has been closely identified with important power companies. If confirmed by the Senate he will be a member of the Commission which will study the engineering problems of the Boulder Dam project. He will also serve as an ex-officio member of the Federal Power Commission, which issues licenses for power development on navigable waters, and which will have to pass upon applications for licenses by companies in which Mr. West is or has recently been interested.

Is it not a fair argument to assume that such an appointment indicates a spirit of unfriendliness, if not hostility, on the part of the Republican Party in the nation to those who stand for public ownership and control of the God-given resources of the nation? Does not such an appointment show a leaning toward those seeking to exploit these resources for their own private gain and profit rather than in the interests of the people themselves?

In the State of New York undoubtedly the most important line of cleavage today between the two great parties is the problem of how to deal with the State's water power. That is, perhaps, the paramount issue in the campaign being waged there. And what does the Republican Party in that State do? It selects as its State Chairman H. Edmund Machold, former Speaker of the Assembly, the most bitter opponent of public ownership and control of water power, who used all his influence and strength in the Legislature to oppose the adoption of a constructive, forward-looking program of State ownership and control and who, until the very day he was selected State Chairman, was affiliated with many of the largest private water power companies in the State.

What can the people of the nation expect from a party that, in one of the greatest water power states in the Union, chooses as its leader the greatest enemy in the State to the development of water power in the interest of the people.

The Federal Trade Commission, in its investigation of public utility corporations, has developed some facts which indicate that Mr. Hoover knew of the existence of this power lobby intended to influence congressional action and legislation. The lobby's executive director, Judge Davis, was formerly Assistant Secretary of Commerce under Mr. Hoover at a salary of $6,000 a year. He resigned this position to accept $35,000 as executive director of the joint committee.

In the testimony it was brought out that Philip H. Gadsden, vice-chairman of the committee, also vice-president of the Gas Improvement group, speaking in Chicago about the selection of Judge Davis, said the following:

"Until June 1st he was counselor and Assistant Secretary of the Department of Commerce. At the special request of

Thousands of Kansans came to Wichita for a glimpse of Governor Smith

Mr. Hoover he was released by our committee so that he could act as chairman of the International Radio Commission, but from now on he is going to be with us."

It is worthy of note that a man named Paul S. Clapp became secretary of the joint committee. Mr. Clapp was and is the executive director of the National Electric Light Association at a salary of $25,000 a year. The National Electric Light Association is one of the three groups which make up the joint committee, the other two being the American Gas Association and the American Street Railway Association.

Mr. Clapp testified that before he was employed by the National Electric Light Association he was a secretary of Mr. Hoover's, and was the secretary also of Mr. Hoover's eastern super-power conference. It is also significant to note that upon the recommendation of Judge Davis, former Senator Lenroot was retained by the joint committee. Senator Lenroot was Mr. Hoover's counsel at the Kansas City convention in the contest over southern delegates.

Why did this committee build up this expensive organization and why did they hire elaborate quarters in the City of Washington? What was the necessity for the expenditure in the year ending June 30, 1927, of $993,000 with a budget for the current year of $1,079,190?

The unquestioned purpose of this organized effort was to discourage public ownership of water power sites for the development of electrical energy and the defeat of pending bills at Washington appropriating public money for such developments. It was accomplished in many ways.

The evidence discloses that the prime purpose of these propagandists was to defeat the Walsh resolution for an investigation of utility corporations, to defeat measures for the construction of the Boulder Canyon Dam, and to defeat legislation for the construction of Muscle Shoals.

The payment of $7,500 was made to one well-known writer for a booklet on Boulder Dam. Ex-Senator Irvine Lenroot was retained as local counsel at a retainer of $20,000 to oppose the Walsh resolution. It was frankly admitted that advertising was inserted in certain newspapers in order to secure from them the printing in their news columns of propaganda against public ownership and against Congressional legislation deemed hostile to the power interests.

To such enormous proportions did this reach that one of the officials testified:

" We discontinued the practice of compiling any figures on the amount of newspaper space obtained for the reason we were afraid they would become public and might be misunderstood."

One hundred and seventy-five thousand dollars was spent to circularize 900,000 holders of public utilities stocks in an effort to cause them to communicate with their representatives at Washington, urging opposition to the measures condemned by the utility companies. So-called boiler plate material was sent out from their headquarters to newspapers all over the country.

The schools were invaded. The people of the United States might well sit up and take notice when the minutes of the National Electric Light Association show a plan to have so-called properly qualified men prepare text books for use in classes and libraries, and by having men prominent in the industry give lectures before the classes in order that the viewpoints of this industry's leaders " may be presented to the oncoming generation."

The dean of a university, on leave of absence, was put upon the payroll at $15,000 a year to ascertain what educational work having a bearing upon the public utility field was being done in schools and colleges. An effort was made to curtail the freedom of speech of university professors by exerting pressure against them. One of the officials wrote:

"The infernal trouble is that these very extension lecturers and chaps who purport to do university service are least likely to be thoughtful and competent men."

He added:

" We can be charged with no interference with academic freedom if we step on it by any honest means in our control."

I think the gentleman was wrong. I thing he can be charged and that he is charged, with interference with academic freedom.

The Federal Trade Commission points out that as far back as 1923 a director of the National Electric Light Association, speaking before their convention, had the following to say:

" I would advise any manager here who lives in the community where there is a college to get the professor of economics interested in your problems. Have him lecture on your subject to his classes once in a while. It will pay you to take such men, getting five or six hundred dollars or a thousand dollars a year, and give them a retainer of one or two hundred dollars for the privilege of letting you study and consult with them. For how in heaven's name can we do anything in the schools of the country with the young people growing up if we have not sold the idea to the college professor?"

The idea they were seeking to sell to children and to college professors was the idea of discouraging public ownership of water power.

It was testified that one of the principal activities of the educational committee of the National Electric Light Association was the censoring and preparation of books for the public schools.

Witness after witness at the hearing of the Federal Trade Commission testified to the nation-wide effort to reach the mind of the child in the public school and in the high school. An example of this is shown in the testimony wherein it was brought out that in one year 65,000 pamphlets were distributed to 289 high schools in New England. Most of these pamphlets went into the question of national legislation and thoroughly condemned the Walsh resolution, the legislation relating to Muscle Shoals, and Boulder Dam.

These men were so much afraid that public ownership and public development would decrease the price of electrical energy, that they spent their money to try to plant in the minds of children, as well as grown-ups, supposed dangers and supposed irregularities that grow out of public owner-ships. In other words, it was an attempt to poison the mind of the American public.

Even if they honestly believed in the validity of their arguments, the methods used were despicable.

I am about to read to you an address by Mr. Hoover delivered before the Forty-eighth Convention of the National Electric Light Association held at San Francisco in June of 1925. Speaking of the men that are responsible for this propaganda, he pins a gold medal on them, in the following language:

"The majority of the men who dominate and control the electrical utilities themselves belong to a new school of public understanding as to the responsibilities of big business to the people."

I prefer to take my stand with Theodore Roosevelt who, speaking of the movement toward monopoly, said as far back as 1909:

"It is still in its infancy and unless it is controlled the history of the oil industry will be repeated in the hydro-electric industry, with results far more oppressive and disastrous for the people."

On the whole question of the conservation of our water-power resources, let me further quote President Roosevelt. In a speech in the City of Watertown only thirteen years ago, he said:

" You have in this section a most valuable asset in your natural water power. You have elected too many men in the past who have taken what belongs to the nation. Coal and oil barons cannot compare to water power barons. Do not let them get a monopoly on what belongs to this State. There has been a persistent effort to give private corporations control of the water power in this country. There has been an effort to give that control to the aluminum trust. If the aluminum trust makes its money fairly, all right. But when it gets money and power by taking the natural resources of the State, it is time for us to object. Do not give up your water power for a promise of quick development. We are poor citizens if we allow the things worth most to get into the hands of a few."

There are pending for consideration two important special waterpower development projects. One is at Boulder Canyon on the Colorado river. The other night at Omaha I wrote out my prescription for the ills from which the farmers of this country are suffering. I would like to put my prescription for Boulder Dam in writing, too, so that there cannot be any misunderstanding about it.

The principles which I have announced apply to the proposed dam at Boulder Canyon. The special need with respect to Boulder Canyon, however, is action, and immediate action. Lands of priceless value, farmhouses and human life in parts of Arizona and California are in imminent danger of destruction from the annual floods of the Colorado river. To allow this situation to continue is a travesty upon government. The floods of the Colorado river must be harnessed to protect not only property, but human life, and make the torrents of that stream not the enemy, but the servant of mankind. There must be no further delay. It is true that all of the seven Colorado river basin states have rights to the use of the water of the Colorado river. The states should enjoy such benefits consistently with the right and duty of

Congress under the Constitution to regulate navigation and the flow of navigable streams. When legislation finally passes through Congress I want to see it produce a dam and not a controversy. It is vital, therefore, that the seven Colorado basin states come to honest and reasonable agreement as to their rights in the Colorado river. At the same time, it is the duty of Congress under the Constitution in such a case to build levees and such impounding dams as may be necessary to regulate the flow of this river, with incidental protection against the destructive forces of floods. Likewise, there is an engineering and an economic problem. A board of distinguished engineers and geologists has been appointed under the authority of Congress to survey, study and report by December 1, 1928, upon the problem relative to the construction of the proposed Boulder Dam.

With that report the states may intelligently cooperate and agree. If in the light of that report and the attitude of the several states involved, it shall appear that the speediest and most effective way to bring about this great improvement is to have the government build it, and Congress should so determine, it would be the duty of the President to abide by that decision and hasten the work upon that dam. If I should be elected President before action had been taken by Congress upon this great question, I would immediately submit to Congress the available data on this subject with the request for immediate action. The situation demands the fair cooperation among the states themselves and between the states and the Federal Government. But, however, this dam shall be constructed, one thing is sure; the site of the dam and the machinery generating this water power must be preserved in public ownership. Never should this priceless right be given away for private exploitation; and, in whatever form the power generated at Boulder Dam shall be distributed, public authority must retain the contractual right to control the rates to be charged to the ultimate consumer, and to control by contract the fair and reasonable distribution of the power to be generated.

Let me say a personal word on this subject. I have had similar problems to this in my own State. The Port of New York includes not only the State of New York but much of the surrounding territory including the waters adjacent to the Jersey shore. We have had the same kind of question there, involving the relations of one State with another. The desirable thing is accomplishment. I brought about results in the Port of New York, by being able to sit down with representatives from the two states and talk reason and justice to them and get reason and justice from them.

If this question is not settled by the time I take the oath of office as President, by that method I am confident that without delay I can succeed in letting you see the men at work building the Boulder Canyon Dam.

As to Muscle Shoals, I believe that the Government should continue the full and complete development of that plant, retaining it under Government ownership and control. The construction of Muscle Shoals was a war measure. Its purpose was to produce nitrates for explosives.

The Republican national administration evidently does not consider this matter of any great importance. In his message to the Sixty-ninth Congress in 1925, President Coolidge said:

" The problem of Muscle Shoals seems to me to have assumed a place out of all proportion with its real importance. It probably does not represent in market value much more than a first-class battleship, yet it has been discussed in the Congress over a period of years and for months at a time."

I disagree most emphatically with the President. The principle involved in the proper disposition of Muscle Shoals means more to the people of this country than one hundred first-class battleships. Only at the last session of the Congress a bill dealing with the problem in a forward-looking manner was included by Mr. Coolidge among his pocket vetoes, not even being worthy, according to his notion, of any explanation for its rejection.

As I stated in my speech of acceptance, it would be the policy of my administration to develop a method of operation for Muscle Shoals under government ownership and control which would reclaim to the government some fair revenue from the enormous expenditure already made for its development. The development of this plant should be completed so that the nation may be reimbursed, agriculture receive the benefit of cheap nitrate production for fertilizer purposes, and the surplus power distributed fairly to the people of the ten states which this plant could serve at rates which should remain under the control of the government.

I have done my best to lay before you tonight what in my opinion is a great national issue. I have, as clearly as I can do it, defined my own views. I am giving you also the benefit of a study of the Democratic platform. I firmly believe that I have shown to you that the Republican platform is meaningless. I have demonstrated that the Republican candidate for President expresses no views on the subject. But you cannot escape the conclusion from the testimony that he is in sympathy with the men who attempted to spread throughout the country propaganda against the progressive idea of public ownership and control of our great water power resources.

It is to be hoped that before the campaign progresses further the Republican candidate will define clearly to the people of our country his stand upon this issue. I await it. Meanwhile, from the public record, from the platform planks, from the speeches of acceptance, the friends of public ownership and public control must cast their lot with the Democratic Party. Study of the platforms and of the speeches of acceptance on all other issues, as well as upon water power, demonstrates that the intelligent, forward-looking, progressive citizenship of the country will make their decision on November 6th in favor of the Democratic Party.

V

ADDRESS AT HELENA

Helena, Montana, September 24, 1928

THE *Denver Post* of last Sunday calls to my attention that the Republican candidate for President, addressing a number of young college men from Maryland, said:

"A new generation must begin now to take over the responsibility of the party and carry it out."

That extract from his brief speech I shall take as my text tonight, and I shall speak to you on the subject of party responsibility.

In the election of 1920 the Republican Party received at the hands of the people of this country an overwhelming vote of confidence. The American people renewed that vote of confidence in 1924.

Let us, therefore, tonight review briefly some of the phases of the Republican administration for the purpose of fixing in our minds the Republican Party's responsibility for some of the happenings since 1921.

Lincoln's ideal was not only government of the people, and by the people, but government for the people. I take it that means all the people, and not the few who use the machinery of government for their personal benefit.

Grover Cleveland said that " public office is a public trust." While that expression came from a Democratic President, it must be agreed to by every honest candidate for public office and by every honest holder of a public office.

The holder of any trust found faithless thereto can be brought before the bar of justice. The faithless political party should likewise be brought before the bar of public opinion. And, let it be said to the everlasting glory of the senior Senator from Montana, Senator Thomas J. Walsh, and his associate, Senator Burton K. Wheeler, that they played a large part in bringing before the bar of public opinion the Republican Party, found faithless to its trust. I feel that the Democratic Party renders a great public service in bringing home to the people the faithlessness of the Republican Party with respect to the conservation of public resources, as represented in their disposition of the oil fields, set aside for the use of the navy of the United States in times of need.

As far back as the administration of President Roosevelt, the President ordered a geological survey of the oil fields of the country and suggested a policy of setting aside certain proven and prospective oil fields within the public domain as a naval oil reserve supply for the United States Navy. He declared, " The preservation of a fuel oil reserve is essential to the very life and future existence of the navy." This policy was carried into effect in the administration of President Taft, and confirmed during the administration of President Wilson.

It is matter of history that during the administration of President Wilson large oil combinations diligently sought to secure leases of these oil reserves from the Secretary of the Navy. The Democratic Secretary of the Navy, Josephus Daniels, was steadfast in his refusal to alienate these great properties, having a keen understanding of their worth to the nation.

This statement, made by Secretary Daniels, sets out his position:

"Any man who would permit the oil reserves of the navy to be tapped is risking the very national existence of the United States. It is outrageous and wicked. Without plenty of oil for future emergency our war vessels will be as useless as a painted ship upon a painted ocean."

Under severe pressure exerted, even by personal friends, the Democratic Secretary of the Navy stood four-square for the preservation of this great resource of the nation.

In 1921, however, the advent of a Republican administration marked a change in attitude of the high officials of the government with respect to these oil reserves. The great oil barons of the country sought leases on what afterward became known to even the children in our public schools as Teapot Dome, in the State of Wyoming, and Elk Hill Reserve, in the State of California. The sworn testimony tells a long story of intrigue, corruption, trickery and chicanery unparalleled in the history of any modern civilization.

On May 31, 1921, the Republican President, by an illegal executive order, transferred the oil reserve from the Department of the Navy to the Department of the Interior and this, according to the sworn testimony, over the vigorous protests of the high officials of the navy.

Following the transfer of the oil reserves to the Department of the Interior, the Republican Secretary of that department, in November of 1921, leased Elk Hills reserve in California to one of the largest oil concerns and, according to sworn testimony, received in cash for himself and for his own use $100,000 that was delivered to him — as the testimony records — in a little black bag.

Does anybody in the United States today desire to say that the Republican Party as an organized political party shares none of the responsibility for that?

In April of the following year, the Teapot Dome reserve was leased to another large oil operator. Following these leases it became known in New Mexico, the home of the Republican Secretary of the Interior — and, for that matter, in Washington — that before this time the Secretary of the Interior was in straightened financial circumstances. Arrearages of taxes on his ranch in New Mexico ran back as far as ten years.

There suddenly became apparent to his neighbors an unusually prosperous appearance to the ranch; roads were built through it, a $45,000 electric light plant erected upon it and various other improvements made. This, following a knowledge of the leasing of Elk Hills, caused some suspicion, to say the least, in the minds of the legislators at Washington, and accordingly, in April of 1922 the Senate ordered an investigation of the oil leases and Senator Walsh of Montana was chosen to direct the probe.

Evidently believing that nothing would be disclosed, the Secretary of the Interior in the following month, with his son-in-law acting as the messenger, received an additional $198,000 bundle of liberty bonds.

It is a matter of history that for a year and a half prominent Republican Senators did what they could to block the investigation and would probably have succeeded were it not for the reawakening of rumors about the extraordinary prosperity of the Secretary of the Interior.

In December of 1923 the Secretary of the Interior was sought by the investigating committee. Feigning illness he wrote to the committee and explained his new prosperity by declaring that he had borrowed $100,000. And further testimony disclosed this to be not the truth. A few weeks later one of the prominent oil men confessed that he had sent the cash to the secretary.

Thereafter the Supreme Court canceled the leases. In its opinion on one of them it said:

"The clandestine and unexplained acquisition of these bonds by Fall confirms the belief generated by other circumstances in the case that he was a faithless public officer. There is nothing in the record that tends to mitigate the sinister significance attaching to that enrichment."

And it further said: "The leases and agreement were made fraudulently by means of collusion and conspiracy."

The sworn statement of an admiral of the navy is to the effect he was informed by one of the Republican Cabinet officers involved that the leasing of these oil reserves was discussed in the Cabinet of the Republican President of the United States.

What was the reason for keeping these oil leases secret for such a long while? What was the reason for making these leases contrary to the established custom without any public bidding and without any publicity?

It is a matter of record that one of the prospective bidders, who desired to make an offer if there had been publication of the proposed letting, was the vice-president of the Texas-Pacific Coal and Oil Company, who wrote a communication protesting against the secret leasing of Teapot Dome.

One of the communications was sent to Secretary Hoover and he turned it over to Secretary Fall after writing thereon the following: "Any reply that you may suggest."

He sent a similar communication of protest to the Republican President himself.

Let us consider some of the other circumstances which caused the Supreme Court of the United States to brand these transactions as corrupt.

The executive order transferring the control of these naval reserves from the Navy to the Interior Department was kept secret long after it was made. Its existence was vehemently denied by officials of both departments. No record of it was filed where executive orders are usually filed. It was held by the courts to be absolutely unwarranted in law.

After it was made the Republican Secretary of the Interior began to move on what the Supreme Court called "a trail of corruption and fraud." High officers of the navy who had been patriotic and diligent in their opposition to these transfers were sent out of Washington. The Republican Secretary of the Interior issued an order on the pretended plea of military necessity that no publicity in old matters was to be given out. He wrote a letter to one of his lessees, assuring him:

" There will be no possibility of any further conflict with the navy officials in this department, as I have notified Secretary Denby that I should conduct the matter of the naval leasing under the direction of the President."

The Supreme Court of the United States refers to this letter as follows:

" This exultant declaration that he was in a position to handle these vast properties as he pleased discredited Fall. His desire to get control of the reservations and then so proclaim that he had it, strongly suggests that he was willing to conspire against the public interest."

With respect to the Teapot Dome lease, there was also a complete secrecy. The Supreme Court said there was never any legitimate reason for this secrecy. The Secretary of the Interior even made false statements about the lease, saying to an inquiring oil man three days after he had signed it that no lease was being contemplated. Long after the leases were made repeated denials were made by government officials of both the Interior and Navy Departments that any such lease had been made.

No wonder, indeed, that when he opened an attack upon the Teapot Dome, Senator La Follette said:

" When all the disgraceful details of his scandalous deals are made public the Senate will be staggered by them."

What the government was to lose and the lessees were to gain from these transactions is evident from the testimony of one of the lessees that it would be a case of ill luck if his company did not make $100,000,000 out of its lease. This was the lease as to which the Supreme Court pointed out that it was " obtained and consummated by means of conspiracy, fraud and bribery."

Here we have as cold-blooded and as deliberate a conspiracy against the United States Government for private gain as can be found recorded at any time in history. It would have been less of treason against the government of the United States to have destroyed her battle fleet, or to have demolished her coast defenses, both of which could have been replaced, whereas these oil reserves established by three Presidents were to be held by the navy for use in time of national emergency and could not be replaced.

Is there anybody in the United States willing to say that the Republican Party is to bear no responsibility for this long tale of corruption, intrigue and treason against the government itself?

I am fully aware that almost all I have here recited was before the American electorate in the presidential election of 1924.

There is one important exception to this, however: The Supreme Court of the United States had in 1924 not yet rendered its decision placing the seal of its condemnation on these wicked transactions. Since the election of 1924, the people have learned on the authority of the highest court in this land that these oil leases were the product of official corruption and fraud.

The Republican Party at that time, judging from the election returns, must have convinced the American people that guilt in this instance was personal, and that it ran against the individuals involved and not against the party. Unless we are willing to accept this theory, we must take another one, which to my mind is unbelievable. It is that the people of this country are callous about these things. That I refuse to believe. However, since the election of 1924 new disclosures put the matter in an entirely different light, assuming that the first premise is correct, and I believe we must assume it.

Since that time testimony has been brought out to show that there was a deficit in the Republican national campaign of some $1,800,000. It was also testified that the Chairman of the Republican National Committee secured from the beneficiaries of the oil leases at least $260,000 in liberty bonds to help liquidate this indebtedness; but being not of itself a straightforward and honest transaction, it had to be canceled, and the testimony shows that the manner and method of concealment was to offer the liberty bonds in large quantities to certain prominent Republicans and have them, in turn, make an equal contribution by check to meet the deficit in the Republican National Committee's treasury.

In a great many instances prominent men in the Republican Party accepted these bonds and gave to the National Committee in their place their checks for equal amounts. It was the handwriting of a dead man that disclosed to the people of the United States to whom these bonds were offered. They were offered to the Republican Secretary of the Treasury in an amount of $50,000. The Secretary of the Treasury was unwilling to be a party to this fraud, and, instead, contributed $50,000 to the Republican National Committee and rejected the bonds.

But this much must be said: That the Senate Committee in search of information as to these bonds could have gotten it from the Republican Secretary of the Treasury long before it was forced out, had he been disposed to aid the Senate of the United States in laying bare this wicked conspiracy against the American people. It stands admitted in the record that for a period of years the Republican Secretary of the Treasury concealed from the Senate investigators his knowledge of the manner in which these bonds were being put into the treasury of the Republican Party.

Is there anybody in the United States that would be willing to make the declaration that for this particular transaction the Republican Party is to bear no responsibility? If there is no responsibility for all of this resting upon the Republican Party, then we must subscribe to the ridiculous theory that the citizenship of this great country is entirely satisfied to allow any political party to fill its treasury with the proceeds of official corruption and crime.

There is no more grateful people in the world than the people of this country when it comes to the proper care of the youth and flower of the land who respond to the call of the President of the United States to uphold the dignity and the majesty of our great republic in time of war.

Following the armistice, the outpouring of the American heart was ready to meet any cost to contribute to the comfort and the well-being of those who were injured in the service of the country. If public money appropriated for the sacred use of caring for the afflicted soldier is wasted and squandered — and I use the stronger word stolen — is there anybody to say that the party in power bears no responsibility for this theft of funds appropriated for the care of wounded soldiers.

The Veterans' Bureau at Washington for the care of disabled veterans, under Republican administration, was brought under investigation by the insistence of Democratic Congressmen and Senators, joined by certain Republican members.

And there was revealed in the course of the investigation and laid bare before the horrified eyes of the American people a record of graft and betrayal of the nation's wards which sent the Republican director of the Veterans' Bureau at Washington to a Federal penitentiary. The responsible official trafficked in hospital sites; located institutions in out of the way, inaccessible places. Millions of dollars' worth of hospital supplies were sold on the theory that they were not needed, at a low price and bought back by the government at five times the price for which they had been sold.

What could be more sordid, what could be worse? And for such performance can it be truthfully said there is no party responsibility?

During the war the property of alien enemies found in this country was seized and held for them in trust under international law. There rested upon the government of the United States the sacred duty of safeguarding these funds and this property. The Republican Alien Property Custodian, appointed by a Republican President, made such disposition of these funds as to bring him within the criminal statutes, and land him in a Federal penitentiary for conspiracy to defraud the government of the United States that he was sworn to sustain. Who in this country would be willing to say that a party must assume no responsibility for that conduct in high public office?

I fully realize that to err is human, and in all governments and at all times individuals will yield to temptation. But the testimony here does not indicate that. It rather indicates a widespread, well thought out, deep-seated conspiracy to defraud the government, participated in by many men of high station, reaching into the very Cabinet of the President of the United States, and into the leadership of the party itself. I am unable to understand by what process of human reasoning it can be said that herein guilt is personal and that the party as a party bears none of the responsibility.

Suppose that any such record as this were laid before the American people as having taken place in the administration of President Wilson. Would not the Republican Party make glorious campaign material of it, insist that the American people believe it to be the record of the Democratic Party, claim it to be legitimate campaign matter, offer it as an abundant reason for the defeat of the Democratic Party and the return to power of their own party?

Could anybody in his wildest imagination believe that the Republican managers would be prepared to say that if such guilt, clearly proven, had existed under the incorruptible administration of President Wilson, it should be regarded as personal and in no way charged against the Democratic Party? Nobody believes that. Nobody thinks it.

The record of the last seven and a half years is as well known to the Republican candidate for President as to any other man in the United States. Nobody will deny that. Mr. Hoover sat in the Cabinet for seven and a half years, yet I search in vain for any word from him of protest, of condemnation or of repudiation of this black chapter in his party's history. On the contrary, in the face of that record, in his speech of acceptance, he said:

"The record of these seven and a half years constitutes a period of rare courage and leadership and constructive action. Never has a political party been able to look back upon a similar period with more satisfaction."

Would Mr. Hoover have the American people believe that in the light of the disclosures I mentioned there was any rare courage, any leadership or any constructive action? Above all things, would he have the American people believe that a political party with that record in office could look upon it with satisfaction? Does Mr. Hoover want the people to believe that he looks back with satisfaction upon that record? It will not satisfy the American people to have him pass that question on to the Chairman of the Republican National Committee; nobody can answer that but himself.

I would regard it as harmful to the country and harmful to the morals of our youth were the people on the 6th of November by their votes to subscribe to the declaration that the last seven years have been fruitful of moral courage and good leadership, and can be looked back upon with satisfaction by any organized political party in the country.

I am satisfied that American citizens, irrespective of party, will not by their votes express their satisfaction with this record of party infidelity and corruption. I am equally satisfied that they will put the stamp of approval on the unimpeachable record of the Democratic Party.

VI

ADDRESS AT ST. PAUL

St. Paul, Minnesota, September 27, 1928

ASIDE from his constitutional duties in connection with the operation of the government, my idea of the President's position is that of a leader of thought of the American people. And if I were asked today what in my opinion was the fundamental weakness of the last two Republican administrations I would be compelled to say it was lack of such leadership.

It is not sufficient, in my opinion, for the President to state his views on great public questions in his annual message to the Congress or in rare formal addresses.

I believe the duty rests upon him of talking to the American people and laying before them the facts, to the end that when they make their determination on big problems of the nation they may be in a position to act intelligently and to have their representatives in the Senate and in the House express their well-reasoned opinion.

I suggest this, following my experience as Governor of my own State: It would have been impossible for me to have secured the governmental reforms that I fought for in the State of New York unless I carried the problems directly to the people themselves.

Reorganization of the State Government, the shortening of the ballot, drastic reform in the manner and method of appropriating public money, rehabilitation of the Department of Health, the establishment of a system of State parks and parkways, legislation in the interest of men, women and children working in factories, salutary amendments to the factory code for the protection of their health and well-being, all came into existence in the State of New York only after a long and vigorous campaign, in the course of which I spoke in practically every city of the State, carrying the message directly to the people themselves, who assisted me in wringing these governmental reforms from a hostile Legislature opposing my proposals only for political reasons.

Because of lack of such leadership in the national administration not one large, constructive achievement can be pointed to in the record of the last seven and a half years; and if the American people will search back through their minds they can see this in sharp contrast with the Wilson and Roosevelt administrations. Wilson and Roosevelt were leaders.

The whole history of the last two Republican administrations suggests that some hidden control, strongly reactionary in its tendencies toward the great questions of the government, has been in a position to dictate party policy from behind the scenes and delay the progress of great public developments which interfered with its plans or program.

For that reason prominent members of the Republican Party have walked out of its ranks and openly declared hostility to their party and disagreement with its reactionary tendencies.

It was that hidden reactionary control that drove the elder Senator La Follette to the creation of a new party for the purpose of giving expression to the progressive views of the State that he represented and the states in sympathy with his point of view on great public questions.

It was a revolt against the same reactionary tendencies of the hidden control which drove Theodore Roosevelt from the ranks of the party that honored him with public office from youth to well past middle age and when he had closed a long public career as President of the United States after nomination by the Republican Party.

What more glaring exhibition of lack of leadership could be found in the Republican administration than its handling of the farm relief problem? That it is a critical problem they have admitted in their platform this year, and they recognized it also in the platform four years ago.

Shortly after the advent of the administration in 1921 the question of relief to agriculture became acute, and from that period down to and including today the Republican Party has been floundering around, with neither the President nor the Republican candidate as his chief adviser on agriculture even able to devise a policy, not to speak of executing one. The Congress of the United States, speaking for all the people, offered a program. The President vetoed it, but offered nothing in its place.

If there was any division of opinion in the United States with regard to the policy of putting agriculture on an economic equality with industry it was the duty of the President to iron out that difficulty. This I feel could have been accomplished by taking the question to the people themselves, and bringing to their attention the cold facts and figures which show that the men engaged in the business of taking from the land the necessities of life are compelled to sell their crops at less than the cost of production.

How many people in this country would deny justice to the farmer if they knew the real facts? Agricultural depression unquestionably reduces substantially the farmer's power of purchase. How long would the business man, the manufacturer and the storekeeper resist governmental aid to agriculture if it were brought to their attention that that depression is interfering with their business prosperity?

Organized labor was quick to realize that agricultural depression drove men from the farm to the cities to take up new lines of endeavor in competition with industrial workers, and therefore approved the principle of agricultural equality.

How many people in the United States are familiar with

the bank and commercial failures directly due to the agricultural depression? And how long would it take the business men of the country to realize that these failures are threatening the whole economic structure?

How many people in the United States today realize that according to the Department of Agriculture it costs the farmer from $1 to $1.72 to produce a bushel of wheat which he is compelled to sell today at much less than a dollar?

It should be brought home to the people that commodities like wheat really bring a higher price, as a rule, in the Canadian unprotected market than they do in the United States, where the farmer has been deceived into the belief that the tariff alone will solve his problems.

The American farmer asks no bounty. He asks no charity or no financial assistance from the government. He asks that the Republican promise of putting his business on an economic equality with industry be carried out. The Republican Party seems unwilling and unable and totally lacking in leadership to make that promise good.

At Omaha a week and a half ago I took a definite position on this matter, and after I spoke of the ills that the farmer is suffering from I read a prescription. I wish tonight to answer certain criticisms of it. So let me read it to you:

" Various people have attempted to misrepresent and confuse my attitude with respect to the McNary-Haugen Bill. I do not propose to leave the slightest doubt in anybody's mind on that subject. As I read the McNary-Haugen Bill its fundamental purpose is to establish an effective control of the sale of exportable surplus with the cost imposed on the commodity benefited. For that principle the Democratic platform squarely stands, and for that principle I squarely stand.

" Mr. Hoover stands squarely opposed to this principle by which the farmer could get the benefit of the tariff. What remains of the McNary-Haugen Bill is a mere matter of method, and I do not limit myself to the exact mechanics and method embodied in that bill.

"Here is a clean-cut issue which the farmers and the voters of this country must decide. It remains but to work out the details by which this principle shall be put into effect, and I have pledged myself to name a nonpartisan commission of farm leaders and students of the problem to work out these details. I shall make that appointment, if I am elected — not when I take the oath of office as President, but immediately after election; and I pledge to the farmers and to the people of this country that no stone will be left unturned to give immediate and adequate farm relief, by legislation carrying into practice the definite principle for which my party and I stand."

The Republican Party candidate in his speeches to date has developed no constructive plan, and I note by the papers that he does not intend to make another speech in the campaign until October 6, and the same papers say that the one following that will be on October 10.

I am not in a position to say whether or not the Chairman of the Republican National Committee speaks for the party, speaks for himself or speaks for the candidate, when he says in criticism of my speech on farm relief delivered at Omaha. I quote from him:

"He enunciated a principle which he says he finds in the McNary-Haugen Bill, but which is not the principle over which the battle has been fought for the last four years."

The Republican chairman displays a lack of knowledge of the whole situation when he attempts to fasten two principles on the plan set forth in the so-called McNary-Haugen Bill. He confuses the machinery for making the principle effective with the principle itself.

The Secretary of Agriculture, Mr. Jardine, made a speech about my program at Riverhead, N. Y., on the 21st. He said:

"Your Governor is in the West to solve the wheat problem and I hope he will do so. I've been trying to do it for seven years and haven't entirely succeeded. Yet, in spite of that, for several years we've managed to get you a pretty good price for wheat and potatoes. I am certain that we will during the next four years if given the opportunity."

He added:

" If you will cut down the acreage of potatoes, then I can help you get together and plant less and get a better price. Always keep in mind the demand. The wheat crop is having the same trouble: Too many acres."

Now there are three points in this speech of Secretary Jardine:

First, he is entirely right when he says that he has not succeeded in solving the wheat problem. Neither has anybody else in his party.

Second, I do not think there is a farmer in this country who will agree with his statements that he has managed to get for the farmer a pretty good price for the wheat. He is the only man I ever knew who would call a price below the cost of production a pretty good price.

Third, he continues to hold out the old plan which was advocated by Mr. Hoover, of cutting down acreage. He continues to advocate this despite the report of the Bureau of Agricultural Economics of his own department, which stated that it was substantially impossible to control the output of wheat by a reduction in acreage.

Mr. Hoover took a similar position back in 1924 when he wrote that surplus crops could " only be corrected by prices low enough to make production unprofitable."

Substantially they both stand for the astounding proposition that the way to help the farmer is to beat him down and drive more men from the farm in addition to the 4,000,000 who have already been compelled to leave them.

Senator Gerald P. Nye of North Dakota, declares for one method of making effective the principle of imposing the cost of surplus control on the commodity benefited, namely, the so-called equalization fee, and then makes the remarkable statement that the people are forced to choose the more definite and available plan Mr. Hoover has outlined.

It is well known that Mr. Hoover, as adviser to the President, declared in no uncertain terms not only against the method known as the equalization fee for control of the exportable surplus with the cost fastened on the commodity benefited, but against the whole principle of assessing the cost to handle the surplus back on the crop benefited.

Senator Nye says that Mr. Hoover has a definite and available plan. What is it? It has so far not been disclosed by the candidate.

In his speech of acceptance he said that the tariff was the foundation of farm relief. That I dispute. The tariff is a help, but everybody familiar with the subject, including Senator Nye, knows that the tariff standing by itself will not bring the relief.

He urges cooperatives. There is no argument about that, they are helpful; but standing by themselves, without machinery by law for making them operate effectively, they will not solve the problem.

He speaks of voluntary stabilization corporations. He knows, and Senator Nye knows, that they, too, are ineffectual. This is apparent from the words of Senator Nye himself, who says:

"I am still partial to the plan (meaning the machinery of the McNary-Haugen Bill) as the best foundation upon which to build a broad and lasting agricultural program."

The criticism of my Omaha speech made by the Republican National Chairman and Senator Nye is met and demolished by the statement made by Senator Norris of Nebraska, the Chairman of the Committee on Agriculture of the United States Senate, and one of the foremost students of this problem in the United States today. He said:

" Men who believe in the theory of the McNary-Haugen Bill should be satisfied with the Omaha speech of Governor Smith. Governor Smith proposes to take care of the surplus and charge the cost to the producer. That is the real object of the McNary-Haugen Bill. He properly reserves the further consideration of the machinery. I do not know, after long study, how anyone can improve on the machinery in the McNary-Haugen Bill, but Governor Smith is to be complimented in holding himself open for a better remedy, if one can be found."

Nothing that I could say would go further to dispose of the statements of Dr. Work and Senator Nye than what I have just read to you from the statement of Senator Norris. They are all members of the same political party, except that Senator Norris believes in progressive leadership and the other two men are content with things as they are.

He sees and understands that the equalization fee is but one method to make effective the principle.

It is noteworthy at this point to recall to mind that Governor Lowden, in the very forefront of the leaders of his party, struggling to assist the farmer, said that if there were any better method to effectuate the principle of surplus control, he would be for it.

Mr. Hoover promises the development of our inland waterways for relief for the farmer.

This subjcet gives us again a glaring example of absolute lack of leadership and constructive thought or action. It parallels the farm relief question as far as promise and performance are concerned on the part of the Republican administration.

Let us go back over the record.

The Republican platform of 1920, eight years ago, said:

" We declare it to be our policy to encourage and develop water transportation and service and facilities in connection with the commerce of the United States."

The report of the Advisory Committee on Policies and Platform of the Republican Party, responsible for that declaration, said:

" The development of inland transportation by water under a broad and comprehensive plan which shall include all the uses of the waters and benefits to be derived from their control is a policy equally of the Republican Party."

It is a matter of history that from 1921, when the Republican Party came into power, until 1924 when they again adopted a platform, nothing was done about a comprehensive plan for the development of inland waterways. Consequently, they found it necessary again in 1924 to make practically the same promise which is to be found in the Republican platform of that year in the following language:

" Fully realizing the vital importance of transportation in both cost and service to all our people, we favor the construction of the most feasible waterways from the Great Lakes to the Atlantic Seaboard and the Gulf of Mexico, and improvement and development of rivers, harbors and waterways, inland and coastwise, to the fullest extent justified by the present and potential tonnage available."

Let us look at the platform of 1928, which again speaks of cheaper transportation for bulk goods from the Mid-West agricultural sections to the sea, and they say that it is recognized by the Republican Party as a vital factor for the relief of agriculture.

They speak of the continued development of waterways. What is meant by the continued development? No comprehensive plan has yet been put forth to develop them, although it was promised in 1920, and promised again in 1924 and now in 1928. They claim to have initiated the systematic development of the Mississippi system. What plan have they for such development, and what have they done to finance it?

I hold in my hand the only substantial piece of legislation I have been able to find with regard to development of the

Mississippi river, and that is entitled: "An Act for the Control of Floods on the Mississippi River, and its Tributaries, and for Other Purposes."

But I can find no other purposes indicated in the bill except flood relief, unless by " other purposes " is meant the preparation of maps required to further the project of flood control. It contains no reference to any comprehensive plan or scheme of inland waterway development. It does not even refer to any substantial development on the upper or northern part of the Mississippi river.

This is as far as we have been able to get on Republican promises after eight years of neglect and delay, and this much has been accomplished only after a great catastrophe, which might well have been avoided had action been promptly taken on the promises.

Even this action is entirely unsatisfactory; and so far as a definite plan is concerned, gets us nowhere. As far as flood relief is concerned, the bill is not thoroughly honest. Leading the people to believe that financial provision has been made for flood relief, the bill appropriates only $15,000,000, although it authorized future appropriations of $325,000,000.

The amount made available, it is unnecessary for me to say, would scarcely scratch the surface of any comprehensive plan or bring about any degree of flood relief.

At this point I call your attention to a policy that has grown up in the Federal administration that can have no other purpose except to deceive the people. Three hundred and twenty-five million dollars authorized but not appropriated is another means of delay. One of the great troubles with this project and with many others is that had adequate appropriations been made for them the Republican Party would be unable to make the boasts of economy in the present administration that they have spread broadcast throughout the length and breadth of the land. You cannot get results promising development as one policy and withholding the funds to carry it out as another policy.

By comparison with the Republican platform, the Democratic platform specifically commits the Democratic Party to the building up of water transportation through the immediate improvement of the inland waterways, and goes further and declares for prompt appropriation of the necessary funds to effectuate a comprehensive plan.

So far as the Mississippi river is concerned, there can be no comprehensive plan that contemplates the development of only a part of that river, as proposed in the Republican legislation I have just referred to. It must include the Mississippi river as a whole and its navigable tributaries. I will carry out that platform in its letter and spirit, and the political expediency of reducing appropriation bills will not stand in the way of making good that promise in the interest of the commerce and agriculture of the whole country.

My attention has been called to an article in the *St. Paul Dispatch* of Wednesday of this week, in which it is claimed that I was advised not to speak on the subject of waterways because it would cause me embarrassment to speak about the St. Lawrence route from the Great Lakes to the sea.

I am never embarrassed talking on any public question. The embarrassment, if it exists, is upon the Republican Party on this question, because the platform of 1928 simply provides " cheaper transportation for bulk goods from the Mid-West agricultural sections to the sea." It says nothing about the route. It does not mention the St. Lawrence river, nor the all-American waterway. It dodges that question. For that matter, it does not speak about a canal at all.

In 1924 the Republican Party dodged the question in the same way when they said that they favored the construction of the most feasible waterways from the Great Lakes to the Atlantic seaboard without mention of the route.

Let us look at the speech of acceptance of the Republican candidate and find out what he says about it. Speaking of the modernization of our inland waterways system, he says:

"It includes not only the great Mississippi system with its joining of the Great Lakes and the heart of the Mid-West agriculture to the Gulf, but also a shipway from the Great Lakes to the Atlantic."

I do not see that he says anything about the St. Lawrence waterway or the all-American route either. If there is embarrassment, according to the record of the Republican Party and the Republican candidate, they are suffering from it, and not I.

I frankly told the people of the United States in my speech of acceptance exactly where I stood on this subject, and I will repeat it here to-night. As Governor of New York State, representing the interests of that State, I took the same position as my Republican predecessor and declared in favor of the all-American route, from Lake Ontario, by way of the Erie Canal and the Mohawk river to the Hudson, and down the Hudson to tidewater.

I frankly stated what everybody knows — that there was a question as to the figures submitted by the engineers with respect to both routes. I would call your attention to the fact that all of the states affected were not in accord on any one route.

I have here a telegram which states that the Mississippi Valley Association, now promoting the candidacy of my opponent, at its convention in St. Louis in November two years ago, adopted a resolution indorsing the all-American route from the Great Lakes to the Atlantic.

If I am called to the office of President by the American people I will make good to the last degree exactly what I said in my speech of acceptance:

"As President of the United States, therefore, it would be my clear duty to re-study this question impartially upon engi-

Waves of cheering rose from this crowd gathered in front of the Hotel English in Indianapolis when Governor Smith appeared on the balcony

neers' reports, the accuracy of which must be above question. When the results of such study are given to Congress I am entirely willing to abide by the decision of Congress."

My interest will be just the same for the Great Northwest territory affected by the improvement as it will be for any other place in the United States, including my own State.

Again I declared that what was needed was action. What is needed is leadership. What is needed is the disposition on the part of the responsible authority to carry these promises into effect. They cannot be dragged from the moth bag every four years and offered as vote-getters to the American people, with no evidence that there ever was any intention of carrying them out.

The whispering forces of the Republican National Committee are at work on this question of the St. Lawrence waterway, and in spite of my clear, plain statement in the speech of acceptance they are attempting to put into the minds of the people the thought that I will be opposed under any circumstances to the St. Lawrence waterway because of my early advocacy of the all-American route. I would be able to meet these arguments if they were made in the open, but it is difficult to answer them when they are whispered. When you again hear them, refer the whisperer to my speech of acceptance and to my remarks from this platform to-night.

In the course of the last two weeks, I have discovered another whispering campaign about my attitude toward the question of immigration.

The Congress of the United States, backed up by the President, has adopted a definite policy of restriction of immigration into this country for the protection of all citizens, both native and foreign-born. The whisperers would have the people believe that I favor a letting-down of the restricting bars and an opening of the floodgates that immigration may pour into the country. Nothing could be further from the truth.

CAMPAIGN ADDRESS

The Democratic platform upon which I stand reads:

"Laws which limit immigration must be preserved in full force and effect."

The Republican Party in different language makes the same declaration in its platform. They speak of amendments to the Immigration Law which would do away with undue hardships that deprive the immigrant of the comfort and society of those bound by close family ties.

The Democratic platform provides for the same thing in a different language. The Republican candidate in his speech of acceptance parallels the Republican platform with relation to unnecessary hardships upon families, but he further says:

"As a member of the commission whose duty it is to determine the quota basis under the National Origins Law, I have found it impossible to do so accurately and without hardship."

With this I agree. Therefore there is no issue between either the parties or the candidates on the question of sustaining and keeping in full force and effect the restrictive features of the present immigration laws. Where they are to be amended for the relief of hardship we are in accord.

I take my hat off to no man in my regard and respect for immigration population. No man can read the history of this country aright and deny the fact that immigrants had a great share in its upbuilding. Certainly, the sturdy stock of Scandinavians and Germans have contributed to the upbuilding of this great Northwest.

As far back as 1915, in the New York State Constitutional Convention, speaking of the character and accomplishments of our immigrants, I said that any man who comes to this country, raises a family, educates them in our public schools and, by his labors and toil helps to keep open the channels of trade and commerce, obeys our laws, takes and respects an oath to sustain our Constitution and flag, is just as good a citizen of this country as the man or group of men who can point to a long and unbroken line of New England ancestry.

Pay no attention to the whisperers. Read the Democratic platform upon which I stand. Consult the record and see if you can find in that record any instance where I have gone back on a promise made to the people during the long years I have been a holder of elective public office.

Notwithstanding the remarks of the self-appointed spokesman of the Republican Party, I think I have clearly shown to you the insincerity of that party on the question of farm relief.

I believe that I have amply demonstrated their insincerity and incapacity when it comes to dealing with the construction and developments of inland waterways in accordance with some comprehensive plan.

I point only to the record to challenge the statement that relief for either of these projects can come from the Republican Party, and I confidently make the declaration that farm relief, development of our inland waterways, development under public ownership and control of our great water powers, can only come from leadership to be won by the victory of the Democratic Party on the 6th of next November.

VII

ADDRESS AT MILWAUKEE

Milwaukee, Wisconsin, September 29, 1928

I AM finishing to-night, so far as speechmaking is concerned, my campaign trip through the west. During the entire trip I have been greatly impressed by the enthusiasm of the people who have greeted me, by the warm welcome which I have received, not only in the places where I spoke but at all stations where the train stopped. In your own State, in a downpour of rain, enthusiasm was not dampened. For this interest and cordial welcome I can only express my sincere appreciation and gratitude.

When I started on my trip through the west I said that I would talk about the great issues of this campaign in a direct, plain and outspoken fashion.

At Omaha I spoke on the important issue of farm relief. I condemned the Republican Party for betraying the interests of agriculture and pledged myself to a constructive program of speedy relief. Newspaper reports indicate that following this speech there were hurried conferences and exchanges of views on the part of the Republican campaign managers. They were worried. They were not accustomed to have this problem dealt with honestly and squarely.

In Oklahoma City I spoke upon the subject of intolerance. I went at length into the question of religion that had so improperly been made the basis of a whispering campaign against me. I spoke with reluctance on this subject because I firmly believe in the absolute separation of Church and State, a principle which cannot, however, be realized if religion is to be injected into a political campaign.

CAMPAIGN ADDRESS

The only official of the government that answered me at all was Mrs. Willebrandt. I shall let the Republican campaign managers worry about her. From comments in the public press all over the country they have abundant reason to do so.

At Denver I spoke on development of our great water power resources and declared definitely, as I have many times before in New York, in favor of the public ownership and the effective public control of these God-given resources of the nation.

At Helena I spoke on party responsibility and disclosed the record of corruption and wrong doing on the part of Republicans of high rank in the last two administrations, and those holding positions of leadership in their party. What I said was not relished by the Republican campaign managers. Your own Senator, La Follette, was equally outspoken in his denunciation of these great wrongs in the minority platform report submitted by him to the Republican National Convention. But you know what was done with that report: It was thrown out of the window. The last thing in the world the Republican leaders want is plain talk upon this subject.

They preferred to gloss over this discreditable record. Indeed, the Republican candidate for President goes so far as to say in his speech of acceptance that no party can look back with greater satisfaction than the Republicans can on the last eight years of Republican rule. I am confident that a large group within the Republican Party does not join the candidate in this expression of satisfaction.

Thursday night at St. Paul I spoke on the subject of leadership, called attention to the lack of leadership in the Republican administration during the past seven and a half years, and pointed out that it was such lack of leadership that prevented the adoption of any constructive program during this period.

AT MILWAUKEE

If there is any one subject above all others concerning which the welfare of the country requires plain speech and constructive leadership, it is the subject of the Eighteenth Amendment and the Volstead Act.

A large part of the difficulty in connection with this important problem is due to the failure on the part of our public officials to talk frankly about it.

I am satisfied that there are thousands of men in public life who think exactly as I do on this subject but who, because of what they believe to be political expediency, keep their mouths shut about it.

I regard this as a great moral issue, and I appeal to the people of America, regardless of party, to put aside any preconceived notions they may have about it and to approach it fairly, without passion and without prejudice, with open eyes and with open minds, to the end that some constructive solution of this important problem may be reached.

For a great many years there was a political party in the United States known as the Prohibition Party. At no time during its existence was it a factor worth reckoning with in our political history. During the war for emergency reasons, Governmental restrictions were put upon the traffic in intoxicating beverages. By governmental order prohibition was enacted against the sale of liquor of any kind to soldiers in uniform. For the preservation of grain and produce needed for the purposes of the war, restrictions were put upon the brewing of malted beverages.

Taking advantage of the frame of mind of the American people, an organization known as the Anti-Saloon League started a drive for national prohibition. In 1917, they succeeded in having adopted by the Congress, for reference to the states, the Eighteenth Amendment to our Federal Constitution. It received a great deal of support through the country by large numbers of our citizens who, as a matter of patriotic duty, had accustomed themselves to accepting restrictions upon their personal liberties during the war.

In 1919 the Eighteenth Amendment was ratified and became part of our fundamental law and, in the same year the National Prohibition Law, commonly known as the Volstead Act, was enacted over the veto of President Wilson.

It goes without saying that back in 1919 and 1920, millions of right-thinking people in this country were firm in their belief that intoxicating alcoholic liquor could be driven out of this country and its use abolished by the American people simply by writing a constitutional amendment prohibiting it, and a Federal statute supporting the amendment. Experience has taught us, and I believe a great majority of the people themselves believe, that this was an erroneous idea. For this reason I hold that the question is not today as between liquor and no liquor, or prohibition and anti-prohibition; rather, the question is what is best for the country to do to relieve a situation that it finds itself in.

We have never had prohibition in this country in the sense that hard liquor was banished from it. No person with knowledge of what is going on in the country would claim that there is no liquor in this country today. I go further than that and say that there is as much, if not more, than there was in the pre-prohibition days, because countless thousands of our citizens today see reason for storing it away.

The question presented, therefore, as to how best to adapt American custom and American habit to a constitutional amendment and a body of sustaining laws that so many millions of our citizens, respecting all other laws and standing high in their communities, are disposed to disregard.

I said a moment ago that this is a moral question and certainly there is no sterner duty resting upon the American people than the preservation of the morals of the youth of this country. In my speech of acceptence I said the following:

"I believe in temperance. We have not achieved temperance under the present system. The mothers and fathers of young men and women throughout this land know the anxiety and worry which has been brought to them by their children's use of liquor in a way which was unknown before prohibition. I believe in reverence for law. Today disregard of the prohibition law is insidiously sapping respect for all law. I raise, therefore, what I profoundly believe to be a great moral issue involving the righteousness of our national conduct and the protection of our children's morals." This statement has been challenged and criticised by the over-zealous among the prohibitionists who appear to be willing to disregard facts and the record.

This was no original thought of mine. I have no personal or intimate knowledge of these conditions among the youth. No man in my position would be expected to know them, but I have abundant evidence to sustain what I said, and it was upon this evidence that I made the statement.

Let us consider some of it. If it were confined to a single section of the United States it would not impress me, but it is nation-wide. It comes from clergymen and educators. Starting with my own State of New York, I have the testimony of the rector of the All Saints' Episcopal Church at Great Neck, L. I., who says:

"I cannot imagine a worse condition than exists at present among the young people who are led to the use of adulterated, strong drink, such as whisky, gin, raw brandies and even plain alcohol, and this because the milder drinks, such as beer, ale and light wines cannot be had for the very simple reason they are difficult for the bootlegger to handle profitably. We are suffering an intolerable situation that means further debauchery of youth beyond anything we have ever imagined."

Let us step into New England. The Rev. P. C. Power, director of the Episcopal home of St. John for children, located in Boston, says:

"Boys and girls and older people habitually in conversation boast of their private and favorite bootleggers."

Rev. J. D. Saunderson, of the Episcopal Church of Christ in Brownsville, Pa., says:

" The moral effect of an unenforced and unenforceable law, particularly on our young people, has been very sad. It soon became, unfortunately, the smart thing to carry something on your hip, to use the cant phrase among boys and girls who, in many cases, had never tasted alcohol until the fad became a habit."

The Rev. R. Johnston Thomas, of Nebraska, says:

"In days gone by it was a disgrace for boys to drink, and especially girls, but now it is the smart thing to do."

Similar letters could be read from all parts of the country.

Miss Ida Tarbell writes:

" Bootleggers and their customers shape their commerce to suit circumstances and in doing so often make drinkers of those who in the old days were protected from direct temptation. Something of that kind is happening in many business offices; the bootlegger serving the man at the top manages to build up a trade among clerks, stenographers and even elevator and office boys."

Nicholas Murray Butler, president of Columbia University, says:

" We have brought about a situation in which we challenge the ingenuity and sporting instinct of millions of young persons to test whether or not they can safely violate a law for which they have no respect. We have invited and induced a spirit and a habit of lawlessness which are quite without precedent and which reach from the highest ranks in the nation's life to the lowest and most humble."

Finally, let me call your attention to the report of the Institute of Social and Religious Research, which has recently completed a study of conditions among undergraduates in twenty-three American colleges. This study was made under the chairmanship of John R. Mott, formerly international president of the Y. M. C. A., and associated with him were men like W. H. P. Faunce, President of Brown University, and Paul Monroe, former professor in Teachers' College, Columbia University, New York.

Fifty-six per cent. of the women undergraduates, who were questioned said:

" The most demoralizing influence in college life as a whole is the use of liquor."

All of this must be known to the people in Washington, but the real truth and the real facts have been concealed.

Let us look at some of the facts. Let us take them from the record. In the first place, I claim that the Eighteenth Amendment and the Volstead Act have produced a condition of wholesale corruption among officials of the government charged with their enforcement, and I call as my witness General Lincoln C. Andrews, a Republican, and a one-time national prohibition director. He told a Senate committee that there was an "astonishing corruption" among prohibition agents; that 875 of them were dismissed for cause. Of these, 121 were dismissed for extortion, bribery or soliciting money, 61 for collusion and conspiracy, and 187 for intoxication and misconduct.

Major Chester P. Mills, former prohibition administrator, of the Second Federal District, of New York, speaking of official corruption, shows in an article in " Collier's Weekly " that bribery was rampant to corrupt enforcement agents who were in the pay of the government to enforce the law and in the pay of the bootleggers to nullify it. Has anybody in official Washington denied this?

Under the Republican Party Major Mills says enforcement of prohibition has , become the " new political pork barrel," and the party workers, throughout the country, have been rewarded for their service to the party by being given a chance at the enforcement of prohibition. He explains that when he first entered the service he was told to organize his own department and to keep politics out of it. He says that gradually these orders to exclude politics were modified, and he was requested to advise with the local party leaders regarding appointments to the force of more than 240 men working under him.

Major Mills learned that his clashes with the local politicians were given nation-wide magnitude, so that the dismissal of dishonest men reached the ear of the President of the United States. Nothing amused me more than to see the telegram of commendation to the Republican leader of New York county, congratulating him on his bold stand for prohibition; for according to Chester Mills, the same gentleman, taking advantage of the patronage system and tapping the pork barrel for the benefit of his followers, supplied four prohibition enforcement agents. In the language of Major Mills:

" These four men, typical of the lowest grade of illiterate henchmen, foisted on the prohibition service by the politicians, were fired."

While that leader apparently was agreeable to the dismissal of one of them, Major Mills says that the underground backwash of their dismissal and his stubborn refusal to reinstate them brought a hurry call to Washington. He then speaks of a conference in the office of the Secretary of the Treasury, in which General Andrews, Chairman Koenig and former Congressman Mills, now under Secretary of the Treasury, took part. After General Andrews had expressed his view that Major Mills was a most efficient dry administrator, Congressman Mills said bluntly:

" No one questions his efficiency, but let us talk patronage."

" Upon my failure to reinstate the man," writes Major Mills, " General Andrews came on to New York to investigate their cases personally, and he urged me to make peace with the politicians by reinstating both the crooks and the bunglers."

I could take up the time of this meeting indefinitely explaining the ramifications that grow out of the injection of politics into the enforcement of the Eighteenth Amendment and the Volstead Act. Suffice it for me to repeat, prohibition has been the great political pork barrel for the Republican Party.

For years all of these positions were out of the classified civil service, so that Republican politicians could name the men of their choice. They were finally placed in the civil service and examination of the men disclosed that two-thirds of the field force were unable to qualify or make reasonable answer to the questions calculated to determine their fitness to perform this work.

The City of Washington itself is governed by a committee of Congress, and the newspapers record the fact that in one year one-third of the members of the entire Washington police force have been up before the officials on charges of being intoxicated while in the performance of their duty.

What other facts must be apparent to the officials at Washington? Again we call on General Andrews. Appearing before a committee of the Senate, he testified that not 5 per cent. of the liquor smuggled into this country was caught by the government; further, that there were 1,720,000 stills operating in the country under prohibition. He further testified that a half-million people are engaged in the making of liquor, that two million people are engaged in the various phases of bootlegging and that occasional or habitual drinking of illicit liquor could be charged against half of our population.

This testimony comes from the Republican Director of the Prohibition Bureau. How long are the officials at Washington going to disregard a condition laid before them by a high official of the government? How long are they going to continue the trick of the ostrich of burying its head in the sand, and assuming that everything is all right? What is the proper thing for them to do — conceal all this or talk it out plainly to the American people?

According to the police records gathered from 403 different municipalities scattered in all parts of the country, and in the states that were dry as well as states that were wet before prohibition, in 1920 there were 237,101 arrests for drunkenness and in 1926, six years after prohibition went into effect, arrests for drunkenness in these same places totaled 559,074. Statistics also show a material increase in deaths from the excessive use of alcohol.

It is further known to be a fact that the drastic and unreasonable definition of what constitutes an intoxicant as contained in the Volstead Act, has driven men and women who heretofore were content with drinking light wines and beer, to the use of strong liquor; and liquor drinking in this country instead of being on the decline, is on the upward move as a direct result of the attempt to prohibit alcoholic beverages entirely.

It is a well known fact that to-night, while I am standing on this platform talking to you, liquor is easily obtainable in every State of this Union, notwithstanding that many of the states are far removed from the seaboard or from countries where liquor is legitimately manufactured. It is a known fact that there is an abundance of liquor in the Capital City itself. Only a short time ago, according to newspaper reports, a waiter in the Senate restuarant dropped a bottle of Scotch whisky on the floor. It broke and its contents spilled over the Capitol, and, according to a New York newspaper, he was discharged the next day for carelessness. Nobody said anything about the crime involved in his possession of it, but it was declared to be the sin of waste by letting it fall on the floor.

So far I have attempted to paint two pictures: First, the picture of the effect of these laws upon the morals of our youth, and, second, the real facts and the real condition, which I claim must be known to the officials of the government. I have taken considerable time to lay this before you in detail, but I could not make a better job of it than to quote what President Harding said about it:

"Constitutional prohibition has been adopted by the nation. It is the supreme law of the land. In plain speaking, there are conditions relating to its enforcement which savor of a nation-wide scandal. It is the most demoralizing factor in our public life."

Let it be said to his credit that President Harding was the one man in high official position in Washington who was prepared to concede that it was the most demoralizing factor in our public life.

What is the answer of the Republican Party to all of this? In the face of this record the platform glosses over the whole thing by quoting the words of George Washington and Abraham Lincoln and again pledges itself and its nominees to the observance and vigorous enforcement of the Eighteenth Amendment; no truth, no candor, not even common honesty. And all of this from a party that for eight years has tried as best it could to be all things to all men. Senator Gore, of Oklahoma, in a speech at Omaha recently summed it up in a few words when he said that the Republican policy was to give the liquor to the wets and give the law to the drys.

The Republican candidate, speaking on the subject, said the following:

"Our country has deliberately undertaken a great social and economic experiment, noble in motive and far-reaching in purpose. It must be worked out constructively.

"Common sense compels us to realize that grave abuses have occurred—abuses which must be remedied."

He thereafter speaks of a searching investigation.

Let me show you a complete record of a searching inquiry made only two years ago, comprising 1,700 pages of testimony, all of which, for reasons of political expediency, were disregarded.

What is the plain common sense of this whole proposition?

Millions of people in this country do not agree with Mr. Hoover that this is a noble experiment. You could get no better testimony for that than to look at the result of the referendum in so many of our thickly populated states.

While it is true that some of the states of the nation have voted against change in the present system, it is at the same time true that in the large populous states the result is the other way, as is evidenced by the referendums.

In New York, people out of sympathy with the law, in a popular election, expressed it by over 1,000,000 majority. In Illinois, by 284,000 majority. In Wisconsin, by 171,000 majority. In Nevada, by 8,300 majority. In Montana, by 10,249 majority.

The point is that a great army of the American people oppose these laws. Nobody can say that that is a healthy condition in our democracy. Nobody can say that people like ours are comfortable when so many of our thinking citizens resist the attempt on the part of the government to regulate their conduct by law. The natural result of it is the breeding throughout the length and breadth of the country a disrespect for all law. Nobody can gainsay the fact that the Prohibition Law and the Volstead Act have found a new line of endeavor for the underworld; they brought to life the bootleggers, and the bootleggers begot the hijackers, and the hijackers the racketeers, so that gangland is interested in the maintenance of prohibition because by its operation they are benefited.

As far as my time permits me, to-night I have painted for you the picture. In my speech of acceptance I suggested a remedy. Let us deal with it for a little while.

First, I recommended an amendment to the Volstead Act which should contain a sane and sensible definition of what constitutes an intoxicating beverage, because upon its face the present definition does not square with common sense or with medical opinion. Each State could then provide for an alcoholic content not greater than that fixed by Congress.

It must be borne in mind that the Eighteenth Amendment does not prohibit alcoholic beverages; it prohibits intoxicating beverages. And no sensible man can truthfully be prepared to say that one-half of 1 per cent. of alcohol constitutes an intoxicant.

I firmly and honestly believe that a great deal of the dangerous and poisonous hard liquor would be driven out of this country if the people could be assured of an alcoholic beverage declared by common sense and by science to be non-intoxicating.

I further recommended an amendment to the Eighteenth Amendment. I placed it squarely upon the basis of the Jeffersonian principle of the right of each State to determine for itself what it wants to do about questions of local habits of life usually covered by local police laws.

I have carefully, however, provided safeguards that will make impossible a return to the old conditions of sale in the saloon, despised, and rightly so, by the American people.

I suggested a referendum for the expression of the will of the people themselves in the first instance. I would then regard it as the right of the State itself, subject to limitations which I outlined, to dispense to its own inhabitants alcoholic beverages as desired by the people of the State.

No man who believes in states' rights, who believes in the fundamental principles of democracy, can find any fault with that. No State should be permitted to impose its will upon another State in matters of local concern. What would the states that desire prohibition think about a proposal to amend the Constitution to forbid them to enact prohibition laws? They would justly resent it. That's the way the people of the other states feel about the Eighteenth Amendment.

The cure for the ills of democracy is more democracy. Hand this back to the people. Let them decide it. And certainly it is not asking too much to let them have something to say about it when an experience of eight years permits me to paint such a dismal picture of failure as I have been able to lay before this gathering to-night.

This I would say to the people of the dry states. I propose nothing which would impose upon them any law which they do not desire within their own states. I propose merely a change which will give to each local community under appropriate safeguards that system of law which it desires.

Speaking of a subject other than prohibition before the American Bar Association at San Francisco, on August 10, 1922, President Coolidge said:

"In a republic, the law reflects, rather than makes the standard of conduct. The attempt to dragoon the body when the need is to convince the soul will end in revolt."

I adopt that statement and I apply it to prohibition. The Prohibition Law should reflect and not make the standard of conduct in each State of this Union. The attempt to dragoon the body of the voters in states which do not believe in this law results in revolt in those states and has brought about conditions of lawlessness and disrepect for law which I believe the people of this country should face and should cure.

It must be borne in mind that under my suggestion Federal prohibition is preserved in its entirety for the states that desire to remain dry. It will remain always the duty of the Federal Government under my proposal to protect the states desiring to remain dry from the introduction or importation into them of alcoholic beverages. It retains all the features of the Eighteenth Amendment and the act sustaining it, except that the State itself, in its sovereign power, may after a vote of its people, decide under strict control to dispense alcoholic beverages.

Now, I am fully aware that the President of the United States cannot bring this about by himself. But, repeating what I said in St. Paul, what we lack in this country is leadership; and if I am elected President of the United States it will be my duty to lay this matter before every community that I can reach and let them make their own decision. If that is not Democratic government, I must confess that I do not understand it.

You can expect nothing from the Republican Party. The long record of eight years indicates that they have used the law for patronage purposes and for political expediency. They tried to be wet when they were with the wets, and dry when they were with the drys. They have silently stood by and permitted the paralysis of the whole machinery of government when it comes to carrying out the mandate of the Constitution and the statute law. It is because of that that after eight years they are compelled to promise again that they will do something about it if given a new lease of life by the American people.

As I said in my speech of acceptance, with respect to prohibition, two constitutional duties devolve upon the President; first, to recommend to Congress what in his opinion is in the interest of this country; second, to enforce the statutes as he finds them. And I told the American people that if I were elected President and I took the oath of office to sustain the Constitution and laws of this country, with one hand on the Bible and the other reaching up to Heaven, that I would make that good and you can take my assurance for it that I will so far as it is humanly possible to do it. I shall likewise discharge my duty to advise the Congress of the changes in the law I deem right.

The Republican Party is helpless. Its record makes no appeal. A sane, sensible solution can only come from a Democratic victory, because the Democratic Party will give this matter its frank and fearless attention and lay it before the American people as it has never been laid before them.

VIII

ADDRESS AT ROCHESTER

Rochester, New York, October 1, 1928

FELLOW citizens: There is something wrong, something wrong. There has been a crossing of the wires or a missing of signals. When the Congressman introduced the chieftain, the band played " The Chocolate Soldier."

As the Congressman said, at some early hour this morning we came across the border into the State of New York after our western tour. Take it from me, I never had such a time in my life.

I enjoyed every minute of it. I took personal pleasure and personal delight in looking into the countenances of so many fellow American citizens, and whether they were on the far northwestern plains or in the central part of the west, they just look like our own neighbors here in New York. I report a little bit short on sleep. They wake up earlier in the morning on the western prairies and they were knocking on the window as early as half-past six and seven o'clock with the familiar shout, " Come out here, Al, and give us a look at you."

I am all even on meals. I brought back an elegant, black and white, harlequin Great Dane. He is down aboard the train waiting for me.

I lost two brown derbies. Outside of that there are no casualties to report.

Here we are tonight in the Democratic State Convention, the supreme body of the party in the State of New York, assembled for the nomination of the State ticket. At midnight on the 31st of December I leave the employ of the State after a period, punctured here and there by intervals of only a few years at a time, going back over a quarter of a century.

In one of my speeches in the west I spoke about party responsibility, and I made up my mind that when I came before the State Convention, as a duty to the party and to the State, there would be no subject so fitting as the subject of party responsibility.

Now unless we are going to hold the parties accountable, unless we are going to fix responsibility on them, we might as well stop going through this idle and senseless and useless performance of meeting in convention and making written promises in the form of platform pledges. We might as well wipe out the party lines, get away from regulation of political parties by the State itself, and make it a free for all and let everybody run for Governor.

The party who gets the greatest number of votes will be elected.

If we are going to have the party system of government, if we are going to have organized political parties regulated by the State itself by statute, we are compelled, if that system is to be successful, to hold the party to strict accountability; and party responsibility should be the keynote when we look back over the record.

The Republican Party in convention assembled about three or four days ago adopted a platform that is as meaningless as anything I ever saw in my life.

Personally, after looking at it, I could get more comfort from a Chinese laundry ticket.

It brought me back over some thirty-five years. All you have to do is pick it up, and you would imagine that you were in the Fulton Market in the dead of winter, picking up a fish.

My purpose here tonight is to compare that platform with the record and give the details of the Republican record. I will be able to demonstrate, if not in the time given me tonight, surely before this campaign is over, that not a single constructive achievement that took place in the government of this State in the last six years had Republican support until they were beaten down to the earth.

Let us take No. 1, the Reorganization of the Government, a great constructive reform that is being copied throughout the commonwealths of the country. In the Republican platform this year they take credit for it. In the platform of two years ago they took the credit for it. And history indicates that from 1920 to the time that it was finally submitted, they opposed it, not only in the Legislature, but they opposed it as a party at the polls.

In 1921 it could have been accomplished, four years earlier than the people got the benefit of it. And what happened? The new Chairman of the Republican State Committee, the Speaker of the Assembly, after it had passed the Senate, threw it into the waste basket. He won't deny that; he can't deny it; it is history.

If you want confirmation of the statement that it was opposed by the Republican Party as a party, look at the returns in the various counties of the State. Look at Livingston county, the home of the United States Senator leading the Republican forces, and you will find that the salutary provision for the reorganization of the government was defeated in that year by over five thousand plurality. How quick they would be ready to apply this test of my sincerity if one of those amendments had been beaten on Oliver street.

After the amendment was adopted it was necessary to appoint a committee to bring the statute law of the State, the department law of the State, into conformity with the Constitution. You all know whom the Republicans desired for chairman of that committee.

They suggested Mr. Machold, the man that tortured it to death, the man that strangled it. I am the one who selected ex-Governor Hughes. I am taking the credit for that because it belongs to me.

Now, let us pass along to another constructive reform. Last election day nine amendments to the Constitution were offered to the people of the State of New York. With discriminating intelligence they accepted eight of them and rejected one. They rejected the four-year term because they discovered that the Republican Party was trying to put something over by law.

What did the Republicans then do? They went back into session in 1928 and in defiance of their own committee and of public sentiment throughout the State, they in effect said to the people of New York, " You will either take it our way or you will not take it at all." Now, that is on the record. You cannot get away from that.

Take the executive budget. Everybody in this State, who knows anything at all about it, knows that the executive budget is probably the most advanced step in the reform of governmental machinery that we have seen during our generation. What is the history with respect to that? Mr. Machold, as Speaker of the Assembly, followed me around this State from one city to the other and argued against it. With a stubbornness almost unbelievable they stood for six solid years against it. What happened? When the Hughes Commission put the departments together under the Constitution they wrote a report that the reorganization could not possibly work without the executive budget, and Mr. Machold himself, who fought it and argued against it, actually signed the report declaring that the only way you could get it was by amendment to the Constitution.

Now, I have a reason for speaking the way I am speaking tonight. I will tell you what it is. I took plain credit for all this for the Democratic Party, but your platform does that, and you know that it was the Democrats that fought for all this. What I am trying to establish tonight is that if the Republican Party, as represented in the Senate and Assembly, had their way about it you would not have a single one of these government reforms. Do you know what the cry down there was? Wait another year, the fellow on the second floor will be out of here next year; wait. " Let us go along another year and take a chance; he cannot come back." But the people of the State of New York fooled our Republican friends, and kept sending me back, and the result is that all these reforms came by what we may call easy stages. If you will look at the year in which they passed, you will find it was always an even numbered year, because that was the year they were going out to the people; that was the year they wanted to make the record as clean as they were able to make it; not so very clean, but as clean as they were able to make it.

It is a matter of fact that the Republican forces in the State, through their organization in the various counties, fought at the polls the executive budget, and Senator Knight, the President pro tem of the Senate, even spoke against it in the campaign. Now, do not let the so-called high-toned Republicans tell you that they have no responsibility for these leaders in Albany. There is no way of ever fixing the responsibility unless you fix it upon the elected officials that carry out what they believe to be the party policy. Take the bond issues. They bitterly fought the issue for public improvements and the issue for the elimination of grade crossings. They came out in the open against the public improvements bond issue and I debated it in the city of Buffalo with Congressman Mills and in Carnegie Hall with former Governor Miller.

And with former Governor Miller they opposed it at the polls, and the vote in the counties indicated it. They also opposed at the polls the bond issue for grade crossings elimination. And what reason do you think they gave for keeping quiet about it? I found it out down in Westchester county, speaking at Briarcliff Lodge. I found out what was the matter. A prominent Republican leader of Westchester county said to one of our women, our Democratic women: " Of course, we don't like to go right out against the grade crossings." She said, "Why not?" "Well," he says, "if there was a great railroad accident ten days or a week before election and a dozen or two dozen people were killed, look at what Smith would say about it."

Not only did they oppose the grade crossings elimination, but they did it in a cowardly way.

Let us take water power. We have had ten years of senseless, stupid opposition to the development of the State's great water power resources. About that there can be no question.

I presented a definite plan. I simply wanted a water power authority set up for the purpose of reporting back to the Legislature a comprehensive scheme for the development of all our great water power, and the Republican answer to it was, "No; we propose to lease them to private individuals so that there may be private profit and private gain."

Wait till I read the water power plank of this year's platform and, if there is anybody in this hall with a sense of humor, they will find in this something almost as good as listening to Moran and Mack.

"Water Power: We adhere to the policy of the Republican Party as heretofore declared in its platform. We oppose the sale or alienation of the State's interest in its water power resources. We favor those sound policies in the development of water power which will adequately protect the consumer. We favor the development of such resources under strict supervision and regulation by law and under full safeguards of the Constitution."

Who can make anything out of that? That does not mean a single thing. What they really did favor was a fifty-year lease; and in the month of December, 1926, before they went out of power they were all prepared to deliver a fifty-year lease to the Frontier Power Company, a subsidiary of the Aluminum Company of America.

The Republican candidate himself, Attorney-General Ottinger, a member of the Water Power Commission by virtue of his office as Attorney-General, examined the lease. He said it was all right, and that they ought to go through with it.

Mind you, they were in full control. I didn't have a thing to do with it — officially. All I had to do was to sit in the Capitol and dare them to do it. And at the last moment they weakened.

Now, they were either right or they were wrong. If they were right they should have driven straight through. And if they were wrong, they should never have started it. And no Attorney-General, protecting the people's right to these great water power resources, should have advised them as he did.

Well, who is the chief opponent, who is the master mind, who sat at the switchboard and plugged in the numbers against State ownership and control for ten years? The new Chairman of the Republican State Committee, who left a lucrative office in the Northeastern Power Company to become Chairman of the Republican State Committee. You can bid goodbye to any State development of water power in the event of Republican success. They will take it as a mandate from the people to lease it for fifty years to a private company.

I am going to step from this to a subject that I am only going to gloss over, because it would take an hour for me to explain it, and that is the general subject of the State's finances. I am going to dispose of the argument of the Republican Committee by their own platform. I am not going to say a word about it. I am going to put the platform in evidence and let the platform say it. Here is the way it works.

Under the heading of State Finances, they find fault with the increase in the cost of government, with the heavy burden that has been put upon the taxpayer, with the increase of the bonded indebtedness of the State.

Now, evidently, this plank was written in one place and the other plank I am going to read was written elsewhere, and they never compared them, because when you get down near the end of the platform they claim credit — for what? For reducing the income tax to 300,000 income taxpayers and they take the credit and demand the credit for reducing the direct State tax from two and a half mills to one-half mill. They are answered in their own platform. There has been no oppressive taxation.

" We, the Republican Party in convention assembled, claim the credit for reducing the taxes to the overburdened taxpayer of the State."

That is what they said in the last part.

And in the first part they said, " We condemn the extravagance of Smith." You cannot have it both ways. You can take your choice there. As the old man who ran the boarding house down in Far Rockaway years ago said, when all the boarders were seated at dinner one night, putting his head out through the little place where they used to hand out the food, " Remember, those that has puddin' can't have pie."

For as long back as I am able to remember, the Republican Party in every campaign makes a special appeal to the farmer. Oh, how they love him in October!

If the farmer could just paraphrase Jimmie Walker's celebrated melody and sing back to them, " Will you Love me in February, March and April as you do in October? "

The one thing that the agricultural interests of this State were interested in last winter in Albany was an appropriation to pay for the breaking down of the Federal census from counties into townships on questions of agricultural production. That is all the interest they had, $25,000. And the Republican Party, in the interest of economy, in the interest of protecting the poor taxpayer, in a budget of $245,000,000, saved that twenty-five and let the farmer go without the census.

One of the great questions in this State, not only for the farmer, but for people generally, is the slaughter of tubercular cattle. The last Republican administration made no appropriation for indemnities to the owners of slaughtered cattle, although the Attorney-General rendered an opinion that the Department of Farms and Markets under the law must proceed with the slaughter.

Consequently, when the Democratic administration came in on the first of January, 1923, not only had we our own program ahead of us, but we had what was left from the two years previous. Accordingly, in six years, we appropriated $20,000,000 as indemnities to the owners of slaughtered cattle. Republican neglect, plus our zeal to do a good, clean job in the matter of cleaning up the cattle herds of the State, meant that those twenty millions were added to the extravagance of the present administration.

You do not hear any of the men who are connected in Albany talking about any of this. They could not keep a straight face. Somebody writes these platforms, the Speakers' Bureau gets together and the orators are turned loose around the State. But the men who are on the inside do not speak about it, because they are afraid that they may be confronted with their responsibility if anything is wrong.

Education: The Republican Party boasts about its assistance to education, and in 1924 they tried one of the meanest tricks that the politics of this State has ever known, when the statement was put out that the Governor was endeavoring to get control of the Department of Education. It was exposed in an editorial in the *Syracuse Herald*, that was afterward printed in every newspaper in this State as a paid advertisement. You can charge the increased cost of government to three activities: The slaughter of cattle for tuberculosis, education, and the road system of the State.

Here are the facts. In 1918 the amount contributed by the State of New York to the various school localities for teachers' salaries was $7,033,555. Last year it was $70,000,000.

Now, let us see where this came from. Do not let the Republican Party have the nerve and the brass to claim credit for this appropriation for public education, because I not only recommended it, but had to fight for it.

Did you ever hear of the Friedsam Bills that came from the so-called Friedsam Committee in New York? They were rejected by the Republican Legislature, turned down. And then they tried to play a smart little trick. They withheld the appropriation, and then in the dying hours of the Legislature put a bill on the calendar increasing the salaries of the school teachers in New York, after refusing to make the money available. But the school teachers were too intelligent. You cannot do that in this State and get away with it. They have too much brains.

What about the rural school problem? We have been talking about that in Albany. I have recommended it eight times. I have sought to give to the children in the country sections in the State the same educational benefits that we give to the children in the cities, but I could get no Republican help with it.

Here we have a situation in this State where out of eleven million people, seven and a half million of them live in five cities, although we have thirty-five cities and a number of large villages. There is no doubt in my mind that the opportunity for a better education for the young has driven a number of people off the farms in the State.

This rural school question has been agitated for the last twelve years, but there it stands, and the Republican Party, the professed friend of the farmer and of education, has been entirely unwilling to do anything about it.

Take the question of the public health. Is it not difficult for you to conceive why anybody would be against doing something to promote the public health? What possible argument can anybody find for opposing anything like that? Yet it is a matter of record that for two years in succession the Republican leadership in the Legislature opposed State aid to the county in setting up county health centers.

They did it when? Only when there was an avalanche of public opinion against them that they were unable to explain.

Oh, every two years, that profession of love and devotion for the laboring man! Oh, how they love him in October of every even-numbered year. He certainly does come in then for his share of patting on the back. The labor plank this year claims credit for everything, even for the Workmen's Compensation Act that was signed by Martin H. Glynn.

The real fact of the matter is that they have done every human thing they could to cripple the Labor Department, to reduce its efficiency and to retard the operation of the Workmen's Compensation Division. In 1925, the first thing that came from the Senate was an Investigating Committee headed by Senator Whitley of Rochester. He went down to New York and made a searching investigation. He came back with the report and said that it was absolutely necessary, if this commission was going to function 100 per cent., that there be two more industrial commissioners and four or five more referees. Why? Because they amended the Workmen's Compensation Act to cut down the waiting period after accidents before compensation commenced. This added over 300,000 new cases to be considered in a year, and what happened? Why, they had a conference, and rather than let the Democratic Governor have the appointment of two people, they would sooner let the workingman wait another year.

Every two years in the off-year there is an attack made upon the Labor Department. In 1923 they used an organization of business men, and I immediately constituted myself a Moreland Commissioner under the Executive Law and sent for all the business men, and said, " What do you know about it," and not one of them knew anything about it.

And when we got all finished, not one of them had a word of complaint to make against the operation of the Labor Department. They started it right off the beginning of this year. Assemblyman Cornaire from Jefferson county said that there was graft and crookedness in the Department of Labor. Just like that. I stepped right on him and appointed Professor Lindsay Rogers of Columbia University a Moreland Commissioner under the Executive Law, and the minute his commission was signed he sent a man up with a subpoena, and he put it in the Assemblyman's hands and said, "Come down here and make that good." And when the Assemblyman came downstairs he said, "The newspaper men did not properly report what I said." He crawled out of it. And the rest of them shut up after that because that was a warning.

Taking the 48-hour law. Just look at the senseless battle that was made against that for eight years. And when they finally did pass it they worded it in such a way that instead of being a 48-hour law it is 49½ hours.

But why battle these things? Why keep putting them off and putting them off and putting them off? Must no odium follow the party that so conducts itself? Is it a wise thing for the people of this State to put the stamp of approval upon the political party that is responsible for that kind of a record? That is the big question. That is what the people of this State have got to think about this fall. Look out about the letter of recommendation that you give them. Be very careful. If that record can be approved by the electorate of this State, it will be the end of any constructive reform during probably the lifetime of a majority of the people that are in this hall tonight. If after eight years of that kind of conduct toward the State, the sovereignty is going into the ballot box and pat them on the back and say, "Well done, my good and noble servant; well done"— if you are going to do that, look out for what the future has in store.

In Rochester, N. Y., this crowd greeted Governor Smith on his way to the
Democratic State Convention

Child Welfare: There is great credit for this in the platform. We have boards of Child Welfare only in such counties where there is a strong local sentiment for their creation. The one thing that would make every county create them would be a State subsidy, so that the county that is not sufficiently interested in caring for orphan children to set up a commission of its own, would find they have to pay for the other commissions that are created. This is the quickest way to make them come into the tent; but could you do that? Not a chance — and no reason against it.

The State Board of Housing: When I suggested first a housing commission, Senator Knight got up on the floor of the Senate and said, "Smith is a Socialist." Well, that was in January, but by the month of March, when Senator Knight began to hear from the people in the big cities, he felt a little differently about it. He said, "Well, maybe he is only half a Socialist, so we will give him about half what he is looking for." But, unfortunately, the half that they retained was the carburetor. They gave me a perfectly good automobile called a State Housing Commission, but before they delivered it they removed the carburetor, and the carburetor in the State Housing plan was the State Land Bank. That was the thing that was to produce the money. That they denied. That they held to be socialistic. The rest of it they gave us. But they dare not go down to New York, or, for that matter, into any city in the State where this problem is understood and ask for a single bit of credit for it, because they do not deserve it.

Now we come to the subject that is near and dear to me, and that is the subject of our parks and parkways. I think the story of the parks and parkway development in the State of New York constitutes as interesting a story as anybody would want to listen to. Prior to 1923 we had no coordinated system of dealing with parks. They were spread out all over the State under commissions here and under trustees there and everybody in the Legislature scrambled around trying to do the best they could to get appropriations for their particular park. In 1923, at my suggestion, we set up a State Council of Parks to supervise appropriations and repair and maintenance work throughout the whole system. In 1924 there was submitted to the people a referendum for $15,000,000 for parks and parkways. In 1923 and 1924 there was appropriated each year $1,000,000 for the purchase of parkways, direct from current revenue. The $15,000,000 was a bond issue.

Everything went along swimmingly. You never heard anything from the Allegany Park region. There was no complaint in the Taconic section; there was nothing as to Westchester county; there was nothing up in Erie, or up at Niagara Falls, nor in the Adirondacks, nor in the Catskill preserves. Everything was going along nicely until the Long Island Park Commission put its eye on a piece of property that could be purchased for $250,000, called the Taylor Estate.

Nobody knew that property could be bought for that price until we went in to buy it, and just as soon as we did a group of young selfish millionaires made up their minds to get it, and they talked the owners out of selling it to the State and said they would give $250,000 for it. I said, " No; you will not do anything of the kind, because we will take it away from you by the right of eminent domain." And down at the County Fair in Dutchess county, in the city of Poughkeepsie, I signed the paper in the month of September. Then there began litigation, fought all the way to the Court of Appeals. The Republican Chairman of the County Committee of Suffolk county made up his mind that he would defeat the State. I went down there to see him and I told him, " You will never beat the State of New York. We will beat you to the ground with all your money."

The issue was finally decided only in the spring of this year by the Court of Appeals, and I had the pleasure of dropping in there this summer to see thousands of people with lunch baskets and with picnic boxes getting the advantages of one of the finest parks there is today on Long Island.

Let me tell you how far the Republican Party went in its effort to defeat the State — to defeat the statute. They postponed for one year, for one solid year, every appropriation from the bond issue that the people in this State ordered in the popular election by over a million plurality. They allowed one solid year to pass without appropriating a single dollar in order to defeat the taking of the Taylor estate in the interest of a small handful of men. And here is the young man who engineered it all, Mr. W. Kingsland Macy, who is the Vice-Assistant Chairman of the Hoover-Curtis Campaign Committee. And they had at all times the assistance of the Attorney-General, now the candidate for Governor. He went out of his way to help the little group of millionaires. Without a bit of knowledge of it at all, he had the nerve to stand up and declare that the Taylor estate offered to the people of the State of New York for $250,000 was worth $400,000, and, therefore, in his opinion, sufficient money was not appropriated for it and that condemnation proceedings could not be legally taken.

Let me give the credit where the credit belongs. Mr. August Heckscher — I called him up on the 'phone and I said to him, " I want $250,000 from you to buy a park."

I told him the story, just what happened down there, and he said, " Let the park authorities come and see me." They went down to see him, and he said, "All right, the money is down in the Empire Trust Company when you want it."

Wait till I read the platform plank this year on parks, after that performance. Listen to this for a minute. It is very short — six lines. They deal with it in six lines. And they say: " For the promotion of the health and recreational interests of the people, we pledge the Republican Party to the continued development and extension of our parks and parkways throughout the State."

Now, I challenge that plank and I make the assertion now, and I will prove it, that they are standing in the way now of the Northern Parkway System to link up the Southern Parkway with the Jones Beach Reservation and Heckscher Park. They are standing in the way of it tonight, and I challenge Hewitt and Hutchinson to come out and say that they are ready to sign the allotment of money.

I looked very carefully through the platform and I was looking for a plank that might say something about the Eighteenth Amendment or the Volstead Act. But we are in a great national campaign and they are quiet this year.

We might as well have a consistent record; we have double dealt, we have double crossed, we have hedged and hedged, and one more year won't do us very much harm. We will take a chance.

I said to a Republican Senator in Albany on one occasion: "Senator, why does the Assembly go through the empty performance of passing an enforcement bill every year when they know the Senate is not going to pass it?" He said, "Well, you know, Al, you have now and then got to make a little gesture for the ladies." Reducing this to ordinary parlance, "It is occasionally necessary to string people."

They might at least have said, "We endorse the sentiment of the Republican candidate for President when he said that the Eighteenth Amendment is a noble experiment."

Now, let me call your attention to something else in the platform. In 1926 the State took over the town bridges that were formerly the property of the townships where they appeared on trunk line highways.

This year they say: "The Republican Legislature first provided for the payment by the State of the cost of construction of bridges on State highways. It has made ample provision for this purpose. Thus far the Democratic administration has deferred and delayed making these appropriations effective." That statement is absolutely and unqualifiedly false.

Here are the facts. Every cent of the $3,000,000 made available in 1927 was expended in that year. The work was progressed within the calendar year. That can be ascertained from the records of the office of the State Comptroller.

This year 325 contracts have been let to date, and we have actually obligated ourselves even beyond the $3,000,000. So that that statement in the Republican platform is absolutely false, and I challenge them to make it good. I defy them to make it good. They can't do it.

Here is another false statement in the platform: Speaking about $500,000 that was appropriated for outside architectural services. This State of New York suffered for twenty years from Republican neglect of our State institutions and necessary State buildings. And when we finally started to catch up after the neglect, absolutely the office of State Architect was flooded. No one single man, even if he were a superman, could begin to take into his office the burden that these bond issues put upon the State Architect. What happened? I called a meeting of the Building and Sites Commission. The Building and Sites Commission has three Democrats and four Republicans on it: The Speaker of the Assembly, the President pro tem of the Senate, Chairman of the Finance Committee, and the Chairman of Ways and Means Committee. And I put this proposition up to them and they absolutely agreed to it. Where did the $500,000 come from? It had to be appropriated by the Republican Legislature. They sat down and agreed to it.

And now in the platform. Wait till I see what they say about it. "More than a score of architects outside of the State, mostly on a fee basis —" Why, certainly, on a fee basis. Joe McGinnies knows that. So does John Knight. So does Eberly Hutchinson. They sat down there and even talked the fee with me. I told them I thought I could appeal to some of the big architects in this State to work for the State for 4 per cent., although the ordinary fee is 6 per cent. They all said, "If you can get it done for that, go ahead. We will put up the money." We got it for 4 per cent. and they knew all about it.

That whole platform plank and what young Mr. Davison, the spokesman of the millionaire blockade group for the Long Island parks, said about this is absolutely false and absolutely wrong. I defy them to make it good. I dare them to even try it.

Now, who is to carry through these great reforms in the government of the State, the party that fought for them and that labored for them, or the party that fought against them and did everything humanly possible to defeat them?

Nothing will be more regretful than to let the record I have laid out before you tonight get the approval of the people of the most populous State in the Union. It would in effect be saying to a political party, "Go ahead, it makes very little difference to the rank and file of the people where you stand on anything; take any kind of position you like and when the time comes, by the force of numbers, we will send you back into office."

This is what it means: It means what Senator Moses of New Hampshire, the permanent Chairman of the Kansas City Convention, said: "Because there are five million more Republicans in this country than there are Democrats, we defy you. Bring on your candidate and we will bury him. We do not care whether his name is Brown, Jones, Robinson or Smith."

This is the attitude of the Republican Party in this State: "We have opposed these things; we do not believe in them; they interfere with members of our party and we are in defiance of you; you have to put us back because there are so many more Republicans than there are Democrats."

Now, it is up to the people of the State. This record of progress can be continued — how? By the election of the candidates that come out of this convention. Irreparable injury can come to the State by any other course, and I earnestly hope and pray that the result on the 6th of November will be a vindication of progressive, Democratic policies and a repudiation of Republican, stand-pat, reactionary policies.

IX

ADDRESS AT NASHVILLE

Nashville, Tennessee, October 12, 1928

SINCE early Thursday morning of this week I have been traveling through our Southland. Campaigning is no new thing with me, but I can say honestly and sincerely that in all of the years that I have been conducting campaigns I have never received a more hearty, or, I might even say, a more affectionate welcome than I have received from the people in the South. At every railroad station and at every large city I have been greeted with an enthusiasm that gives me a new confidence in the righteousness of the cause that I am fighting for.

In accordance with the program of the National Committee, my next speech is to be at Louisville, Ky. I was to pass through the State of Tennessee, but I did not feel like leaving the State that gave to the nation that great leader of Democracy, Andrew Jackson, without saying something in appreciation of the warm welcome that I have received.

In Omaha, a little over three weeks ago, with a national radio hookup, I outlined the Democratic attitude on farm relief. I contrasted the platforms of the two parties, and the speeches of acceptance of the two candidates, and I definitely impressed upon the people that a speedy constructive program of farm relief could only come from the Democratic Party.

Republican orators, the Republican National Committee and, for that matter, the Republican candidate himself, have been very hard pressed to answer my Omaha speech on farm relief.

CAMPAIGN ADDRESS

Senator Curtis, the candidate for Vice-President of the Republican ticket, takes a chance with it, and in his speech at St. Paul he says:

" Tariff protection on farm products is an important means by which to relieve the present depression in agriculture and to place the farmer in a position of economic equality with our other industries."

The Senator keeps repeating that, with the hope that if he says it often enough, somebody will begin to believe it. He knows as well as I do that the tariff standing by itself is not the remedy for the present depressed condition in agriculture. That he recognizes this to be the fact is shown by another sentence from his same speech when he says:

" But in considering tariff rates as a means for improving the problems of agriculture, the danger of undue reliance on the effectiveness of this method must be avoided."

What does he mean by that? Since when has he discovered that? The Republican Party four years ago promised measures that would put agriculture on an economic equality with industry. It is a matter of history that nothing was done to carry out that promise for four long years. For that reason we see the same promise repeated in this year's platform, word for word, sentence for sentence; and at the end of four years Senator Curtis volunteers the information that we must not put undue reliance upon the effectiveness of the tariff.

That is not in keeping with the candidate of his party, Mr. Hoover, who distinctly says in his speech of acceptance that the tariff is the foundation of farm relief.

Senator Curtis knows what the farmer needs. One method calculated to bring about economic equality with industry was suggested in the form of a legislative enactment. Senator Curtis voted for it when it was before the Senate and voted against it after it was vetoed by the President. In other words, he was with the farmer one day and against him the next. He could not have been right both times. He, above all men, is in no position to promote the interest of the candidate of his party, because his own record of farm relief does not stand the test.

The Republican candidate for President, speaking in Tennessee a short time ago, spoke about the far-reaching and specific proposal made by his political party on behalf of the farmers. I read the speech carefully, and I failed to see wherein he makes any definite suggestions to meet the difficulties that the farmer and the cotton grower must overcome in order to share in the general prosperity that the Republican Party claims to have brought to the country.

He repeats the language of his speech of acceptance about farmer-owned and farmer-controlled stabilization corporations intended, as he claims, to protect the farmer from depressions and demoralization of summer and periodic surpluses; and, while he definitely says that he does not propose a subsidy or a fee or a tax upon the farmer, he speaks about clothing the Federal Farm Board with power and resources with which to back up farmers' cooperatives. No mention is made by him of what the resources are.

No proposal is made that is to allow for not only the periodical and the summer surpluses but the annual surpluses in crop, which, being in excess of domestic consumption and offered in a domestic market, fix the price of the whole crop. He fails to understand that the great fundamental principle of control of the exportable surplus is the prime solution of the problem.

This great principle is lost sight of, not only in the plan advanced by the candidate, but in the platform of the Republican Party; and he, in turn, following the lead of Senator Curtis, repeats the time-worn language of economic equality as between agriculture and industry. If that means anything, to my way of thinking, it means making effective the tariff for agriculture as it is effective for industry. That can only be done by control of the exportable surplus; and unless the cost of disposing of that surplus is charged back upon the crops benefited the Republican candidate cannot in truth say that there is to be no subsidy, no fee or no tax upon the farmer.

Never in the history of political campaigning has an issue been as closely drawn as the one affecting farm relief. The Democratic Party in its platform and myself in my speech of acceptance have definitely laid down, first, the recognition of the principle, and second, the promise to work out the mechanics necessary to carry it into effect.

On the other hand, neither in its platform nor in the speech of acceptance of its candidate, nor in anything that the Republican orators have so far said, does the Republican Party suggest even the basis of a plan calculated to bring about the necessary relief, and the farmers of the country must look to the Democratic Party if they are to be relieved from some of the burdens of the situation in which they find themselves.

Let me quote the Republican President on the farm question. Speaking about it in his message to Congress in 1926, he referred to the burden of debts and taxes resting upon the shoulders of the farmer, too heavy for him to carry, and concluded by saying:

"If a sound solution of a permanent nature can be found for this problem the Congress ought not to hesitate to adopt it."

Congress sought and offered to the President a solution. Senator Curtis originally voted for it. The President vetoed it, and it is a matter of history and record that he offered nothing in its place, although he admitted in the same message that the subject was given more attention by the Federal Government than was given to any other subject.

The Republican candidate, known to be the President's chief adviser upon this subject, in one part of his speech of acceptance approves of the Coolidge policies and in another part proposes farm relief; and in Tennessee he said:

" We must continue our endeavor to restore economic equality to those farm families who have lagged behind in the march of progress."

If the endeavors of the past are continued as promised by Mr. Hoover, the farmer has nothing to hope for. I know if I were a farmer that is the way I would be compelled to take it, unless I were ready to admit that I have no understanding of the English language.

There is no question of such far-reaching importance to the people of this country today as the development of electrical energy from falling water, commonly referred to as water power. It is the last of our great natural resources and it is threatened with invasion at the hands of the power trust and private monopoly that would use it for private profit and for private gain. Early in this campaign I spoke about talking plainly to the people. In my speech at Denver some two weeks ago I made a definite, clean-cut, concise declaration of what I believe to be the proper public policy with regard to the development of public water powers.

I said that they should be developed by the government if under government control, by a State if under State control, or by a group of states if under such control. I have been patiently waiting, as must also be the people of the country, for a declaration from the Republican candidate of just where he stands with regard to the ownership of the great publicly-owned water powers of the country.

I believed and had the right to expect that, speaking in Tennessee, a State to be greatly benefited by public operation and control of Muscle Shoals, he would say something upon the subject that would give the American people an understanding of his attitude. To my great surprise he did not even mention Muscle Shoals, but contented himself with the following general observation:

" There are local instances where the government must enter the business field as a by-product of some great major purpose such as improvement in navigation, flood control, scientific research or national defense."

I do not know what he can mean by " by-product," unless it is the generation of hydro-electric energy.

In another part of the speech he said that violations of public interest by individuals or corporations should not induce us to abandon progressive principles and substitute in their place deadly and destructive doctrines.

I would like to know what Mr. Hoover means by " deadly and destructive doctrines." Does he refer to government ownership and control of water power sites? If so, why not say it? What is to be gained by clothing it in language that the man on the street is unable to understand?

Is public ownership and public development of water power deadly? Is it a destructive doctrine? If so, why not let Mr. Hoover come right out and say, " I believe in leasing or in selling or in disposing of, to private corporations for private development and for private profit, the great water power resources that belong to all the people?"

That would define the issue. But why evade it? Why conceal it behind a wall of high-sounding phrases that leave in the minds of so many thousands of our people the element of doubt as to his exact position on this issue?

Mr. Hoover found that his reference to this problem was considered to be so vague and ambiguous that he subsequently felt obliged to issue two statements regarding Muscle Shoals and, if anything at all happened, his position became more involved than ever.

I have clearly defined my attitude. It will be found in my speech of acceptance.

So far as Muscle Shoals is concerned, I said in my speech at Denver that I believe that the government should continue the full and complete development of that plant, retaining it under government ownership, operation and control. While it is true that it was a war measure and its purpose was to produce nitrates for explosives, the by-product of electrical energy can be used to promote industry and give cheap and reasonable rates for home, small store and farm consumption.

The Republican candidate for President has promised to follow the Coolidge policy. That policy is best set forth in his message to the Sixty-ninth Congress in 1925, when he said:

" The problem of Muscle Shoals seems to me to have assumed a place out of all proportion with its real importance. It probably does not represent in market value much more than a first-class battleship, yet it has been discussed in Congress over a period of years and for months at a time."

Let me add, "and disposed of by Congress." But the disposition, being favorable to the rank and file of the people, met with executive veto, and with that policy Mr. Hoover says he agrees.

As against that, I promise the completion of the development under government ownership and control, which would reclaim to the government some fair revenue from the enormous expenditure already made for its improvement. When completed, the nation will be reimbursed, agriculture will receive the benefit of cheap nitrate production for fertilizer purposes and the surplus water power can be distributed fairly to the people of the ten states which this plant could serve at rates which should remain under the control of the government and be fair and equitable.

The people of the country have their choice between my clear, clean-cut policy and the clear, clean-cut, straightforward policy of the Democratic platform, and the evasion, ducking and dodging of the Republican platform and the Republican candidate.

While I have the Republican candidate's speech before me, let me nail down hard and fast an old-time Republican campaign trick. Mr. Hoover says:

" I do not favor an increase in immigration."

Let me say, most emphatically, neither do I and neither does the Democratic platform.

He says: "At the same time we must humanize the laws but only within the present quotas." That is exactly what I say, and is exactly what the Democratic platform says. What is the necessity for the Republican candidate making that statement? Nobody disagrees with him.

Reading further in the speech of Mr. Hoover I find that he says:

"The purpose of the Eighteenth Amendment is to protect the American home."

In his speech of acceptance he said that he looked back with satisfaction over the Republican record during the last seven and a half years.

In view of that record, can he conscientiously say that the Republican administration has so enforced the Eighteenth Amendment as to make it any degree whatever of protection to the home?

The Republican Party has made prohibition the football of politics. A former Republican enforcement agent referred to it as the new political pork barrel. Graft, corruption, bribery, on a large scale, have been the history of attempted enforcement under Republican auspices. The record shows that we have never had prohibition in this country in the sense that hard liquor was banished from it. There is as much, if not more, liquor in this country today than there was in the pre-prohibition days. We have not achieved temperance under the present system. On the contrary, the widespread disregard of the Prohibition Law is today undermining respect for all law.

The Republican candidate himself admits the abuses that have grown up around it; but instead of suggesting a remedy, which he is either unwilling or unable to do, he expresses just the faint hope for its future success.

AT NASHVILLE

I have definite ideas about the Eighteenth Amendment and the Volstead Law and, as a husband and a father, I have as much interest in protecting the American home as any man in the United States. I ask that the prohibition question be treated in accordance with the Jeffersonian theory of states' rights. This great section of the country through which I have been traveling for the last two days during all of its history has been devoted to the Jeffersonian principle of states' rights. Why not apply it to this question? I think you must admit the great difficulty of securing co-operation from the rank and file of our people for a reasonable, fair and just enforcement of the Prohibition Law when large numbers of the people of so many states are out of tune and out of sympathy with the law.

If you have any doubt about this consult the popular referendums that have been had in so many states that stand in opposition to the existing prohibition statutes, and ask yourselves this question: What would you or the people of any dry State think about a proposal to amend the Constitution to forbid you to enact prohibition laws? You would resent any such proposal, and justly so. That is just the way the people of other states feel about the Eighteenth Amendment in its present form.

In my speech of acceptance I laid down a clear, definite program. In the first place I said that I do not believe the present definition of what constitutes an intoxicant is an honest one. I simply ask that Congress, after proper advice and after proper medical and scientific research, provide a definition of an intoxicant more in keeping with the fact and the truth. I firmly feel that a great deal of the poisonous hard liquor that we now have in this country would be driven out of existence if people who desired to do so would, under appropriate restrictions, be permitted to use beverages not in fact intoxicating.

In the second place, I said that I personally believed in an amendment to the Eighteenth Amendment, which would give to each individual State itself, after approval by a referendum popular vote of its people, the right wholly within its borders to import, manufacture or cause to be manufactured, and sell alcoholic beverages, the sale to be made only by the State itself and not for consumption in any public place. That would mean that it would be impossible to return to the old conditions of the saloon, despised, and rightly so by the American people.

Such an amendment would permit a dry State to be as dry as it liked. It would preserve for the dry states all the benefit now growing from national prohibition and would give them the benefit of a national law on the subject.

It would always remain the duty of the Federal Government, under my proposal, to protect states desiring to remain dry from the introduction or importation into them of alcoholic beverages. At the same time is would permit a State which, after a vote of its people, did not wish to be dry, to dispense alcoholic beverages under the strict control and limitations that I have outlined.

If that is not good, old fashioned honest democracy, if that is not in keeping with the Jeffersonian theory and principle of State's rights, then I do not understand what those words mean. I stated in my speech of acceptance that with respect to prohibition the President had two duties imposed upon him by the Constitution. First, to recommend to Congress what in his opinion would promote the best interests and the welfare of the country. I have indicated briefly here to-night, and more fully in my speech of acceptance and in my speech at Milwaukee, the recommendations that I propose to make to the Congress on the subject of national prohibition.

The second duty imposed upon the President is to enforce the law as he finds it. When I told the American people that if I were elected President and, with one hand on the Bible and the other hand reaching up to Heaven, I promised that I would faithfully execute the office of President of the United States and to the best of my ability preserve, protect and defend the Constitution of the United States, you may take my word for it that I shall make that assurance good, and shall wipe out the corruption and the bribery that have been so widespread in connection with prohibition enforcement during the last seven and a half years of Republican administration.

I am glad to be with you tonight and pleased to have this opportunity to talk to you. On the few issues that I could touch upon I have talked plainly. That was my purpose in the beginning of the campaign. That is what I have been trying to get my opponent to do, upon the theory that when the American people make their decision they will make it with the full knowledge of all the facts. And if that kind of a campaign can be conducted throughout the length and breadth of this land, I have not in my mind any doubt that the Democratic Party on the sixth of November will ride to a great national victory.

X

ADDRESS AT LOUISVILLE

Louisville, Kentucky, October 13, 1928

TO my personal knowledge, the Republican Party for thirty-five years, lacking an issue and unable to defend its past performances, has always fallen back upon the familiar cry of Republican prosperity, claiming credit for prosperous business conditions and attempting to saddle upon the Democratic Party all blame for industrial depression and business conditions over which no political party could exercise any control. Running true to form, they are today making dire predictions as to what will happen to the country in the event of Democratic victory.

If the American people will think back over history, they will find financial panics and business depressions have been as frequent in Republican administrations as they have been in Democratic administrations. If in the administration of Grover Cleveland the country passed through some trying moments, it must be borne in mind that the crash came too soon after inauguration to be recognized as anything else than a heritage from President Harrison. A panic occurred in the administration of President Roosevelt in 1907, three years after his election. The fact is that the most effective guaranty against panics ever enacted by law was the Federal Reserve Act, passed in the Wilson administration, which the present Republican Secretary of the Treasury acknowledges "gave to the country the soundest financial structure in its history" and "is one of the most important factors in the effort toward world stabilization."

Incidentally, let me say that the Republicans gave but little encouragement to this great measure. When it came up in the

Senate originally for passage, only three Republican Senators voted for it and but one came from a State east of the Mississippi.

The Republican Party seems to be unable to avoid the temptation to misrepresent this condition. There was no business depression in the first four years of the administration of President Wilson. The fact is, business was sufficiently prosperous to warrant the American people in re-electing President Wilson.

The long history of the Republican Party discloses that its tariff argument is used to cover a multitude of sins. When presented with any other great issue the Republican Party does not seriously stress the tariff. Let us look at the tariff plank of the Republican platform in 1920. It contains but seven lines, and it refers to the time-worn expression of protection to American industry as though that were something that belonged exclusively to the Republican Party.

Four years later, however, there is an entirely different story to tell. Looking for a campaign issue and in an endeavor to smoke-screen the black record from 1920 to 1924, we find whole pages of the Republican platform devoted to the plank on tariff. In 1928 we find them again claiming credit for business prosperity beyond a point where it would be possible for any political party to claim the credit for it. Pages of the platform are again devoted to the subject of the tariff, and the old-time bugaboo is again resurrected in an attempt to scare business men and workingmen generally and to threaten dire results to the country and its business prosperity in the event of Democratic success.

The old gentleman with his Prince Albert coat, symbolizing the G. O. P., is found in the garret of the Republican household shining up the old " full dinner pail " and acting as though in the last thirty-five years the American people have gained no knowledge upon this subject and contenting himself with the belief that the American public continues to pay attention to the fallacy that Democratic success means general business depression.

The Republican Party and the Republican candidate would have us believe that the fact that we have a comparatively high level of wages in industry today is the barometer of prosperity in this country. This I deny and I take the Republican candidate's word for it when in his speech of acceptance he said:

"Although the agricultural, coal and textile industries still lag in their recovery and still require our solicitude and assistance, they have made substantial progress."

What is the progress and where has it been noted? Certainly not in agriculture if the Republican platform is right, because it recognizes the dire distress of our citizens engaged in that industry, incidentally, one-third of the whole population of the United States. The Republican slogan "no Republican tariff ever mortgaged a farm" does not make much of a hit in the corn belt and in the wheat country.

The textile industries are in straightened financial circumstances, and it is rumored that the proposed speech of the Republican candidate in the city of Boston is intended as an attempt to comfort those engaged in that industry in the New England states.

Whatever may be our wealth in spots, nobody can claim with any degree of justice that our whole people are passing through a great period of prosperity when a debate in the Senate last winter brought to the front a statement not successfully challenged or contradicted that four million men out of work, representing with their dependents upward of fifteen million people, were suffering distress because of unemployment.

Certainly nobody can say that we are passing through a period of wonderful prosperity when there is recorded 830 bank failures last year, with total liabilities of over $270,-000,000, almost entirely in the agricultural regions, as compared with forty-nine such failures during the last year of the Wilson administration, and when ruined farm people are being driven from their homes at the rate of about one million per annum.

The Republican Party struggles hard to make us believe that they are entitled to the credit for the new standard of American wages and American living conditions. It requires but the exercise of ordinary common sense to know that this standard of wages and of living conditions was fixed during the war and during the administration of President Wilson.

In the first place, the war meant a cessation of immigration. That naturally narrowed the American labor market. In the second place, the war paralyzed foreign competition and that left a free field for American production. From both conditions there grew a new American prosperity and an unexpected enlargement of our domestic market. In the meantime, the prosperity of the rest of the world vanished.

The result was that the whole American economic structure during the Wilson administration was raised to a new plane of prosperity and created a marked difference between American standards of living and American wages and those of other countries.

To preserve this American standard against ruinous inflow from the depressed world two things were necessary: First, a restriction upon immigration and, second, a tariff sufficiently high to protect American industry and American labor from the starvation wages of less fortunate countries. This new standard was created under Wilson and the Republican Party had absolutely nothing to do with it, and no person in possession of his natural faculties would believe for a moment that by any act the Democratic Party would attempt to tear down these standards.

On the other hand, while the Republicans offer nothing to safeguard or increase future prosperity, the Democratic Party is pledged to a policy to restore farm-buying power. This hope of an addition to our markets of such an "increased" domestic demand is the most hopeful sign in the business sky.

Of course it is not surprising that in September and October, in the midst of a national campaign, the Republican campaign managers should claim credit for what prosperity there exists in this country. However, in June, 1928, President Coolidge, the leader of the Republican Party, in addressing a meeting of government officials, made no such claim. He is reported in the seventh annual report of the Director of the Bureau of the Budget to have said:

"It would be unfortunate if out of these discussions the impression should be gained that it is the obligation of the government to furnish the people with prosperity. They are entitled," the President said, "to such an administration of their affairs as will give them every fair opportunity, but if there was to be prosperity they must furnish it themselves."

Naturally, the Republican Party attempts to link prosperity to the tariff with the hope that they may create alarm in the business world by forecasting imaginary reductions of the tariff following Democratic success and by appealing for support to special and favored interests that might improperly benefit by an increase in some of the tariff schedules.

Let us briefly review the history of tariff legislation in the past, and I am satisfied that it will demonstrate the insincerity of the Republican position on this question. Every person who has given thought to the subject knows how unsatisfactory has been the method of both political parties in the past in dealing with this important problem.

No tariff bills found their way into the statute books of the country as the result of fair, impartial and scientific inquiry. No tariff bill has ever been produced as a result of a report of an impartial fact-finding body. The tariff has been in politics and tariff bills have uniformly been the result of what we call legislative log-rolling. Special interests represented at Washington have been in a position to write their own schedules.

The final product has been a compromise and clearly indicates that even the most conscientious members of Congress were without the necessary information on which to pass an intelligent, business-like tariff measure.

One of the leading authorities on the tariff in this country, Prof. F. W. Taussig, of Harvard University, former chairman of the United States Tariff Commission, speaking of the traditional method of framing tariff legislation, said:

" Influential persons could ' fix ' legislation and work jokers in and eventually bring into effect provisions which could not be said to be intended by Congress or by anyone except an occasional conniving member of Congress. Our tariffs have been settled in ignorant and irresponsible fashion. Of this we have become painfully aware."

Complaint of tariff bills was so pronounced that the progressive members of both political parties twenty years ago recommended that there be some scientific basis for tariff legislation and sought means by which the facts necessary for the information of Congress on this subject might be procured by an impartial fact-finding body.

As far back as 1909 several bills for the creation of such a commission were introduced in the National Congress but went to death in committee. Under a clause of the tariff act of 1909 the President was given the power to appoint a board to advise him with respect to foreign tariffs discriminating against American products. Under this provision President Taft appointed a board made up of three Republicans.

The following year there was proposed a bill to establish a bi-partisan commission to deal generally with the tariff but it was killed in a filibuster on the last day of the session, it being noted at the time that a majority of Congress actually approved it. When I say that it was lost in a filibuster that means that it was beaten by indirection and not on its merits.

Notwithstanding its defeat, the President added two Democratic members to the existing tariff board to the end that he might carry out what he regarded as the intent of Congress.

In a message to Congress on December 7, 1909, referring to his authority to appoint a Tariff Board, President Taft said:

" I believe the work of this board to be of prime utility and importance whenever Congress shall deem it wise again to readjust the custom duties. Nothing halts business and interferes with the growth of prosperity so much as the threatened revision of the tariff, and until the facts are at hand, after careful and deliberate investigation, upon which such revision can properly be undertaken, it seems to me unwise to attempt it. The amount of misinformation that creeps into arguments pro and con in respect to tariff rates is such as to require the kind of investigation that I have directed the Tariff Board to make."

Again he emphasized the necessity for a tariff commission in an address at Portland, Ore., on October 2, 1909, in which he said:

" You hear a great deal about the tariff, but I would like to have you take up a tariff bill and go through it and then tell me what it means. Why, it is just like so much Choctaw to a man who is not an expert."

It will be readily understood that this expression from President Taft did not indicate on his part a great deal of respect for the common sense of the average tariff bill. I have taken occasion to look up his reference to Choctaw and find that it is one of the largest Indian tribes with a most difficult language.

It is a matter of history that President Taft was unable to cope with the leaders of his own party in carrying out the principle of fact finding by a tariff commission before the passage of a general tariff. He was astounded when he found how unpopular was the Payne-Aldridge Bill, accepted by him, and not based upon any reliable information such as could be furnished by a tariff commission.

The bi-partisan board named by President Taft went out of existence in 1912 when a Democratic Congress failed to make an appropriation for its continuance. The staff of the board and in effect its duties were transferred to a bureau created in the Department of Commerce and known as the Bureau of Foreign and Domestic Commerce.

The abolition of the tariff board as an independent agency of the government was, to my way of thinking, a mistake. This mistake, however, was later rectified when in 1916 there was created under the administration of President Wilson a permanent tariff commission. The creation of this commission received considerable support in business circles, and was strongly urged by the United States Chamber of Commerce.

The commission as appointed consisted of six members named by the President by and with the advice and consent of the Senate. The original members were to serve for overlapping terms and thereafter for terms of twelve years each and to receive a salary of $7,500 a year. Not more than three of the members were to belong to the same political party. Each member was to give substantially his entire time to the work.

The permanent tariff commission created under the act of 1916 held out to the people of this country the hope that the ambitions and ideals of Taft and Wilson would be carried out. Under President Harding, however, the Tariff Commission was paralyzed, rendered useless and relegated to a back seat when the Republican administration decided again to put the tariff into politics and enacted the Fordney-McCumber Tariff Bill, under the old worn-out method of log-rolling and star chamber proceedings.

It is a matter of record that the representatives of special interests paraded through the lobbies of the national capitol and secured for those whom they represented tariff schedules that they desired, enacted largely in return for campaign contributions — the pre-election slogan being — small favors thankfully received, larger ones with a proportionate amount of gratitude.

I could offer a great deal of evidence to back up what I just said. Let it be sufficient for me to refer to Dr. William Starr Myers, professor of politics of Princeton University, himself a Republican, writing the history of his own party when he said:

" The Fordney-McCumber tariff was worked out in a spirit of log-rolling that was anything but edifying to the country. It required a long and bitter fight before this piece of legislation finally passed the two houses of Congress and was signed by President Harding on September 21, 1922. It stands as one of the most ill-drawn pieces of legislation in recent political history. It is probably near the actual truth to say that, taking for granted some principle of protection of American business and industry, the country has prospered due to post-war conditions abroad and in spite of rather than on account of, the Fordney-McCumber tariff. Mr. Fordney himself was of the vintage of the Republican campaign textbook for 1888 and apparently had learned nothing and forgotten nothing since that time."

Later on in the campaign, if time permits it, I will go into detail regarding the treatment accorded to the Tariff Commission under the Republican administrations of the last seven and half years.

As indicating clearly what President Coolidge's attitude was to this important agency of the government, I shall refer to one of the Democratic members, David J. Lewis, of Maryland. In his case President Coolidge went so far as to ask that a letter of resignation be left with him before he would reappoint Mr. Lewis on the commission.

The record shows this Mr. Culbertson, Republican member of the commission, had an interview with the President. He says:

" I received a request over the telephone to come to the

White House to see the President. I went over immediately. The President was reasonably cordial. The President stated he intended to reappoint Mr. Lewis, but that he desired Mr. Lewis to prepare and give to him a letter of resignation as a member of the Tariff Commission. At first I did not fully comprehended the nature of the request. I spoke of Mr. Lewis's term having already expired — then the President explained that he wanted Mr. Lewis to submit his resignation under the new commission, to be effective in case he (the President) desired at any time in the future to accept it. The President then handed me a sheet of White House paper so that I would take down the tenor of the letter which he wished Mr. Lewis to write. I wrote down the following words, 'I hereby resign as a member of the Tariff Commission to take effect upon your acceptance.'"

When Mr. Culbertson explained this situation to Mr. Lewis, the latter was surprised and indignant. Mr. Lewis, in his testimony before the Senate committee investigating the Tariff Commission, then said:

"As I entered the office of the President he greeted me cordially and said in his quiet way: 'Mr. Lewis, I am going to reappoint you.' As he said that he reached over on his desk for a large paper, which turned out to be the commission, and was proceeding to sign it. So far as I can judge, when he had gotten about half way through the signature, he asked me: 'Did you bring that letter with you?' Referring to the letter of resignation. I said: 'No, Mr. President. From such consideration as I have been able to give to the matter, I do not feel free to sign such a letter.' He stopped momentarily and seemed much displeased and then resumed the signature, saying: 'Well, it does not matter; you will hold office only at my pleasure in any event.' Noticing his disappointment, I said: 'Mr. President, perhaps if you were to hear the considerations which determined me to this conclusion, you might agree with my point of view.'

"He said: 'Oh, no, I would not.' By this time the paper was finished and he pushed it over toward my position near the desk. Compelled to notice his continued displeasure, I said: ' Well, now, Mr. President, you and I are the only men in the world who know that paper has been signed. Just destroy it. I do not want to be unfair or dishonorable with you. Just destroy it.' He said: ' Oh, no, I won't do that. I had no present intention or thought of using it at all. My only idea was that if a separation became necessary between us it might be accomplished more pleasantly in this way.' "

The President did not send Mr. Lewis's name to the Senate for confirmation and consequently his recess appointment expired on March 4, 1925, when Congress adjourned.

In connection with this treatment of Commissioner Lewis by President Coolidge, it is worth while to quote what Dr. Thomas Walker Page, chairman of the Tariff Commission, under Presidents Wilson and Harding, and chairman of the Institute of Economics at Washington, says as to how a tariff commission ought to function:

" For accomplishing any effective reform the maintenance of a permanent tariff commission is indispensable. It is absolutely essential that a tariff commission should carry out its work without prejudice. Nothing can so completely destroy the usefulness of such an agency as the taint of favoritism or partiality or political bias."

The best proof of the utter neglect of the Tariff Commission by the Republican Administration is that under pretense of economy their appropriations were reduced to a point where they were compelled to stop a great many of their studies.

The Republican Party so successfully buried every hope offered by the Tariff Commission recommended by their own President Taft that the Republican platform of 1928 contains not one single word about the Tariff Commission. From a Republican point of view it is dead and gone, and it would be interesting to ask the Republican candidate if he views that performance with satisfaction. In his speech of acceptance he makes no mention of it. Is that performance on the part of the Republican Party a part of the record of the last seven and a half years that he praises and looks back upon with great satisfaction? Nobody can answer that but himself. It will not do to pass that on to Dr. Work or Secretary Jardine.

Running true to form the Republican Party in the present campaign is grossly misrepresenting the Democratic attitude to the question of tariff. I predicted that there would be an attempt made to distort my attitude, and I have lived to see the prediction realized. In the course of one of his speeches the Secretary of Agriculture, Mr. Jardine, is reported in the press to have said:

" If Governor Smith is elected and tariff rates are reduced to the schedules of the Underwood Act as the Governor forecasts in his speech of acceptance, the entire farm industry will be thrown into a state of utter demoralization. In his speech accepting the Democratic nomination, Mr. Smith spoke of the Underwood Act as a measure embodying all that is best in tariff principles."

In making that statement the Secretary of Agriculture deliberately and wilfully misrepresented my views to the American people. I challenge him or any other member of his party to point to anything I said in my speech of acceptance that would in any way warrant the statements attributed to me by Secretary Jardine.

I made no mention of the approval of the Underwood Act and at no time did I forecast the reduction of tariff rates to the schedules of the Underwood Act; I said absolutely nothing that would suggest even an inference by any one to that effect unless it be by a person who was deliberately seeking to put me in a false position for the purpose of misleading the people.

The trouble with Secretary Jardine is that he is not a very careful man and does not seem to be very particular about what is said or done by himself or any of his subordinates. If

At Helena, Montana, Indians adopted Governor Smith as a member of
their tribe (above)
In Louisville, Ky., a brown derby parade of young Democrats featured
the nominee's welcome

he had been a little more careful, if he had paid more attention to the duties of his office, a situation would not have been brought about such as resulted from a cotton price prediction issued by the Bureau of Agricultural Economics on September 15, 1927.

The prediction from his department that the price of cotton was likely to decline was found by the Senate Committee which investigated the subject to be " mainly responsible for the breaking of the market at the time and made it extremely easy for those who were organized and ready to realize and profit by this break to take advantage of the situation to press the market to the disastrous low level that it reached." Secretary Jardine's department was directly responsible for great financial loss to the cotton growers of the south. The carelessness which permitted such a situation is reflected in his comment upon my speech of acceptance.

In my speech at Omaha on the farm problem, in order to curb misrepresentation, I wrote out a prescription and I read it to the American people and placed it on file in the newspaper offices so that there would be no opportunity for Secretary Jardine, Chairman Work or any other individual to get in any of his fine work of misrepresentation.

I have written a prescription that to my mind meets the situation with regard to tariff, and here it is:

First: I believe that the tariff should be taken out of politics and should be treated as a business and economic problem. I am opposed to politics in tariff making.

Second: I believe in the Democratic platform, which recognizes that the high wages and constructive policies established by Woodrow Wilson and the business prosperity resulting from them in America, coupled with the economic ruin of the rest of the world, brought about a new condition that committed the Democratic Party to a definite stand in favor of such tariff schedules as will to the very limit protect legitimate business enterprise, as well as American labor from ruinous competition of foreign-made goods produced under conditions far below the American standard.

Third: I condemn the Republican policy of leaving the farmer outside our protective walls. On import crops he must be given equal protection with that afforded industry. On his other products means must be adopted to give him, as well as industry, the benefit of tariff protection.

Fourth: I state definitely that the Democratic Party if entrusted with power will be opposed to any general tariff bill. Personally, I regard general tariff legislation as productive of log-rolling, business confusion and uncertainty. I consider the method of general tariff revision to be inherently unsound and I definitely pledge that the only change I will consider in the tariff will be specific revisions in specific schedules, each considered on its own merits on the basis of investigation by an impartial tariff commission and a careful hearing before Congress of all concerned.

Fifth: No revision of any specific schedule will have the approval of the Democratic Party which in any way interferes with the American standard of living and level of wages. In other words I say to the American workingman that the Democratic Party will not do a single thing that will take from his weekly pay envelope a five-cent piece. To the American farmer I say that the Democratic Party will do everything in its power to put back into his pocket all that belongs there. And we further say that nothing will be done that will embarrass or interfere in any way with the legitimate progress of business, big or small.

Sixth: I favor a tariff commission made up as hereinafter referred to with ample facilities and resources, with broadened powers, and with provision for the prompt and periodical publication of its report which shall be in such form as to present serviceable and practical information.

In the belief that provision for a bi-partisan tariff commission promotes rather than eliminates politics, I would ask

Congress to give me authority to appoint a commission of five members from among the best qualified in the country to deal with the problem, irrespective of party affiliations, with a salary sufficiently large to induce them to devote themselves exclusively to this important work.

I would consider it my duty to see that this commission was left absolutely free to perform the important duties imposed upon it by law without the slightest suggestion or interference from any outside agency, official or otherwise. I would believe it to be my duty to build up the commission in public confidence and support.

Seventh: I will oppose with all the vigor that I can bring to my command the making of the tariff a shelter of extortion and favoritism of any attempt to use the favor of government for the purpose of repaying political debts or obligations.

Eighth: To the very last degree I believe in safeguarding the public against monopoly created by special tariff favors.

Ninth: I can relieve the Republican Party and its managers of the necessity of spreading false propaganda about the Democratic attitude on the tariff by stating that neither the Underwood nor any other tariff bill will be the pattern for carrying into effect the principles herein set forth.

With this prescription honestly put forth, with a clear-cut and definite promise to make it effective, I assert with confidence that neither labor, nor industry, nor agriculture, nor business has anything to fear from Democratic success at the polls in November. On the contrary, the carrying of these policies into effect will result in widespread and more equal distribution of prosperity that will not be confined to any limited groups in the community, but in which all will have an equal opportunity to participate.

XI

ADDRESS AT SEDALIA

Sedalia, Missouri, October 16, 1928

N O political party is entitled to the confidence of the people if it conducts a campaign of misrepresentation. Throughout the country the Republican Party is conducting such a campaign. In the last three weeks I have exposed a large part of it. To-night I propose to expose the grossest misrepresentation so far made by the Republican Party as a reason why it should remain in control of the government.

Lacking an issue and unable to point to any constructive achievement the Republican Party has, through its orators, its public officials, its press bureau and through its National Committee, attempted to put into the minds of the people of this country that, by what they are pleased to term Coolidge economy, they have actually reduced the cost of operating the government.

I shall paint here for you to-night three pictures. Picture No. 1 is what the Republican Party would like to have you believe. This picture was started as far back as 1924, when the Republican platform and the Republican campaign text book of that year started their propaganda and made the claim of reducing the cost of operating the government. At that time the statement was technically correct, because the figures in the 1924 book were based on a comparison between peace time and wartime appropriations, expenditures and revenues.

The picture shows one fact and that is a substantial reduction in 1924 as against 1921, because in 1921 the government was still paying, and paying dearly, for necessary expenses incident to the war. It took years to disband and return to their homes the two million soldiers who were abroad when the Armistice was declared. It took years to muster out of the service and return to their homes the two million men in camp in this country. It took years to reduce the navy to a peace time status and to disband the various other costly agencies set up by the government for the purpose of prosecuting the war.

It is, therefore, quite natural that during 1921, 1922 and 1923 the enormous wartime expenditures began to drop; and because of that fact entire pages of the campaign book of the Republican Party of 1924 were devoted to a recital of the great reduction in the cost of government. The campaign text book of that year did not, however, give the true cause of the reduction, to wit, the completed change from a wartime to a peace basis, but ascribed it for political purposes to what they claimed to be Coolidge economy. In that manner the economy myth since made so much of by the Republican Party had its origin.

The children in our public schools know that it costs a great deal less to run the government in time of peace than it does in time of war.

To show how this false picture was built up, we have to consider some of the public statements intended to lead the people to believe that Republican economy is responsible for reducing the cost of government.

In a recent speech over the radio Under-Secretary of the Treasury Mills said, when comparing 1921 with its great war expenditures and 1928:

" We spent $1,895,000,000 less."

The statement was undoubtedly intended to make the people believe that there has been a reduction in the cost of government under the two Republican administrations. Nothing could be further from the truth.

The Republican National Committee in an attack made upon me after the delivery of my speech of acceptance, said:

" While Federal expenses were being reduced, New York State expenditures were almost tripled."

There again we find an attempt to fix in the minds of the people that the Republican Party reduced the cost of the government. It is strange to see in the very same statement that, in attempting to explain increases in Federal expenditures, they criticise me because they claim I ignored a $3,000 increase in the vice-president's salary. Three thousand dollars is a very small amount in a saving claimed to be as high as two billion dollars.

They also said I overlooked a large item of expense to make the White House a safe place in which to live. I hope they did not expect me to criticise that item. I would be in favor of that. Certainly, if there is a man in the United States who wants the White House safe to live in, I am that man.

I could go on here for hours recalling the different public statements and public speeches made by Republican orators during the last four years, all stressing their claim that Coolidge economy was reducing the cost of the government. They went so far as to find fault with states and municipalities for not following what they called the good example of the Federal Government when these various states and civil divisions required more money for the operation of government. By constant repetition they hoped to induce a great many people in this country to think there was something to their contention.

The chief orator on this subject is the Director of the Budget himself, General Lord. I personally heard him say at Poland Springs in June, 1925, while I was attending the conference of Governors that because of the Budget Bureau established under President Harding it was possible to come within $48,000,000 of reducing the cost of government by two billion dollars, between 1921 and 1925. The true explanation of this reduction, however, he did not discuss.

How a man of General Lord's ability could get it into his mind the people of this country would be prepared to believe that you could reduce the cost of government by two billions of dollars simply by the introduction of a Budget Bureau is more than I am able to understand. It was necessary, however, for the Director of the Budget to try and make these figures stand up, and consequently there were printed and distributed all over the United States some extraordinary statements about alleged Coolidge economy. Some of the samples from his report are both interesting and amusing.

He speaks about a messenger in the navy storeroom in Washington going through the waste paper basket and saving pins, paper clips and pieces of pencils. He tells the story of the American Consul in Java who rearranged the lighting of his office so as to save $45.21 a year.

He speaks of the American Consul at Curacao, in the West Indian Islands, cutting out office lights sufficient to save the government $14 a year.

He spoke at great length about the blue stripes that we see on mail bags and figured how much the government would save by leaving the blue stripe off the bag; at the same time taking no account of the great loss in money and inconvenience to the people of Chicago only last Christmas when, according to the postmaster in that city, there was not a sufficient number of mail bags to distribute the Christmas mail. While he was talking about stripes he also eliminated the red stripe in government towels.

He explained about seven barrels of spoiled soused seal shoulders shipped from Alaska that were unfit for consumption. I do not know to whom the shoulders were shipped, but they were spoiled en route and, by great economy, they were sold for crab bait and brought the government twenty dollars.

In every publication of the Budget Bureau, claims are made of billions of dollars saved and, in order to back them up, there are always some small economies listed. Here is a shining example:

In the 1925 report the Director said:

" The use of both sides of the paper in printing mimeographed publication and administrative orders and circulars, where there is no compelling reason why only one side of the paper should be used, has been recommended."

In order to give color to the great saving of billions, there was organized among government employees the Loyal Order of Woodpeckers. Let me quote the language of General Lord himself:

"All hail to the Loyal Order of Woodpeckers, whose persistent tapping away at waste will make cheerful music in government offices and workshops the coming year. No reports will be required, and only such records kept as the agencies themselves think necessary or desirable."

There is another item of great saving at the Augusta Arsenal. After reducing his personnel, the Commander sought further economy, and he turned off the electricity used for lighting the roads and walks on moonlight nights.

Now, let it not be understood for a moment by the American people who will hear or read this speech that I am attempting to belittle economy in the management of the government. I would be the last man to suggest that, because I have insisted on it in the operation of the government in my own State. What I do want to bring to your attention in the painting of this picture is the attempt that is being made to lead the people to believe that by the elimination of these insignificant expenditures the government is being more cheaply operated today than it was when President Coolidge first took office.

The Republican candidate, Mr. Hoover, had a large share in the painting of this false picture when, in his speech of acceptance, he said:

" By rigorous economy Federal expenses have been reduced by two billion dollars per annum."

No more misleading statement could be made in a campaign than this statement taken from the speech of acceptance of the Republican candidate. He knows better, or should know better. He knows, or he should know, that the two billion dollar reduction is the difference between the peace time cost of government and the wartime cost of government. If he were talking out straightforwardly and fairly to the American people, that is what he would say. He chooses, however, to attempt to conceal the true state of facts. I challenge him to make good his statement that Republican economy made a difference of two billion dollars in the cost of running the government. He knows that is not so, and he could never in his lifetime make good his misleading claim.

The finishing touches were put to the false picture by the Secretary of the Treasury, Mr. Mellon, in a talk over the radio only a few nights ago, when he said that Governor Smith and the other Democratic speakers were seeking to withhold credit from the Coolidge administration for reducing expenditures. Well, we certainly are, because there has been no reduction. In fact, the expenditures have been increased. And Mr. Mellon and Mr. Hoover know that to be the fact.

Now that I have finished the false picture, let me paint for you the real picture. Anticipating just such a speech as this, the Republican campaign managers produced their alibi in advance. They destroy the false picture when in their campaign book of 1928 they say the following:

" Neither is there any denial that more money is being appropriated to operate the government than was appropriated three or four years ago."

In painting the real picture, it is obvious that a comparison between 1921 when the country was on a wartime basis and the peace time of 1928 would in no way reflect the true situation.

In the real picture, let me first call your attention to the fact that $2,600,000,000 worth of assets acquired during the Wilson administration for the purpose of progressing the war were turned into cash in peace time by the succeeding Republican administrations and no credit given on the Wilson side of the ledger. This the Secretary of the Treasury admits in his annual reports.

The annual report of the Secretary of the Treasury for the year 1927 shows that if it had not been for the assets left behind by the Wilson administration there would have been deficits in the years 1923 and 1925, and very substantial reductions in the surplus in the years 1924, 1926, 1927 and 1928. The public, to discover this, would be compelled to delve into the Treasury reports. We would never hear of it from Republican campaign orators. We would never learn this from the political bookkeeping of Mr. Hoover and Mr. Mills, or the Republican National Committee. But, of course, when you are painting a false picture, overlooking a little item like $2,600,000,000 is not of much consequence.

In painting the real picture, let us go first into the office of the great apostle of economy, the President himself, and we find that in 1921 the Executive Department, limited to the office of President and Vice-President, cost the people $210,000. In 1927, that figure moved up to $686,000, but as long as the National Committee says that this increase was caused by an expenditure for putting a new roof on the White House to make it safe, we will let it go at that. But what about 1928, when there was no roof to be paid for, and the appropriation moved from $210,000, the first year of President Harding's administration, to $528,000 in 1928, considerably more than 100 per cent. increase?

Let us take the District of Columbia, which is a city run by the Federal Government. In the first year of the Harding administration it cost the people of the country $21,921,000. In 1928 it jumped to $40,058,000, almost a 100 per cent.

increase, and this in the face of the Republican claim that cities and municipalities of the country outside of the District of Columbia were responsible for destroying the effects of alleged Federal economy.

If Coolidge economy has reduced the cost of government, it should be reflected in the expenditures in the various departments of government. Let us take a look at the figures.

The cost of operating the Department of Agriculture jumped from $143,000,000 in 1924 to $156,000,000 in 1927; the Department of Commerce from $25,000,000 in 1924 to $31,000,000 in 1927; the Department of the Treasury from $117,000,000 in 1924 to $144,000,000 in 1927. And so goes the whole story. For the purpose of painting the picture properly, let us take all the departments of the government, and we will find an increase in expenditures in 1927 as against 1924 of about $200,000,000; and the appropriation acts of 1928 so far signed by the President show that expenditures for this fiscal year will be greater than in 1927.

There is nothing there that makes good the first picture. It destroys it entirely. And it was because of that, the Republican managers saw fit to set up an alibi in the Republican campaign book.

At this point let me say that the fiscal reports of the United States Government come as near to a Chinese puzzle as anything I have ever seen. They were in the same condition in my own State until I devised a system of direct accounting to the people in plain, ordinary words and figures that the man on the street can readily understand. The fiscal reports of the United States Government challenge even the ingenuity of accountants, and for that reason they readily lend themselves to misrepresentation. The Federal procedure in appropriating and expending money is hard to follow and difficult to analyze. It looks almost as though the whole system was devised to confuse and mystify. Certainly that has been the effect.

When Congress convenes in December, according to the Director of the Budget, it will be compelled to meet a deficiency of approximately $100,000,000. That means money that should have been appropriated at the regular session, but was not, and I see a certain significance in that, entering a presidential campaign, when there is a desire on the part of the Republican Party to paint for the people of the country a false and misleading picture of economy.

You may be sure, however, of the figures I gave you tonight, because they are correct. I have given you the real picture as it would be given by any man who desired to talk plainly and honestly to the American people.

There is still a third picture that I would like to paint tonight and lay before the American people. That is a picture of what should have been done and was either neglected entirely or postponed, or was started with a grossly inadequate appropriation so that the administration could get the credit in the election of doing something without paying for it. In order to put this picture properly before you I must first call your attention to what I consider to be trick bookkeeping. Under the system in Washington we have what is known as deferred appropriations. This is a device under which undertakings are started with small appropriations and the government is committed to large appropriations in succeeding years, thereby passing the buck to the next administration after election.

There is no greater waste in the country today than the annual rent roll of the Federal Government, which is about $20,000,000. Can you imagine an administration claiming credit for great economy that expends in rent in one year $20,000,000? I am informed that in some instances the rental paid gives a yield to the property owners in excess of 12 per cent. per annum. There is no economy in that. That is cold-blooded waste.

Let me put into this picture exactly what is going on in

the government at Washington with respect to property acquired for public buildings of various kinds throughout the country, and as against the first picture of alleged economy let me show a picture of wilful waste. Bear in mind that when the government acquires property for public use, it is immediately lifted out of the taxable values of the community wherein it is situated. That means that if the government acquires a plot of land in any city, town or village, the municipality loses the tax revenue of that piece of land. Consider what a waste it is, not only to the city, but to the government itself, to have parcels of land standing idle for years with no buildings on them.

In your own State of Missouri there are several sites, all acquired in 1917 and 1918, for which no construction has yet been provided. They remain idle. There is no economy in that.

Let us take a few shining examples. In the borough of Brooklyn in the city of New York a site was acquired as far back as 1915 at a cost of $290,000, and not a single thing has been done to put a building on it. In the meanwhile the government is renting outside quarters at an annual cost of $60,000. This is not economy. This is deliberate waste.

In Binghamton, New York, as far back as 1916, a site was acquired at a cost of $100,000. Not a single thing has been done to put a building on it.

Over a year ago a site was acquired in Chicago at a cost of close to four millions of dollars. The new Federal building there is designed to cost $14,250,000. The last session of Congress appropriated just $300,000, not enough for the foundation, and the government is paying in rent for postal facilities in the city of Chicago $243,000 a year. This is not economy. It is gross waste. Aside from that, the Postmaster General in a recent report said that a large part of the increased cost of operating the postal service of this country was directly chargeable to antiquated facilities. Withholding appropriations for up-to-date facilities is not economy; it is loss, and would not be permitted for a moment in any well-organized private business.

In Richmond, Virginia, the government, as far back as 1916, acquired a site for a post office that cost $450,000, and not a single dollar has since been appropriated in all that time to put a building on the land.

In the city of Pittsburgh, Pennsylvania, the government expended $2,077,000 for a site for a post office. The post office is designed to cost $6,425,000; and this year they appropriated $300,000, not sufficient to make any kind of a start on the building. In the meanwhile they are paying $173,000 a year rent, and losing in addition $95,000 a year which the Assistant Postmaster General testified could be saved in the operation of the post office when the new building is completed.

I could go through the list and take your time for the rest of the night. Let me sum up by saying that there are almost 100 sites acquired for Federal buildings since 1915, and also a number of sites acquired between 1913 and 1915, on which no buildings have as yet been constructed. These sites are laying idle. The interest on their cost is running against the government and they are lifted out of local taxation. In the meanwhile the government is spending large amounts of money in rent. This is not economy. It is waste, and it is worse than that — it is inefficiency.

One of the glaring effects of the failure to provide post office facilities is illustrated in a letter from the Postmaster General to the Chairman of the Joint Commission on the Postal Service. In this letter the Postmaster General said, as far back as 1921:

" Let me call your attention to the fact that the business of the Post Office, doubling every ten years, can never be placed on an efficient and stabilized basis until the erection of suitable buildings in suitable places is planned, not only on an economical basis but from a scientific and service viewpoint."

In this connection it is also worth while to point out that the Postmaster General rents furniture on the basis of a twenty-year lease. This has been done in order to keep up the fiction of economy in spite of the fact that the Postmaster General admitted in 1927, in the hearings before the House Appropriations Committee, that if a sufficient appropriation were made to buy furniture, a saving of 72 per cent. could be effected in the course of twenty years, amounting in the aggregate to over $530,000. Where is there any economy in doing business that way? No business concern in the country could last that would attempt to conduct its business the way the Federal Government does.

Let me take up a subject in which the State of Missouri is vitally interested. That is the Mississippi Flood Control Bill. It constitutes as fine an illustration as you can get of Republican shifting of the burden. While they have been discussing pro and con and back and forth the share that should be borne by the government and by the states for flood control on the Mississippi, millions and millions of dollars worth of property, and even human life, have been in jeopardy. The improvement of the Mississippi river, to my way of thinking, is a matter of national concern, and should be paid for by the Federal Government. It is not sensible to assume that the rest of the country is not sufficiently interested in the lives and property of millions of its citizens that it would tolerate long and useless discussion, instead of going ahead with the work and completing it.

The Republican administration is looking for a great deal of credit for bringing relief to the flood sufferers and effecting a cure for floods in the future. While the Mississippi Flood Control Bill authorizes an appropriation of $325,000,000, it actually appropriates only $15,000,000. The rest is to be passed along to the next administration.

Instead of trifling with the situation, we should at once bring our great drainage system under control and the enor‧ mous amount of water now running to waste in destructive floods should be harnessed and made to work for us instead of working against us.

Let me give you a few illustrations of palpable neglect, brought about through a false economy which in my opinion amounts to a national disgrace. The United States Government owes a duty to the American Indian, and last May Dr. Work, then Secretary of the Interior, issued to the public a report which shows that owing to neglect by the Federal Government and failure to make adequate appropriations, the Indian wards of the government are rapidly dying of disease, due to the low standard of living. In the schools for Indian children the average spent per day per child for food was as low as nine cents, and malnutrition was evident. I do not ask you to take my word for it. Let us take the report of the Secretary of the Interior himself in 1927, when he said:

" Years of financial neglect require larger appropriations if the Government is to perform its full duty to the American Indian."

This neglect complained of by Dr. Work resulted in inadequate school and hospital facilities for the Indians and their children.

What has Dr. Work got to say about this today when, as head of the Republican National Committee, he is a party to the false picture of economy in the fall of the year, when the Republican Party is seeking a return to power, and one of its severe critics, when he is talking as the head of the great Department of the Interior? What explanation can be made by any of the members of the Republican Party who helped to paint the false picture, for this palpable neglect of the health and comfort of the helpless children of these Indians?

Going over the Federal records is a hard and tiresome job, but if a man has a sense of humor he can occasionally get a laugh out of it. Here is something that gave me a real one and I want to share it with you. In the files of the Department of the Interior there was found a letter from Albert B. Fall, Secretary of the Interior. I will read it to you. It is addressed to President Harding:

" My dear Mr. President:

" I thank you very much for handing me the letters of General Dawes, commenting upon my letters to you with reference to the savings of this Department. It is very gratifying to know that General Dawes is in accord with myself in the matter of true efficiency, as I perfectly well know that he must be when he understood the subject of my departmental activity from my standpoint. Through you I would like to convey to him my appreciation of both the tone of and the assurance contained in his letters which I am returning for your files as requested.

" Very sincerely yours,

"ALBERT B. FALL."

Here is the laugh. This letter about efficiency and economy in the Department of the Interior was written at the very time that the Secretary was taking the first steps to get control of the naval oil reserves so that he might lease them to private interests from which, according to the record, the private interests were to make one hundred million dollars. There is economy and efficiency for you, running wild.

In all the record of the public business at Washington there is no more papable evidence of neglect than the treatment by the Republican administration of the question of proper housing for the army.

I could go into this at very great length to show a wilful and a known neglect of the property of the Federal Government used for housing our soldiers. Suffice it for me to say that no well-organized business institution in the world would tolerate for one week what has been going on in the government at Washington during the present administration. Page after page of public hearings on the War Department appropriation bills testified to it in language stronger than I could use. For the time being, let me quote the Secretary of War, who said:

" I have not hesitated to say quite frequently that I think the condition of our housing is a very serious matter and almost amounts to a national scandal."

These words come directly from a member of the administration. In order to try to make the first picture stand up, a member of the administration is compelled to say that the conduct of his own party in power at Washington on the question of housing our soldiers amounts to a national scandal. It is also a matter of record that army officers of high rank, have been reprimanded because they have publicly referred to the disgraceful housing conditions in the army. What does Mr. Hoover think of that kind of economy? He should not pass that question along to Dr. Work. The American people are entitled to know from his own words whether or not he approves of an economy that starves Indian children and fails to provide adequate housing and proper eating and sleeping quarters for the American soldier.

In a later speech in the campaign I propose to take up the question of the reorganization of the government, a great reform designed to bring about real economy, and promised by both President Harding and President Coolidge, and by spokesmen for both of their administrations and which, because of weakness and lack of leadership and questions of patronage involved, was never carried out, even in the slightest degree.

I have painted for you tonight three pictures:

First, the picture that the Republican Party would like to have the American people believe as showing great efficiency and great economy, always with the hope of making you believe that because of their wonderful handling of the government it is costing less today than it did in the first year of President Coolidge's administration. I have made this picture full and complete.

I have painted for you a second picture setting up real facts which show that the government is costing more this year than it did the first year of President Coolidge, and which show that the small, petty economies used to bolster up the false claim of economy are but a drop in the bucket and really mean nothing as against what could be done.

I painted a third picture of Republican lack of ability, lack of efficiency and lack of business methods.

Mr. Hoover has been identified with the administration of our government for many years. If he is unable to see these three pictures in their true light, I am forced to the conclusion that he does not understand the operations of the government. If he does see these three pictures, I am unable to understand how he could have made that exaggerated and grossly misleading statement that by " rigorous economy Federal expenses have been reduced by two billions per annum."

Real economy, as applied to national affairs, is not only prudent management and expenditure but far-sighted planning in the interest, not only of the people of today, but of those of the future. It involves the protection and the development of our natural resources of all kinds. It means facing the problems of the country and meeting the cost — whatever it may be. While it is fundamentally true that not a single dollar should be wasted, it is also true that no obligation or known want of the government should be postponed or hidden, nor should conditions be allowed to arise and continue which are a disgrace to a great nation.

According to my ideas of economy, the last two administrations have been as wasteful as any the country has ever seen. They attempted to give away our natural resources. They have postponed and neglected the most pressing needs.

AT SEDALIA

When I take my place at the head of this great nation I will meet these problems squarely and without the waste of a single dollar. I will explain to the people the financial needs of the country with frankness and honesty. On the record the Republican Party is helpless. Relief can only come by Democratic victory on the 6th of November.

XII

ADDRESS AT CHICAGO

Chicago, Illinois, October 19, 1928

"THE record of the present administration is a guarantee of what may be expected of the next."

The words that I just read are taken from the Republican platform adopted in Kansas City last June.

Why did the Republican platform drafters limit the guarantee to the present administration? They have been in power since the fourth of March, 1921. I can see no other reason for it except a deliberate effort to get away from the record of the previous administration.

However, the Republican candidate in his speech of acceptance said:

" The record of these seven and a half years constitutes a period of rare courage in leadership and constructive action. Never has a political party been able to look back upon a similar period with more satisfaction."

Let us, therefore, deal tonight with that record, a record which the candidate looks upon with satisfaction and a record which the Republican Party offers as a guarantee of what may be expected in the next four years if it is continued in power.

Let us take first the record with regard to the nation-wide question of relief for agriculture. As far back as 1924 the Republican Party in its platform definitely promised such legislation as would give to agriculture the benefit of the tariff and place it on an economic equality with industry. They so signally failed in that promise that they found it necessary to repeat it word for word in the platform of 1928.

The Republican candidate, who is the chief adviser to President Coolidge on matters affecting agriculture and its promotion, holds out no hope to the farmer in his speech of acceptance.

Senator Borah, today the chief spokesman of the Republican Party, is making a special appeal to the farming sections of the country for a renewal of their support, so freely and so cheerfully given to the Republican Party in years gone by.

Let us consult the record and find out how much help Senator Borah gave to make good their previous promises. As far back as 1925, speaking of the farmer, he said:

"His problem is still with him, and Congress should, before many months, pass a law to give him the relief to which he is entitled."

Senator Borah, now pleading for farm support for his party, voted against the only bill suggested to bring that relief, and at the same time offered no solution of his own.

A further extract from his speech is amusing and entertaining, and I shall read it to you:

"Don't forget that both major parties promised this relief when they asked the farmer for his vote last year (meaning 1924). Both parties always show a great love for the farmer just before election time. Now the hour to make good is at hand."

When that hour struck, neither Senator Borah nor his party was prepared to make good and, as a matter of fact, did not. We find the Senator out now, just before election time, again promising that relief and again expressing that great love and devotion to the cause of the American farmer. He is himself engaged in doing the very thing that he accused both parties of doing. He is going a step further and misrepresenting the situation to the American farmer in an effort to make him believe that Mr. Hoover kept up farm prices during the war and in the reconstruction period thereafter.

I read a cablegram addressed to one of the farm leaders by Mr. Hoover, in which he said he was keeping the prices down. Who is right, Senator Borah or Mr. Hoover? Let them explain the matter to the American farmer.

I am convinced that the farmer is not taking the Senator very seriously. For a great many years he had the reputation of being a progressive representative of the great farming sections of the country. This campaign, however, discloses that he is more anxious for the success of his party than he is for the vindication of any great principle that he has heretofore enunciated.

Let us see how he dealt with the candidate of his party when that candidate was not leading the Republican forces, but was at the head of the Food Administration Bureau under President Wilson.

In the course of his speech in the Senate on a bill to appropriate one hundred million dollars for food for suffering Europe, Senator Borah, in opposition to the appropriation, had the following remarks to make about Mr. Hoover, then Food Administrator. I read them from the record as he spoke them:

" I challenge successful contradiction that three of the vast monopolies which control food in this country have, with relation to their commodities, directed and controlled the Food Administration since its organization."

Speaking further of Mr. Hoover, he said:

" He permits these people to in effect fix their own prices. It is a case of an individual dealing with himself."

Further on in the speech, speaking about the food monopolies, he said:

" Their profits under Mr. Hoover amounted to all the way from 20 to 40 per cent. for the last two years. Shall I be called upon under my oath as a Senator here to turn over one hundred million dollars to feed the poor of Europe when I am notified that out of that one hundred million dollars those that control the food products of this country will ask — and probably receive — from 25 to 40 per cent. profit on their investments? "

This, to my way of thinking, was quite an indictment of the efficiency and the ability of Mr. Hoover to administer the fund for foreign relief. Further on in his speech, speaking about the appropriation of one hundred million dollars, he used this remarkable language:

"No man who has such perverted views of decency ought to be trusted with unlimited power to deal with one hundred million dollars."

I ask Senator Borah this question: To whom did he refer? What man did he have in his mind when he made that statement?

On a subsequent occasion Senator Borah said:

"Mr. Hoover, who violated the most fundamental principles of the Constitution of this country, will not have very much regard for a statute in Europe."

That, to my mind, is a polite way of calling a man a law-breaker. That was only nine years ago, and today Senator Borah is busily engaged in explaining to the American people that Mr. Hoover is the greatest man in the country and should be entrusted with the care of the government for the next four years.

Senator Borah was either right in 1919 or he is right today. Which is it? He cannot have his pie and eat it. That cannot be done. If he was wrong in 1919, he was reckless in speech; and that raises, naturally, the question of how much importance ought to be attached to the speeches in this campaign of a man so palpably careless in his public utterances.

Contrast the attitude of Senator Borah with that of the former distinguished Governor of Illinois, Governor Lowden, who was a formidable contender for the Republican nomination for the presidency, and who, I have no doubt, read the guarantee that I tonight quoted from the platform, when he sent this message to the convention:

"I have stated publicly that I did not want the nomination unless the Republican Party was prepared to meet fully and fairly the agricultural problem. I have waited upon no particular remedy, but I have stated at all times if there was a better method than the so-called equalization fee, I would gladly accept it. I have urged, however, that it is the duty of the Republican Party to find some way to rescue agriculture from the ruin that threatens it. This, in my judgment, the convention by its platform just adopted has failed to do. I therefore authorize the withdrawal of my name from before the Convention."

Governor Lowden's knowledge of this subject is broad enough to suggest to him, as it does to me, that when the buying power of those engaged in the pursuit of agriculture is paralyzed, not only does agriculture suffer, but business suffers. A paralysis of the buying power of the American farmer is reflected in all the rest of the business that is conducted in this country. Poverty on the farm is disastrous to the storekeeper, the merchant, the manufacturer, and to the laborer engaged in industry.

If the platform of the Republican Party was not good enough for Governor Lowden to run on, what must the American farmer think about it, because he was devoted to their interests first, last and all the time.

The difference between Senator Borah and Governor Lowden is the difference between a politician seeking success at the polls and a statesman devoted to a principle. The American public can distinguish between the two men. I hold that Governor Lowden is the statesman.

If the record of the last seven and a half years is a guarantee of what the farmer may expect in the next four — in the event of Republican victory — then let us look forward to more bank failures in the farm districts, millions more of men leaving the farm for the cities and, as Governor Lowden predicted, the realization of the ruin that threatens agriculture.

The Republican Party, with the full knowledge of the record, in full possession of all the facts, says in unmistakable language to the American farmer: The record of which you so bitterly and so justly complain is the Republican guarantee of what you may expect in the next four years.

On the other hand, the Democratic Party, in a clear-cut, concise, and definite platform plank, recognizes the great underlying and fundamental difficulty confronting agriculture, and promises immediate solution of the problem with a constructive program for its relief.

I stand hard and fast by that platform, and I promise you that if I am elected President of the United States, it will be entirely unnecessary for me to seek excuses for nonperformance in the carrying out of that pledge, because I shall make good that promise, and I shall not be scurrying around the United States to look for words to build up the reason why it was not done.

Let us look into the record for a minute and see if we can find a reason why the platform builders of the Republican National Convention desired to confine themselves to the present administration as against the last seven and a half years. There is no doubt in my mind that they were endeavoring to get away from the black, disgraceful record of public corruption disclosed in connection with the oil reserves of the country, the administration of the Veterans' Bureau and the office of the Alien Property Custodian. The Republican candidate, however, was not in accord with the purpose of the platform builders, because he said that the party could look back with satisfaction on the record of the last seven and a half years.

It is true that certain operations with regard to the oil scandal were before the American people in 1924. The Republican Party in that year was successful in inducing the electorate to believe that the guilt was personal and that the responsibility for it should fall upon unfaithful members of the party entrusted with high public office. However, since the last presidential election, Senator Walsh of Montana has brought to the public attention the fact that a large part of the money growing out of the oil scandal found its way into the treasury of the Republican National Committee, and liberty bonds coming from the oil operators were exchanged with prominent members of the party for their checks as a contribution to meet the deficit in the Republican campaign chest. The effect of this testimony was to bring the responsibility right to the leaders of the party. The bonds were offered by no less a person than the Chairman of the Republican National Committee.

Here we have Senator Borah again assuming one attitude in the spring of the year and an entirely different one in the fall of the year. Last winter during the session of the United States Senate, the Senator borrowed a halo and a pair of wings and, standing on the floor of the Senate, he said:

" No political party is responsible as a party for the wrongful transaction of individual members who in secret betray it. But when the transaction becomes known to the party it must necessarily become responsible if it fails to repudiate the transaction and return the fruits thereof."

I have been a fairly close student of what took place. I have no recollection that the President or the candidate for President or any prominent official of the Republican Party used any language to repudiate the transaction, and certainly they have not returned the fruits of it. Senator Borah himself suggested a conscience fund and ventured the opinion that there were plenty of Republicans who would be glad to contribute from a dollar up in order to clear their party of this humiliating stigma. I refer to it as a conscience fund. The amount required to remove the stigma from the Republican Party was $260,000.

When it came to the conscience fund, widely heralded by the winged apostle of reform, lo, the mountain labored and brought forth a mouse. Instead of $260,000, they got one dollar and thirty-six cents.

That apparently satisfied the Senator, because he is now on the stump vigorously advocating the retention in power of the Republican Party, stigma or no stigma.

Dr. Work, Chairman of the Republican National Committee, only yesterday said:

" The people are tired of hearing of these oil leases."

The Chairman of the Republican National Committee told the truth, but he could have gone a little bit further; he could have said they are not only tired but they are disgusted.

What gave rise to this statement by the chairman? The discovery that an improper and illegal sale of the Federal oil royalties in the Salt Creek oil fields was executed in behalf of the government by the Secretary of the Interior in December, 1922.

The present Chairman of the Republican National Committee, when Secretary of the Interior, renewed that contract in January of this year. Shortly after its renewal the question of its validity was submitted to the Attorney-General who, in an opinion within the last four days, declared it to be invalid in that it was improperly and illegally executed. While it purported to offer the valuable oil rights to the highest bidder, the bids were so rigged as to let one individual bidder have a distinct advantage as against all the rest.

When these rights were advertised for public bidding, the advertisements for the bids called for the purchase of the oil for a period of five or ten years. The company that won the contract did not bid according to the advertisement but, on the other hand, bid for a five-year term with an option of renewal, thus placing the company in the position of being able to walk away from their contract at the end of five years, if it was unprofitable to the company, and leaving it in a position to continue the contract for ten years provided it was unprofitable to the government. That bid was accepted as against the other companies and as against the form of advertising, and that led the Attorney-General of the United States to say the following about it:

" It is well established law that a public officer given power by statute to enter into a contract on behalf of the public with the best bidder has no power to grant that bidder any term materially advantageous to him which was not announced in the advertisement for bids. The contract entered into must be a contract offered to the highest responsible bidder by advertisement. This being so, I think the Secretary has no power to enter into a contract with the highest bidder containing an option of renewal provision, when such provision was not offered to all the bidders in the advertisement for bids."

On March 2d of this year President Coolidge forwarded to the Attorney-General correspondence and papers sent to him in relation to this matter by Senator Walsh of Montana. What happened between the 2d of March and the 15th of October? This is a simple question of law that could be determined in one hour by any lawyer in the country. I do not know how the American people feel about it, but I am forced to the conclusion that there was an attempt to suppress this decision until after election, and I am satisfied that it would never be given out in the heat of a political campaign if it was not forced into the open by the insistence of Senator Walsh, and newspaper activity, both designed to bring the facts to the American public at the earliest possible moment.

The public official responsible for the renewal of this invalid and illegal lease is no less a personage than the Chairman of the Republican National Committee and, according to the newspapers, his only explanation is:

" I have no comment to make. Those things are past. People are tired of hearing of these oil leases."

The record of the present administration is a guarantee of what may be expected of the next, and the candidate said:

" The record of these seven and a half years constitutes a

period of rare courage and leadership and constructive action. Never has a political party been able to look back upon a similar period with more satisfaction."

In 1920 the Republican platform, speaking of World War veterans, said the following:

" We hold in imperishable remembrance the valor and the patriotism of the soldiers and the sailors who fought in the great war for human liberty, and we pledge ourselves to discharge to the fullest the obligations which a grateful nation justly should fulfill in appreciation of the services rendered by its defenders on sea and on land."

This plank from the Republican platform was a declaration of a noble purpose. It was patriotic and it was humane. It was what might be expected from an American political party voicing as it does the sentiment of the American people to the men that offered themselves to the country in her hour of need. What happened afterward, however, constitutes one of the darkest pages of American history when it was discovered by an investigating committee that a large part of the money taken from the treasury of the United States to pay only in part American gratitude to the soldier was so misapplied that the Republican Director of the Veterans' Bureau served a term in Atlanta Penitentiary. When speaking of the evidence adduced before that committee, General O'Ryan, Commanding Officer of the Twenty-seventh Division, summed it all up when he said:

" No American can read it without a feeling of disgust of the manner in which the great work of aiding the disabled was prostituted for self-aggrandizement and greed. No soldier can consider it without feelings of rage and shame that the disabled among them should be so callously exploited. The testimony of witnesses and exhibits of the Bureau all tell a story of almost unparalleled waste, recklessness and misconduct. This transaction resembles more the work of buccaneers

A small portion of the thousands who jammed the Union Station at Chicago when Governor Smith arrived on his campaign tour

in the looting and scuttling of a ship than the mere neglect of trusted government officials."

I could add nothing to that. And while the platform of the Republican Party attempts to evade responsibility for that, let it be borne in mind that the candidate looks back with satisfaction upon the record of the last seven and a half years.

While we are on this subject of fair and proper treatment of our veteran soldiers, let me call your attention to a telegram received by me since I arrived in the city of Chicago. The United States Government maintains a sanitorium for the cure of tubercular soldiers at Tupper Lake in the Adirondack mountains in my own State. I am in possession of information that the Republican Inspectors of Election refused to permit World War veterans in that sanitorium to enter their names upon the register as electors. The Democratic State Committee resorted to the courts. No matter what may be the decision of the courts, it stands, nevertheless, upon the record that the Republican election officials in that section of New York State are attempting to deny to the afflicted soldier that offered his life to the country the right to cast his ballot in the coming election.

Let me say a word to you about water power. The country's water power possibilities are practically the very last of our great natural resources that have not fallen into the hands of private monopoly. It is the contention of the Democratic Party as outlined in its platform and in my speech of acceptance that these great God-given resources belong to the people and should never be alienated, and should be developed under public ownership and under public control, to the end that a public agency, whether State or Federal, may be in a position, by supplying the energy under contract, to fix the rates to the ultimate consumer, and also to provide for its just and equitable distribution. The Democratic Party has taken the big, broad, progressive view of developing electrical energy from water power. The Republican Party, on the other hand, bowing in obedience before the power trust, evades the subject, offers no definite program, and the Republican candidate in his speech of acceptance refers to it so vaguely that nobody understands his position. When recently speaking at Elizabethton, in the State of Tennessee, he made some mention of dangerous and destructive doctrines in relation to this problem. I can spell nothing from his language except opposition to public development and public control. By their very action they have aligned themselves with the great interests that seek to wrest this last resource from the hands of the people themselves. That they lend moral support to the propaganda of the lighting companies, spread broadcast through the country to discourage public ownership and control, there can be no question. No satisfactory explanation can ever be made of the appointment of Roy O. West as Secretary of the Interior, in which position he is ex-officio a member of the Federal Power Commission, in view of his long history of connection with private power companies.

Boulder Dam, with its great possibilities of electrical energy, remains undeveloped. Muscle Shoals, constructed with government funds during the war and capable of building up a large section of the country by the production of electrical energy at reasonable prices, is standing idle. A bill for its further development and its operation under governmental control met with a veto at the hands of President Coolidge and he rebuked the Congress for spending so much time talking about it, on the theory, as he himself said, that it was not worth any more than the price of one first-class battleship. At the end of seven and a half years public development has not only been arrested, but there is every sign on the Republican political horizon that these great natural resources will, if left to the Republican Party, finally find their way into the hands of private individuals and private corporations for private gain and for private profit.

That is the record of the present administration as far as water power is concerned, and that record is offered to the American people as the guarantee of what they can expect in the next four years in the event of Republican success.

Development of our inland waterways is promised every four years by the Republican Party, and 1928 sees us without even a plan, not to speak of a development, and so far as these arteries of trade and commerce are concerned the record of the present administration is the guarantee of what we may expect from another Republican administration.

In my speech at Louisville last Saturday night I offered from the record absolute proof that the Republican administration paralyzed the Tariff Commission recommended by President Taft twenty years ago and later by President Wilson. The purpose, and only purpose, of the Tariff Commission is to lay before Congress the facts and figures from which an intelligent and understandable tariff bill can be drawn. Immediately following my speech the Republican candidate entirely distorted my remarks and attempted to make the American public believe that I desired to transfer the law-making power from Congress to a Tariff Commission, when no such suggestion came from me. I merely asked that there be made effective and that there be strengthened the thought and the idea of a fact-finding Tariff Commission originally advanced by President Taft. I read from the record and I showed how President Coolidge did his full share to paralyze the Tariff Commission and render it useless.

This is the record as far as the Tariff Commission is concerned and it constitutes the Republican guarantee of what may be expected in the next four years in the event of Republican success.

It is a matter of common knowledge throughout the length and breadth of this land that the Republican Party in the last seven and a half years has entirely closed its eyes to the problem of prohibition. Its record is one of double-dealing and of double-crossing. It has attempted the impossible by trying to carry water on both shoulders. It has tried to be dry among the drys and wet among the wets. I have the testimony of a Republican official that it was used for Republican patronage purposes.

The long record of corruption connected with its attempted enforcement indicates that men paid from the pockets of the taxpayers to sustain the law exacted payment from those who were permitted to wink at it. As to the fundamentals of the problem, the Republican administration, like the ostrich, has buried its head in the sand and has assumed that everything is all right.

The Republican candidate says it must be worked out constructively. What he means by that no living person can tell. It is a matter of record, however, that no attempt has been made by the Republican administration over seven and a half years to work it out in any fashion. While referring to it as a noble experiment, the Republican candidate speaks of the grave abuses that have crept into its administration. There is nothing on the record that indicates that the Republican Party has done a single thing in the last seven and a half years to eradicate these abuses. If they did anything, they helped to promote them by the character of the men that they insisted, for patronage purposes, be charged with the enforcement of this law.

This is the record, and they cannot escape it, and this record they offer as a guarantee of what is going to happen in the next four years. The poor, weak, vacillating, broken down Republican machine is unable to offer a constructive suggestion for the relief of the present intolerable condition.

Against this I offer to the country a constructive policy.

I have two duties as President with regard to prohibition. First, to enforce the law as I find it. The American public may rest assured that if I take the oath of office as President of the United States on the 4th of next March, I will sustain the Constitution and the laws of this country with all the force and all the vigor I am able to bring to my command. My second duty is to advise Congress as to what, in my opinion, is in the best interest of this country. With respect to prohibition, I shall advise an amendment of the Volstead Act that will give a sane, sensible, scientific definition of what constitutes an intoxicant. Thinking people throughout the United States are all in accord with the fact that the present definition is a dishonest one and not in keeping with fact or truth.

I shall also recommend an amendment of the Eighteenth Amendment that will permit a sovereign State, after an affirmative vote of its people, to dispense alcoholic beverages to its own inhabitants under such regulation as will prohibit its sale in any public place.

I predicate this recommendation upon the Jeffersonian theory of State rights. I would leave to the dry states the full protection of the Eighteenth Amendment and the Volstead Act. I would, on the other hand, where a majority of all the people of a State demanded it, allow a State to handle the question by itself under the restrictions and safeguards laid down in my speech of acceptance.

I believe that in this way we could make this law responsive to the will of the people in the various states of the country, bring back respect for law, promote the cause of real temperance and, at the same time, put an end to the corruption, the lawlessness and the bootlegging which have become so widespread in this land today.

Time will not permit me tonight to lay before the public the full record of the present administration, which I am thoroughly satisfied they would be unwilling to accept as a guarantee of the way they want this government conducted in the next four years.

The more I analyze that statement in the Republican platform the more I become convinced that it is entirely and thoroughly characteristic of the Republican Party. They never see anything new; they never make any progress; they never make any advance; they never attempt to meet new conditions; they never attempt an up-to-date solution of the problems of government. Reactionary to the last degree, steeped in bourbonism,— which learns nothing and forgets nothing,— they frankly say that the record of the present administration is a guarantee of what may be expected from them in the next. That holds out no hope to the American people of a sane or sensible solution of any of the problems pressing them at this time.

As far as I am concerned, government should be constructive and not destructive; progressive, not reactionary. I am entirely unwilling to accept the old order of things as the best unless and until I become convinced that it cannot be made better.

This I stated in my speech of acceptance and it sums up in a few words my attitude to the progressive reforms that I think must be adopted in the interest of progressive government. The Republican Party disagrees with the Democratic platform and disagrees with my declaration, and frankly says to the American people: Nothing new; nothing will happen; look forward to no progress in government; look for no betterment of conditions as they exist, because the record of the last four years is all that you can expect in the next four, if we win.

If I understand aright the thought of the American people, the Republican guarantee is so far from sufficient to meet the needs of today, that the forces of progress in the country will reject the Republican platform, the Republican guarantee and the Republican candidate and turn to the Democratic Party for vigorous and progressive leadership.

XIII

ADDRESS AT BOSTON

Boston, Massachusetts, October 24, 1928

"WE shall use words to convey our meaning, not to hide it."

On August 11th of this year in the State of California the Republican candidate, in his speech of acceptance, made use of the words that I have just spoken and held out a high hope to the people of the United States that in the course of the campaign plain speaking would give the American people an opportunity to render their verdict on the sixth of November in the light of a thorough understanding of where the candidate stood on all of the great questions upon which this contest must be decided. If lived up to, it would be an innovation in Republican campaigning.

Let us take up some of the subjects before the electorate and see how far the Republican candidate has used words to convey his meaning.

Take, first, the question of the development of our great natural water power resources.

Let me first state the question at issue. Throughout the length and breadth of this country today there are great possible water power developments. The Democratic platform refers to them as the last line of public resources not yet in the hands of private companies for private gain and private profit.

The question is: How are they to be developed? By the government itself, retaining ownership and control for the purpose of putting the government in a position by contractual agreements to guarantee fair rates and equitable distribution to the users of electrical energy, developed as a result of their ownership of these resources? Or are they to be alienated and fall into the hands of the private power companies eagerly seeking an opportunity to use the natural resources of the country, the property of all the people, for their own profit?

Early in the campaign I exposed the operations of the power lobby and their attempts for many years to discourage public development and ownership. We are dealing with no new question, but with one that has been before the country for quite some time.

There can be no mistake about the Democratic position or about my own attitude. I am endeavoring to apply to the nation the principles that I applied in the State of New York, where probably the largest and the greatest of these water powers now resides. Only two years ago I successfully defeated the aspirations of the power trust by calling public attention to the fact that the public-controlled water power commission of New York State was prepared to turn over the potential water power possibilities of the St. Lawrence river to a subsidiary of the Aluminum Company of America.

Properly developed, there is enough publicly owned water power in the State of New York to light New England, and it is running to waste tonight while we are gathered in this hall, simply because it has been impossible up to date to get any agreement as to the manner and method of dealing with it. The private power companies have been successful in blocking all attempts at public development.

All this is known to Mr. Hoover, as it is to the Republican leaders of the country generally.

There can only be two sides to the question: Either the people are to retain these water power sites under public ownership and public control, or they are to lease them to private companies for private profit. It should be, in the ordinary course of events, a perfectly easy thing for any public man to declare without equivocation just where he stands on the fundamental principle involved.

Take the very speech of acceptance in which appears the text of my speech tonight. In so far as it deals with water power, this is what he said:

"Nearly all of our greater drainages contain within themselves possibilities of cheapened transportation, irrigation, reclamation, domestic water supply, hydro-electrc power and, frequently, the necessities of flood control. But this development of our waters requires more definite national policies in the systematic coordination of these different works upon each drainage area."

What does all this mean? I am unable to make anything out of it and, if the American public can, I would like to know what it is. Where could you find in any political campaign of the past a better example of the use of words to hide rather than to convey a meaning?

Following his speech of acceptance, the Republican candidate was confronted with a nation-wide demand that he use words to convey his meaning and not to hide it. As a result, on the 18th of August, one week after his speech of acceptance, he spoke at Los Angeles. I carefully read the speech and all that he said about the fundamental principle of control of the sources of supply was that he was in accord with the engineers at Boulder Dam on the Colorado river; that they ought to build a high dam; in fact, he favored a dam as high as the engineers would approve.

This has to do with construction. The fundamental principle he carefully avoided.

He next touched upon water power in the State of Tennessee, a State which would be particularly benefited by complete development of a water power on the Tennessee river at Muscle Shoals and, strange to say, in his entire speech he never even mentioned the words "Muscle Shoals."

CAMPAIGN ADDRESS

The following is an extract from his speech:

"Violations of public interest by individuals or corporations should be followed by the condemnation and punishment they deserve, but this should not induce us to abandon progressive principles and substitute in their place deadly and destructive doctrines."

What did he mean by "deadly and destructive doctrines?" Did that mean public ownership and public control? If so, why not use words to convey the meaning? And what did he have in his mind when he tried to hide it?

Let me read further from the speech:

"There are local instances where the government must enter the business field as a by-product of some great major purpose, such as improvement in navigation, flood control, scientific research or national defense, but they do not vitiate the general policy to which we should adhere."

What is the general policy to which we should adhere? What is the candidate's policy with regard to the development of water power?

The candidate's statement at Elizabethton was so far from conveying any meaning that a chain of newspapers throughout the United States supporting his candidacy had one of its men call upon him to find out exactly what he meant, and it is reported that in a private conversation with one of the newspaper editors on the subject of Muscle Shoals he said:

"You may say that means Muscle Shoals."

Even after the newspaper interview, upon his return to Washington, he made a third statement with relation to Muscle Shoals, and the last and final statement was more complicated than the first.

I am not simple-minded on this subject. I knew all along exactly where the Republican candidate stood. What I have been trying to do is to drag him into the open.

From August 11th until October 22nd, Mr. Hoover succeeded in using words to hide his meaning, but on last Mon-

day night the cat got out of the bag and, at Madison Square
Garden in New York city, he told the progressive members of
his own party, as well as the Democrats of the country, that
their proposals would " cause us to turn to State socialism."

If what he says in his Madison Square Garden speech is
true, then all the members of Congress, Republican and
Democratic, who voted for the Muscle Shoals Bill — vetoed
by President Coolidge — are Socialists.

Where did I hear this before?   Where did this expression
of " State socialism " originate as applied to State ownership
and development of water power?   It is the stock argument
of the power trust and was used against my power plans by
the power lobby in the State of New York.   It was the very
same argument made by the present chairman of the Republican State Committee of New York who, until the day he was
selected to be the leader of his party in the State, was at the
head of the Northeastern Power Company and who, as
Speaker of the Assembly, stood against every proposal for
State development and State ownership.

I can almost picture the Republican candidate saying to
Chairman Machold: " What argument did you use against
Smith's water power proposal in New York?"   And
Machold's reply: " Refer to it as State socialism; that is
best calculated to scare business men, large and small."

I am pretty sure, however, that Chairman Machold did not
explain to the candidate that there are some distinguished
men, some of them members of his own party in the State of
New York, who, so far as the power subject is concerned, lined
themselves up with what he is pleased to call a socialistic
doctrine.   Let us see who they are.

Former President Theodore Roosevelt, speaking about the
power possibilities on the St. Lawrence river, said the following:

" You have in this section a most valuable asset in your
natural water power.   You have elected too many men in the

past who have taken what belongs to the nation. Coal and oil barons cannot compare to water power barons. Do not let them get a monopoly on what belongs to this State. There has been a persistent effort to give private corporations control of the water power in this country. There has been an effort to give that control to the aluminum trust. If the aluminum trust makes its money fairly, all right. But when it gets money and power by taking the natural resources of the State, it is time for us to object. Do not give up your water power for a promise of quick development. We are poor citizens if we allow the things worth most to get into the hands of a few."

Another distinguished Socialist — according to the Republican candidate and the Republican chairman — is former Governor Hughes, ex-Justice of the United States Supreme Court, ex-Secretary of State and candidate of the Republican Party for the presidency in 1916. As far back as 1907, twenty-one years ago, he first advocated the development of public waters in the State of New York under State ownership and State control. These words I have taken directly from the title of an act passed in that year placing upon the then existing Water Power Commission the duty of drawing a comprehensive plan, and the words " State ownership and State control " are written into the law.

Nathan L. Miller, former Judge of the Court of Appeals and former Governor of the State of New York, advocated the erection of State-owned and State-controlled power plants on the Erie canal and, while we are here in this hall tonight, they are operating, generating electrical energy and earning for the State a large return upon the State's investment.

If Mr. Machold and Mr. Hoover are right, former Governor Miller takes his place among the Socialists on the question of water power development.

Owen D. Young, Chairman of the board of directors of the General Electric Company, an advocate of State owned and

State controlled power sites must, according to the language of the Republican candidate, take his place in the rank of State Socialists.

Taking the candidate at his own word, why does he not, instead of hiding behind the catch phrase of " State Socialism," come right out and say: " I believe in leasing or selling or otherwise alienating the water power of this country in the interest of private power companies for development by them for private profit and private gain, and I am opposed to government ownership, government control and government development?" Why not be as frank and open as he was in the speech that he delivered before the Annual Convention of the National Electric Light Association in 1925, wherein he went so far to discourage public ownership and public development that this association issued his speech in a pamphlet as part of the propaganda that they spread throughout the country against all proposals for public development?

No more palpable example of using words to hide a meaning can be found than the candidate's own statement in his speech at Madison Square Garden on Monday night when, at great length, he attempted to lead the American people to believe that public ownership and public development of water power meant putting the government in business and, to bolster up his claim, he quoted from a speech delivered by Samuel Gompers at Montreal as far back as 1920, and attempted to make that speech apply to water power when it was really made against government ownership and operation of railroads of the country.

There is a wide difference between a privately owned railroad and a water power site, the ownership of which in the first instance, resides directly with the people of the country. Mr. Hoover failed to differentiate between the development of a natural resource and the operation of a privately built-up business.

This is using words not only to hide the meaning but to attempt to distract public attention from the main issue.

"In the past years there has been corruption, participated in by individual officials and members of both political parties, in national, State and municipal affairs. Too often this corruption has been viewed with indifference by a great number of our people."

I just read to you again from the speech of acceptance of the Republican candidate for the purpose of calling to your attention that here also we find words used to conceal rather than to convey a meaning. This is a national campaign. Why any reference to State or municipal affairs? And if words are to be used to convey our meaning, and the candidate is dealing with corruption, why not speak about the oil scandals and the frauds in the office of the Alien Property Custodian? Why not condemn the disgraceful thefts in the Veterans' Bureau, unearthed largely through the efforts of your distinguished Senator Walsh?

I disagree with the candidate that the people generally view with indifference stories of official corruption made public as far back as 1923. If there has been any indifference to official corruption it is more noticeable among the leaders of the Republican Party than among the rank and file of the people. The rank and file of the American people, Republicans as well as Democrats, are thoroughly disgusted with the whole oil question, and they naturally look to the Republican leaders and to the Republican candidate for strong denunciation of the Republican officials and party managers in any degree involved.

The American people in 1924 believed that they had heard the last of this dark chapter in American history, but were greatly stirred when, subsequent to the 1924 election, it developed that a part of the oil money found its way into the campaign funds of the Republican Party itself, linking not only dishonest public officials with the oil scandals but also the Chairman of the Republican National Committee and such members of the party as were willing to assist him in having the oil money find its way into their party treasury. That incident closed, the American people hoped that they had heard the last of it, and now it crops up again in 1928, when the Chairman of the Republican National Committee, the former Secretary of the Interior, renewed for five years the contract of the Sinclair Oil Company for the royalty oil in the Salt Creek oil region.

The original sale was made by Secretary Fall for a five year period with the option of a five year renewal. Reference to this matter during the trial of one of the oil magnates, and in the Senate investigation, should have been sufficient to put Dr. Work, the Secretary of the Interior, on notice, so that at least before renewing the option he would get an opinion of the Attorney-General as to its validity. This, however, was not done and the renewal was executed in January of 1928 and branded by the Attorney-General as illegal and improper, in the middle of October of this year, after the matter had been on his desk since the 2nd of last March.

What more palpable exhibition of indifference on the part of a party leader could you find than the newspaper interview with Dr. Work reported in the daily press? I shall read it:

" Why didn't you inquire of the Attorney-General's office about the validity of the lease before its renewal?"

" There was no question of its validity. Get this clear: There was nothing to do with making a lease or examining its validity. A lease had existed five years. There was an option for a five years' renewal. It was only a legal question of renewal and the Department acted on the solicitor's advice."

" Weren't matters in the Interior Department ever referred to the Department of Justice?"

" Yes. When there was occasion to. There was no occasion in this matter."

"Doesn't it seem queer to you that the Attorney-General should have cancelled the lease immediately upon disclosure of the facts by The World?"

"No. It's all over. I have nothing to do with it. Furthermore, I've nothing to say."

"But weren't you inclined to be suspicious or curious because this was a government oil lease with the Sinclair Company?"

"No. Why should I be?"

Dr. Work suddenly looked up and said: "You understand I'm not being interviewed. I won't be interviewed on this matter at all."

"Very well. I can only quote what you've said so far, then."

"You can't quote me at all. I'm not being interviewed."

"You said nothing of the kind, sir."

"Well, ——————— you're a gentleman, aren't you?"

"If you had told me you were speaking in confidence I should have been bound, sir. But I told you who I was and where from at the outset and asked questions directly, which you answered."

"What is you name?"

He was told the reporter's name.

"Well," concluded the former Secretary of the Interior, "I have nothing at all to say on this matter. I have nothing to do with it. And it is all a matter of record now, not discussion."

Talking about indifference, here is a report of an interview with Mr. Hoover himself. One newspaperman said to him:

"Do you agree with Dr. Work that the people are tired of hearing about oil?"

"I will not discuss that matter," said Mr. Hoover.

Let the American people judge what meaning Mr. Hoover meant to convey or to conceal by this silence.

In the early part of my speech in reference to water power

I clearly showed that the Republican candidate left the minds of the public in darkness for two and a half months and finally disposed of the public water power development by calling it "State Socialism." He has taken that identical course on the subject of farm relief. In his speech of acceptance and in all of his speeches in which he has touched upon the question of farm relief, he used words to hide his real meaning but, at New York on Monday night, he declared my plan for farm relief to be State Socialism, although the fundamental principle of my plan was twice recognized by the Congress of the United States and twice approved by an overwhelming vote of Democrats and Republicans in both Houses, and twice submitted to the President of the United States and twice vetoed by him, despite the fact that he had no plan of his own to offer in its place.

Let us see whom we can add to the ranks of the Socialists as the result of that vote.

The vice-presidential candidate is a 50 per cent Socialist. He voted for it when it came before the Senate originally, but refused to vote for it over the veto of the President.

We materially add to the ranks of the State Socialist Party when we take in the members of Congress of both parties in both Houses at Washington who twice voted for the principle set forth in my stand for farm relief.

Former Governor Lowden of Illinois, according to the candidate's Monday night declaration, is an active and militant member of the State Socialistic Party.

Let me not at this time overlook the Vice-President of the United States who, because of his advocacy of the principle set forth in my speech of acceptance, would become a member of the State Socialist Party.

How must it ring in the ears of the farmers in the wheat and corn belt of the country to have the Republican candidate on Monday night at Madison Square Garden line them all up with the State Socialist Party?

CAMPAIGN ADDRESS

The Republican platform adopted at Kansas City says:
" The agricultural problem is national in scope."

With that we are all in accord, because there is no denying the fact that when one-third of the whole population of America is in distress and their buying power is paralyzed, the other two-thirds must feel it. That New England does feel it there can be no doubt, although the Republican candidate, when speaking in the city of Boston, referred to the wages paid in the textile industry as indicating a great prosperity evenly spread all over the country.

While in Boston the candidate spoke of the prosperity of New England, but in his speech of acceptance he said that agriculture, coal and textile industries are still lagging behind.

What are the facts? In one manufacturing city alone in this State the number of wage earners in industry dropped from 33,300 in 1921 to 24,800 in 1927, a loss of work for 8,500 men and women, particularly in the woolen and cotton mills. In that same period the amount of wages earned in a year had fallen from $36,904,884 to $28,961,874, or a loss in wages of $8,000,000 a year.

These figures come from the Massachusetts State Department of Labor and Industry.

In his Boston speech Mr. Hoover offered the textile workers of New England the consolation that they earned on an average 40 cents an hour and, for that reason, they were much better off than textile workers in other parts of the world.

For a little over a 53-hour week, 40 cents an hour would make the weekly wage of a full time textile worker $21.36 a week. Even this small amount is not agreed to by the Bureau of Labor Statistics in Washington, which only recently issued a statement declaring that a survey of the cotton textile industry showed that for a little over a 53-hour week the worker received $17.30.

Let us see how the report of the Bureau of Labor Statistics

at Washington squares with the advertisement inserted in the newspapers by the Republican Party. The advertisement says:

"Republican prosperity has reduced hours and increased earning capacity."

That cannot be made to apply to the farmer and because it cannot is one of the reasons why it cannot be made to apply to the textile workers of New England, for the reason that the buying power of one-third of the American people has been paralyzed. The advertisement says that "Republican prosperity has put a chicken in every pot and a car in every back yard." The textile workers of New England, at $17.30, cannot buy very many chickens nor very much gasoline.

"Republican efficiency has filled the workingmen's dinner pail and his gasoline tank besides, and placed the whole nation in the silk-stocking class."

I should like to have a picture of a $17.30 a week textile worker riding out to dinner in his own automobile with his silk stockings on.

In face of the candidate's own statement, in the face of the Republican Party's own declaration that agriculture is prostrate and that the buying power of one-third of the people of the nation has been paralyzed, the Republican candidate at Madison Square Garden on Monday night of this week declared the Democratic remedy for the economic ills of agriculture to be State Socialism, without offering anything in the way of a remedy for their solution. Unfounded statements of that kind go further to build up the ranks of Socialism in this country than anything else.

As far as these problems are concerned, certainly words have not been used to convey a meaning but have been used to hide it.

Talking about using words to hide a meaning, let us take the gem of the speech of acceptance of the Republican candidate. Speaking of prohibition, he said:

"Our country has deliberately undertaken a great social

and economic experiment, noble in motive and far-reaching in purpose. It must be worked out constructively."

What does that mean? What is the matter with the noble experiment that, after eight years of trial, it is necessary for the Republican candidate to say it must be worked out constructively? Is it working now? If not, what is the matter? And what is his remedy? Why not use words to convey the meaning and not to hide it?

Further in his speech he says:

" Common sense compels us to realize that grave abuses have occurred."

What are they, and what is the remedy for them?

Speaking in Milwaukee, in great detail I laid before the American people the abuses of prohibition: Bootlegging, official corruption, and general disrespect for law. And I offered a remedy. Strange to say, at Madison Square Garden on Monday night, my remedy — modification of the Volstead Act and the application of states' rights to the solution of the problem — is referred to by the Republican candidate as State Socialism. It cannot be possible that Mr. Hoover means seriously to try to lead the American people to believe that the cure of these evils by the application of the principle of states' rights can be attacked as Socialism.

Where does Mr. Hoover's do-nothing policy with respect to prohibition get us? For anything that he has to suggest we shall continue to live under the present grave abuses. If my plan of liquor control is State Socialism, the present condition of bootlegging, hijacking, racketeering, corruption and lawlessness is governmental anarchy.

Is this cry of Socialism anything new? Not to a man with my experience. I have heard it raised by the reactionary element of the Republican Party in my own State over a period of a quarter of a century. Every forward-looking, progressive, up-to-date legislative enactment in New York was at some time or another referred to by reactionary Republican leaders as State Socialism.

I recall vividly to mind the debate in the Assembly when I was the leader of the Democratic Party on the floor of that house on the question of pensions for widowed mothers. The Republican leader referred to it as paternalism and as Socialism. The Workmen's Compensation Act, enacted by a Democratic Legislature and signed by a Democratic Governor, was referred to as paternalistic and Socialistic. All of the salutary amendments to the factory code intended to promote the health and well being of women and children in industry were decried as being Socialistic and paternalistic.

As early as 1922 a large part of the argument made against me and my campaign for the governorship was predicated on the theory that I favored paternalistic legislation because I argued for the strengthening of the child labor laws, the laws for the protection of women in industry, and the extension of the benefits of the Widows' Pension Act. And in the present campaign in New York State the Republican candidate is building a large part of his argument on a promise to extend the benefits of all these laws, notwithstanding that at the time of their original introduction they were all decried by the reactionary element of the Republican Party as Socialistic and paternalistic.

The cry of Socialism has been patented by the powerful interests that desire to put a damper on progressive legislation.

Failing to meet the arguments fairly and squarely, " Special Interest " falls back on the old stock phrase of Socialism. The people of New York State are tired of the stock argument, have discovered that it means nothing, that it is simply subterfuge and camouflage, and I am satisfied that the people of the nation in their wisdom will so appraise it.

As far as all these problems are concerned, I have certainly used words to convey my meaning and I have not attempted to conceal it, and it made no difference in what part of the country I was talking. To refer to the remedies for all these evils as State Socialism is not constructive statesmanship, it is not leadership; and leadership is what this country is hungry for today. It has not had it in the last eight years, and it has little prospect of it in the four to come, in the event of Republican success.

The solution of these problems along sane, sensible, progressive lines can only come from the restoration of the Democratic Party to power under a leadership that I promise will be active, alert, forward-looking and successful.

XIV

ADDRESS AT PHILADELPHIA

Philadelphia, Pennsylvania, October 27, 1928

I SHALL begin tonight by disposing of some statements made by the Republican candidate and some of his prominent supporters which in my opinion are beclouding the issues and are intended to mislead the American public.

In his speech in Missouri last Monday night former Governor Hughes, in discussing the prohibition issue, said:

" We have a sham battle over prohibition."

A sham battle? What does Governor Hughes mean by that? Does he take the position that the American people are not concerned about prohibition? Does he mean to indicate that they are satisfied with conditions as they exist today? Further on in the same speech he said:

" I do not say that the election of Governor Smith would not greatly intensify the demand for a change."

Now, if my election will in fact intensify throughout the country a demand for a change in the Prohibition Law, by what process of reasoning does Governor Hughes believe it to be a sham battle? If I understand aright the public sentiment in this country there is nothing sham about this issue. It is a real one and comes very close to the heart and to the conscience of the American people. It involves bribery, corruption, lawlessness, intemperance and violation of and disrespect for all law. Leading men in the business world, presidents of colleges and universities, clergymen of various denominations, men and women in all walks of life, are openly and fearlessly on record, irrespective of their political affiliations, in opposition to the condition in which the country finds itself today as the result of the Eighteenth Amendment and the Volstead Act.

On this subject former President Hadley of Yale University, in the fewest possible words, voiced the feeling of millions of right-thinking men and women when he said:

" The object of the Eighteenth Amendment was to stop drunkenness and promote public order. This object has not been attained. The amendment and its enforcing statute, the Volstead Act, have not only failed to secure either of these results, but have failed so conspicuously as to produce disrespect for law among private citizens and public officials alike. For the last five years it has been the paramount duty of the party in power to recognize this situation and deal with it intelligently. This obligation it has failed to meet."

Leaders of the American people who had vision and knowledge of human nature predicted what would result from the attempt to write a police statute into the fundamental law of the land.

Former President Taft in 1918 said:

" I am opposed to national prohibition. I am opposed to it because I think it is a mixing of the national government in a matter that should be one of local settlement.

"I am opposed to the presence of laws on the statute books that cannot be enforced and as such demoralize the enforcement of all laws. . . .

" I am not in favor of a national amendment which should force twelve or fifteen great states into a sumptuary system which the public opinion and the real practices of the people of those states would not support."

To my way of thinking, he seems to have hit the nail exactly on the head when he said:

" The regulation of the sale and use of intoxicating liquors should be retained by the states. They can experiment and improve. They have the full power and the Federal Government has helped them by making it a Federal offense to import liquor into their borders if they forbid it. If the power of regulation is irrevocably committed to the general government, the next generation will live deeply to regret it."

President Wilson, referring to prohibition, said:

" You cannot regulate the morals and habits of a great cosmopolitan people by placing unreasonable restrictions upon their liberty and freedom. All such attempts can only end in failure and disappointment. In the last analysis, in these matters that seek to regulate personal habits and customs, public opinion is the great regulator."

All this must be known to Mr. Hughes, and I am unable to say by what process of reasoning he believes that a constructive policy, put forward by me to meet the situation which these great leaders foresaw, is a sham battle. It is a fair question to ask whether Mr. Hughes himself is satisfied with the results of prohibition in this country.

Let us see if Mr. Hoover knows anything about it. As far back as 1918, when Food Administrator, he said:

" If we stop brewing, the saloons of the country will still be open, but confined practically to a whiskey and gin basis. Any true advocate of temperance and of national efficiency in these times will shrink from this situation, for the national danger in it is greater than the use of some four million bushels of grain monthly in the breweries."

He further said:

" It is mighty difficult to get drunk on two and three-quar-ters per cent. beer. It will be easy enough if we force a sub-stitution of distilled drinks for it."

That is exactly what prohibition has brought about.

While there are no public saloons today, no person of any common sense will deny the fact that hard liquor can be pro-cured in any part of this country and is being illegally trans-ported and illegally sold.

We have the sworn testimony of the officials of the govern-ment to make good this statement. Exactly what Mr. Hoover warned about ten years ago is taking place in the United States today. Still he says it is "a noble experiment," and Mr. Hughes says that the man who offers a suggestion to cure these evils is carrying on a sham battle.

Mr. Hoover speaks about appointing a commission to find out what abuses there are in the administration of the prohibition laws. The Senate studied this whole matter only a short time ago and they have before them the sworn testimony of the head of the Prohibition Enforcement Agency in the whole country; and I quoted from it at great length in a speech that I delivered in Milwaukee.

Mr. Hoover shows from his own lips that he knows about it. He appeared before a committee appointed to bring in a plan for the reorganization of the executive departments of the Federal Government. The Chairman of the Commission asked him this question:

"Mr. Secretary, was your attention called to the fact that the Secretary of the Treasury stated that in his judgment the coast guard and the lifesaving service were necessary now in the enforcement of prohibition?"

What reply did Secretary Hoover make to that question? Here is what he said:

"That I would agree with, in the matter of the coast guard but not the lifesaving service. I think it would be a great misfortune if the lifesaving men were brought into prohibition enforcement. The same thing has been suggested with regard to the lighthouse service. I cannot conceive anything that would corrupt the fine traditions and personnel of those groups of men more than by having them plunge into police duty of that character."

What did he have in his mind? The lighthouse and the lifesaving men were under his command and under his control. He was telling the chairman of the committee that he did not want them corrupted by the blighting influence of prohibition enforcement. However, he was entirely satisfied and willing that the coast guard under the Secretary of the Treasury, and for which he had no responsibility, be put in a position where they might be corrupted. This is what he refers to as " a noble experiment." But he did not want any of his men to have anything to do with it.

Lately I have heard a great deal of Republican gossip to the effect that " Smith could do nothing about the prohibition laws if he were elected." Governor Hughes voices that thought. Where did I hear that before? That was the stock argument made against me in the State of New York for years in the attempt to draw Republican support away from my candidacy for the governorship when I advocated drastic changes in the structure and form of the government in the interest of economy and efficiency.

Under our New York State Constitution it is practically impossible to elect a Democratic Assembly. In 1922, when I carried the State by 387,000 plurality, I was confronted with a Republican Assembly. The word had been spread around by the Republican organization workers and leaders that " there is no use of voting for Smith. He can't do anything to benefit the government of New York State because the Legislature won't be with him."

The Republican platform itself openly declared against a constitutional executive budget. They were bound by a solemn party promise not to do anything about it. And that lent force to the argument that Smith would not be able to accomplish his constructive reforms.

They have all been accomplished: Reorganization of the government; shortening of the ballot; executive budget by constitutional law; bond issues for the elimination of dangerous railroad crossings at grade; bond issues for parks and parkways, looking to the health and comfort of future generations; bond issues for the rehabilitation of the State's hospitals, plants and structures. After a quarter of a century of Republican neglect these have all been accomplished in the

State of New York in spite of the argument that "Smith couldn't do anything with a hostile Legislature." And how were they accomplished? By direct appeal to the people, by the marshaling of public sentiment, by the focusing of public demand for these things directly upon the legislative bodies. It is a matter of history that these reforms were taken by the Republican Party reluctantly, although after once having been accomplished they sought the credit for them.

Suppose the kind of argument now made by Governor Hughes had prevailed in the minds of the people of New York, we would have had no reorganization, we would have had no improvement in the government, things would have stood still. Nevertheless, that is a part of the argument that Mr. Hughes now offers, and it is a part of the whispering campaign to the effect that "Smith can accomplish nothing so far as prohibition is concerned."

What did Mr. Hughes do himself when he was Governor of New York? When he suggested something to the Legislature of his own party which they rejected, using his own words, he appealed to the people. He did not believe that he was carrying on any sham battle. He stated that he was in a real fight and he carried it directly to the rank and file of the people of the State of New York. And they backed him up.

He knows what I say is true, because he admits that my election will intensify the demand for a change in the prohibition laws.

Governor Hughes says that he feels that my election would impede the efforts at enforcement. What efforts? The situation could not be worse than it is today all over the country. Is he satisfied with it? Is he willing to take his place alongside Mr. Hoover and do nothing about it, except to call it a noble experiment?

If I had to admit that the American people were helpless to change the intolerable conditions which exist today, I would be forced in the next breath to deny the efficiency of Democratic representative government.

I believe that with the facts clearly before them the American people will express their dissatisfaction with the present condition. I believe they are ready to remedy it.

If elected, I shall discharge my constitutional duty and enforce the existing law to the very best of my ability. At the same time, I shall carry this matter straight to the American people and lay it before them frankly and clearly. I have suggested a remedy which, in my opinion, will wipe out the evils of corruption and bootlegging, promote real temperance and restore respect for law. It rests upon the fundamental doctrine of states' rights. It would give to the people of each State the power under the conditions set forth in my acceptance speech to determine for themselves the position they wish their State to take with respect to prohibition. It would make the law again responsive to the will of the people themselves, and I am satisfied that the people themselves, under constructive and intelligent leadership, can be relied upon to effect this reform. Governor Hughes need not worry — this is no sham battle.

While we are correcting statements calculated to becloud the issues of the campaign, let me correct a statement by Mr. Hoover himself made in his speech at Boston. After referring to the fact that " the Tariff Commission is a most valuable arm of the government," and that "it can be strengthened and made more useful in several ways," he said:

" But the American people will never consent to delegating authority over the tariff to any commission, whether non-partisan or bi-partisan. Our people have a right to express themselves at the ballot box upon so vital a question as this. There is only one commission to which delegation of that authority can be made. That is the great Commission of their own choosing, the Congress of the United States and the President."

Mr. Hoover could only have used these words for the purpose of beclouding the issue. No suggestion was made by me
that the Tariff Commission should take the place of Congress,
nor is there a single line in the Democratic platform to that
effect. I definitely referred to the Tariff Commission as a
fact-finding body to lay before the Congress of the United
States the facts in detail so that Congress may intelligently
exercise its power to make tariff bills. I quoted former President Taft, who said that the members of Congress themselves
did not understand the tariff bills. He challenged anybody
to tell what they meant after a reading of them. The only
proposal that came from me with regard to the Tariff Commission was that it ought to be rehabilitated, it ought to be
strengthened, it ought to be put into the hands of the most
capable persons that can be procured in this country. Mr.
Hoover well knows that the proposal he seeks to inject into
the controversy would require an amendment to the Constitution of the United States. Nobody ever even remotely suggested any such thing. He knows what a Tariff Commission
is. He says it is a most valuable arm of the government;
but he neglects to say that his own party palsied that valuable
arm and rendered it useless. He knows that. And he further
knows that when he intimated that I proposed to limit the
power of Congress, he was doing it to muddy up the water.

Former Governor Hughes, speaking of me in Missouri,
commented on my statement that I want to take the tariff out
of politics. He said:

"If history is clear about anything it is that you can't take
the tariff out of politics."

Does Governor Hughes really want to continue to have the
tariff treated as the football of politics? Is he in accord with
the present system of tariff-making by compromise and log-
rolling? The American people themselves will take the tariff
out of politics when they get the facts. The trouble today
is that they have not got them and, as President Taft said, not

even the members of Congress know what is in the tariff bill. Governor Hughes did not make a very good point when he challenged my declaration that the tariff should be taken out of politics. If Charles E. Hughes thinks that the present system of tariff-making has any widespread approval in this country he does not keep track of the proceedings among business groups as outlined in the *Journal of Commerce* only two days ago. The National Manufacturers' Association, according to the *Journal of Commerce*, in session here, passed resolutions declaring against the old-fashioned log-rolling method of drawing up the tariff bill. And I read from the headline:

" They recommend that the Commission be taken entirely out of politics."

His party won't try it. I will.

Governor Hughes argues, "nothing can be done." He found fault with me because I referred to the reactionary Republican leaders as Bourbons, who learn nothing and forget nothing. It seems to me he is making good my statement for me. I do not have to offer any evidence; I will take his —
" You cannot do anything about it." A man with constructive ideas for the betterment of conditions is either fighting a sham battle or he is trying to do something which cannot be done, or, as Mr. Hoover said, he is a Socialist.

In his Chicago speech Governor Hughes said that the Democratic Party would have to eat crow to modify its tariff policy to meet the changed conditions of today. I do not see what license he has to make a statement of that kind. Why, even the Republican Party sometimes changes its position. It changed its position on the Federal Reserve Law. When that bill was pending before Congress, during the administration of President Wilson, only three Republican Senators voted for it. Senator Borah, the great Republican Progressive, as he likes to hear himself called, voted in the negative. The speeches in the Senate indicate that the Republican Party then feared that the government was being put into business and that it was probably a little journey into Socialistic territory. In fact, Senator Borah, speaking against the Federal Reserve Act, said the following:

" The wisdom of the matter I do not discuss, but it is just as Socialistic to assemble the banking powers and turn them over to the government as it would be the railroads."

Where did we hear that before? That was the theory put forth in Madison Square Garden by the Republican candidate only last Monday, speaking with reference to the Democratic solution of the farm, water power and prohibition questions. But read what they say about it today. Observe their change of attitude. Secretary Mellon today says about the Federal Reserve System:

" In the few years of their existence, the Federal Reserve Banks have demonstrated beyond any doubt their value to the country. During these years the country has come safely through a great war not only without a panic but with a minimum of strain upon its financial structure. The credit for this achievement is due in a large measure to the steadying influence exerted by the Federal Reserve System."

The Democratic Party all during its history has been able to meet the popular need and the popular will. Under the administration of President Wilson there was set a new standard of American living and of American wages, and the Democratic Party is only living up to its history and to its tradition when it declares that it will maintain that standard. Governor Hughes attempts to make the point that the members of Congress will hold to tariff ideas that prevailed before the war and would be unwilling to follow my leadership in the declaration that I made at Louisville. Tonight I will ease his mind on that subject and set to rest the fears generally of the Republican leaders as to what will happen in the event of Democratic success.

A telegram has been sent to every Democratic member of Congress and every Democratic candidate for Congress, for

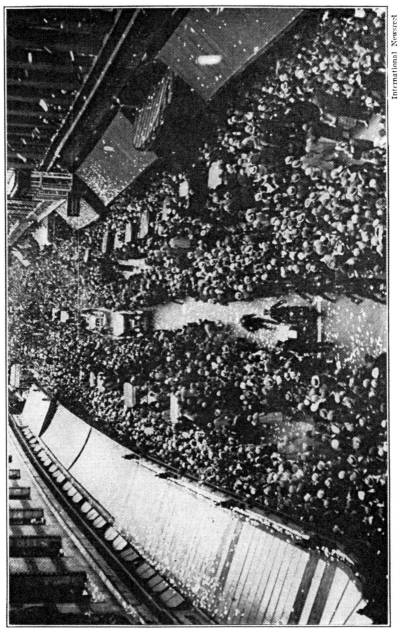

Boston's populace all but blocked the streets in their greeting to Governor Smith and his campaign party

the House and the Senate, asking their attitude with respect to my tariff declaration at Louisville. Eighty per cent. of them have replied thus far. A few have not yet replied because of absence from home in campaign work. Every one who has replied has authorized his signature to the following declaration:

" We, the undersigned Democratic candidates for the House and Senate, reaffirm the allegiance of our party to a non-partisan tariff commission as enunciated in the Democratic platform adopted at Houston and declare our approval of the constructive interpretation placed on the tariff plank by our standard bearer, Governor Smith, in his Louisville speech when he said, ' I definitely pledge that the only change I will consider in the tariff will be specific revisions in specific schedules, each considered on its own merits on the basis of investigation by an impartial tariff commission and a careful hearing before Congress of all concerned. That no revision of any specific schedule will have approval of Democratic Party which in any way interferes with American standard of living and level of wages. In other words, I say to the American working man that the Democratic Party will not do a single thing that will take from his weekly pay envelope a five cent piece. To the American farmer I say that the Democratic Party will do everything in its power to put back into his pocket all that belongs there. And we further say that nothing will be done that will embarrass or interfere in any way with the legitimate progress of business, big or small. With this prescription honestly put forth with a clear-cut and definite promise to make it effective, I assert with confidence that neither Labor nor Industry, nor Agriculture nor Business has anything to fear from Democratic success at the polls in November.' And we hereby pledge our cooperation in carrying out the principles and policies therein set forth."

That puts an end to the effort of Governor Hughes and his Republican colleagues to disturb the business of this country by predictions of business upheaval in the event of my election because of the Democratic attitude to the tariff.

Week before last, in the State of Missouri, I spoke on Federal finances and I clearly showed that the Republican administration at Washington was painting for the people of the country a false picture, calculated to make them believe that the present administration had reduced the cost of operating the government. I clearly showed from figures taken from the public record that in 1927 and 1928 the government cost more to operate than it did in the first year of the Coolidge administration.

Secretary Mellon immediately came to the rescue of the administration and made the statement that I had distorted the figures. Let us see what he offered to back up this statement.

In the first place, he admitted that there was an increase in the cost of government in the Coolidge administration, although in a radio speech delivered several weeks ago he claimed it had been decreased. He says, however, that the figures which I gave, showing an increase of two hundred million dollars between 1924 and 1927, were wrong, and he says the increase is only $29,000,000. In order to get this figure, for some reason known only to himself, he left out of consideration the Post Office Department. Since when did that cease to be a part of the Federal Government? It is true it earns a revenue. The fact that postal revenue is earmarked for the use of the postal service no more justifies leaving post office expenditures out of a statement of Federal finances than I would be justified in leaving out the expenditures of the New York State Motor Vehicle Bureau, because the thirty odd million dollars received from motor vehicle licenses are earmarked for highway purposes.

AT PHILADELPHIA

This is a little more of the trick bookkeeping that I spoke about, designed to withhold the truth about the increase in the cost of government under the present Republican administration. I said in Missouri, and I say again tonight in Pennsylvania, that the cost of government between 1924 and 1927 increased two hundred million dollars.

Secretary Mellon in his own reports shows that expenditures were higher in 1925 than in 1924, and in 1926 they were still higher, and that in the two years the increase amounted to almost eighty million dollars.

In my speech in Missouri I spoke about the failure of the Republican administration to make adequate appropriations for the housing of our soldiers. Secretary Davis said that the complaint I made about inadequate housing had been taken care of and, as a matter of protection, added that what was not already attended to would be taken care of by the next Congress.

He knows nothing about what the next Congress will do, and it is not an answer to a statement of fact with regard to neglect to say that in the next Congress or some following one something undoubtedly is going to be done about it. Only a year ago, before the House Committee on Appropriations, Secretary Davis testified that it would require one hundred million dollars to finance the army housing program, and that only a small fraction of this amount could be obtained from the sale of existing sites. He further said:

" I have not hesitated to say quite frequently that I think the condition of our housing is a very serious matter and almost amounts to a national scandal, and if money was available certainly an additional amount could and should be expended on that item."

Was the one hundred million dollars appropriated? Secretary Davis knows that it was not, and he further knows that he rushed to the rescue of the Republican administration with a misleading statement.

CAMPAIGN ADDRESS

The same situation obtains in the navy. Everybody remembers that Admiral Magruder wrote an article for the *Saturday Evening Post*, entitled " The Navy and Economy," in which he charged that the navy had failed to demobilize after the World War, that it was overorganized and overstaffed and still on a war-time basis. He said there were too many yards and that they were being maintained for political purposes; that in one fiscal year the cost of maintenance of the yards was $61,000,000, although only $16,000,000 worth of repairs was done. Immediately after making these charges Admiral Magruder was called to the Navy Department to justify his claim. He was then called before the House Committee on Naval Affairs and questioned about this article. He reiterated all of his charges of extravagance, failure to demobilize and excessive cost of maintenance. The result was that he was relieved of his post as Commandant of the Philadelphia Navy Yard by the Secretary of the Navy. He appealed to President Coolidge. The President rejected his appeal. He is still on the waiting list.

This is what happens to a man who ventures a suggestion for real enonomy when it interferes with political patronage.

Governor Hughes at Chicago distorted my Missouri speech into a criticism of economy. I carefully said in the State of Missouri that I gave the Federal Government full credit for every economy in government it effected, and I went so far as to say that I not only approved that but that I insisted on it in the government of New York State. What I criticised was the attempt to use a few petty economies to lead the American people to believe that there has been a reduction in the cost of government under Mr. Coolidge.

This brings me to something which, if put into effect, would have resulted in a real economy. A real economy means a benefit not only to every taxpayer but to every citizen, because the burden of the cost of government rests not only on those who pay taxes directly but on all the citizens of the country. The tax burden has a way of being passed along and being borne finally by the people who pay the rent and buy the necessaries of life. Economical administration of the government is, therefore, a matter of vital importance to every one of us.

Let us take a look at the Republican platform for 1920:

" We advocate a thorough investigation of the present organization of the Federal departments and bureaus with a view to securing consolidation, a more businesslike distribution of functions, the elimination of duplication, delays and overlapping of work, and the establishment of an up to date and efficient administrative organization."

The present makeup of Federal departments in Washington comprises at least 200 units. Not all of these fall within the ten departments whose heads sit in the President's Cabinet. Forty or more of the units, involving upwards of 50,000 employees, are independent in the sense that they report to no member of the Cabinet.

I could give no better explanation of the present disorganized and disjointed governmental system at Washington than that given by former Postmaster-General Hays in a speech that he delivered to the Fifth Avenue Association of New York as far back as November, 1921, when he said:

" When President Harding began his administration he found deplorable conditions in what I may term the housekeeping part or the business management part of the government, everywhere throughout Washington, aggravated of course by the war situation; yet the inefficiency was not the result of the last few years. It goes to the heart of the government. The government has been growing for 132 years, but its growth has not been symmetrical like the growth of a tree nor has it been built up like your own great business institutions. It has been a growth of adding a bureau here and a department there, without any regard for relevancy, appropriateness, efficiency or economy. The result is that if you could visualize the government as a business or administrative unit, you would see something much like one of these grotesque spectacles of a big oyster shell, to which in the course of years big and irregular masses of barnacles have attached themselves without symmetry or relevancy."

Mr. Hays recalled what he called a laughable lack of system, and he said that Mr. Hoover himself had called it to his attention. He talked about conservation of wild life in so far as it applies to bears. Arctic bears come under the Secretary of Commerce; grizzly bears are cared for by the Secretary of the Interior and brown bears are looked after by the Department of Agriculture. He also referred to the business man who came to Washington to sell road dressing to the government only to find out he had to see eight different department heads because the building of roads was under the jurisdiction of eight people. He told the story of the three hundred lifesaving stations under the coast guard service which, by the way, is in the Treasury Department while the lighthouse service, with many of the lighthouses located within a few steps of the lifesaving station, is in the Department of Commerce.

A half dozen separate agencies of the government disseminate intelligence to the navigation interests of the country. Charts of the American sections of the Great Lakes are prepared and furnished by the Lake Survey Water Department. Charts of the Canada sections of the Great Lakes and of foreign waters are furnished by the Navy Department. Charts of our Atlantic and Pacific coasts and of territorial waters are prepared and furnished by the Department of Commerce. Storm warnings are sent out by the Weather Bureau of the Department of Agriculaure. Nautical Almanacs are provided by the Naval Observatory.

Mr. Hays further said:

" It is not necessary to point out the numerous duplications of overhead, of plant, equipment and of personnel which unavoidably accompany this scattering of similar work among different departments. To all intents and purposes the ten great executive departments have been functioning independently of each other, and forty odd establishments not under any cabinet officer conduct their business practically without any coordinating influence whatever."

This speech by the Postmaster-General, made as early as 1921, and the definite platform pledge of 1920, held a hope out to the people of the country that they could look forward at an early date to a reorganization of the machinery of the Federal Government in the interest of a greater efficiency and economy.

During the Harding administration nothing happened. The platform plank and the eloquent speech were entirely forgotten.

In 1924, following its old-time trick, we find the Republican Party back again with a renewal of the promise. Their platform said:

" We favor a comprehensive reorganization of the Executive Departments and bureaus along the lines of the plan recently submitted by a joint committee of the Congress which has the unqualified support of President Coolidge."

What happened in the last four years? The plan approved by that platform declaration was thrown in the waste basket, and in its place just two consolidations were effected. The Bureau of Mines and the Patent Office were transferred from the Department of the Interior to the Department of Commerce. That is the sum total of the reorganization, in pursuance of that pledge. And the United States Chamber of Commerce at its sixteenth annual meeting in May of this year said:

" No progress has been made on the plan of reorganization of the government departments as advocated by the Chamber."

That brings us down to date.

I have searched through the Republican platform of 1928, and it does not even mention reorganization. As far as the Republican Party is concerned, they not only broke their word from 1921 to 1928, but they hold out not even a future promise. And in the face of this, in the platform of 1928, they say to the people of America:

" Our words have been made deeds. We offer no promises but accomplishments."

So far as reorganization of the government is concerned, they can point to no accomplishment, and they don't even make another promise. On the other hand, the Democratic Party specifically pledges a businesslike reorganization of all the departments of the government, the elimination of duplication, waste and, overlapping and the substitution of modern, businesslike methods for existing obsolete and antiquated conditions.

In all that I have stated here tonight I believe that I have made out a case for a just statement on my part that the Republican Party is seeking to continue control of this country under false pretenses. It misstates and misrepresents the Democratic attitude; misstates and misrepresents its own attitude; and boasts of accomplishment that in fact never took place.

It is for the American electorate on the sixth of November to decide how much longer they are ready to stand for broken promises and misstatements.

To bring the government into harmony with modern progress and efficiency, it will be necessary to restore the Democratic Party to power; and tonight in Philadelphia I confidently assert that that will be the decision of the American people on election day.

XV

ADDRESS AT BALTIMORE

Baltimore, Maryland, October 29, 1928

IN my speech accepting the Democratic nomination for the Presidency I used the following language:

"Government should be progressive, not reactionary. I am entirely unwilling to accept the old order of things as the best unless and until I become convinced that it cannot be made better."

When I spoke these words I had something in mind, something born of a quarter of a century of experience in elective public office. During that time I found men elected to office who were entirely satisfied with what I referred to as the old order of things and were entirely willing to accept the honor and the glory of public office, but who were unwilling to devote their time, their ability and their energy into making government more responsive and more progressive. On the other hand, in my time I have seen men elected to public office who discharged their duties with a sincere desire for progress and betterment.

The last quarter of a century has seen the greatest material advance that the world has probably ever witnessed, and a large part of the credit for it belongs to modern and progressive business ideas. The government alone seems to be lagging in the march of progress. It seems to be fastened down to the older order of things. As a boy I heard of the standpatter as one who wanted nothing done, the man who was entirely satisfied with things as he found them, the man who followed the line of least resistance.

There has been less improvement in national government in the last seven and a half years than in any similar period during my public life. In our country government is the agency of the people for making effective the popular will. The man at the head of the government is the servant of the people to direct and shape and execute the policies that spring from the will of the great majority.

In my speech of acceptance I said that any foreign policy must come from the people themselves. I go a step further and say that the Constitutional requirement of a vote in the Senate of two-thirds of that body for the ratification of a treaty showed that it was the intent of the framers of our Constitution that treaties with foreign powers must be approved by the overwhelming sentiment and wish of the American people. It evidently was the intent of the framers of the Constitution that agreements between our country and foreign nations be distinguished from ordinary legislative questions and be lifted out of the realm of partisan politics.

Since our experience in the recent World War, unquestionably the fathers and mothers of this country desire peaceful and friendly relationships with every other nation. The man on the street not accustomed to the high-sounding phrases of international diplomacy desires to have the government apply the simple rule of " do unto others as you would have others do unto you."

In my speech of acceptance I amplified the declaration of principles concerning foreign relations set forth in the Democratic platform and, with election day only one week off, I have yet to hear a word in criticism or reply from the Republican candidate or his spokesmen.

It is extremely difficult to make a hard and fast rule with regard to our relations with other countries. I have often been prompted to the belief that the administration of foreign affairs is largely based on the personal equation, the sincere desire to be as just and fair to other nations as we would have them be to us. Beyond that we must have an administration able to adhere to such definite policy as can be clearly enunciated. I know of no better policy so far as our Latin-American relations are concerned, than the one set forth by Elihu Root, Republican Secretary of State, when he said:

"We consider that the independence and equal rights of the smallest and weakest member of the family of nations deserve as much respect as those of the great empires. We pretend to no right, privilege or power that we do not freely concede to each one of the American republics."

That definite statement of policy, so far as Latin-America is concerned, unquestionably received the widespread approval of the American people.

If you desire to know how far the Republican Party departed from that principle and policy, ask Senator Borah, for example, what he thinks of the foreign policy of the present Republican administration in so far as it applies to our intervention in an election dispute in Nicaragua. I am satisfied that the protection of life and property of American citizens in all countries should be a matter of national concern, but, on the other hand, I am satisfied that the American people will no longer tolerate interference with the international affairs of the South American republics.

Under my administration there will be no diplomacy practiced that will permit the exploitation of weaker nations. You cannot preach one doctrine of foreign relations in Europe and practice another doctrine in Latin-America.

Believing, as I do, in the great brotherhood of man under the fatherhood of God, I am satisfied that the American people will always be ready and willing to assume their fair share of responsibility for the administration of the world of which they are a part, without political alliance with any foreign nation. In that belief, I am prepared to make a real endeavor to make the outlawry of war effective by removing its causes and to substitute the methods of conciliation, conference, arbitration and judicial determination.

CAMPAIGN ADDRESS

The Republican Party holds out but little hope to the American people for a forward-looking foreign policy, in view of the fact that Mr. Hoover promises to follow the Coolidge policies, which policies have been uniformly, in season and out of season, denounced on the floor of the Senate by the Republican chairman of the Committee on Foreign Relations.

Only by executive leadership, Congressional co-operation and the support of the people can we hope to deal with the great questions that lie ahead of us. Only by this method can we hope to make the outlawry of war a reality. Only then can we hope to regain the confidence of our neighbors in Latin-America. Only then can we hope to restore the Monroe Doctrine to what it once was and always ought to be — a mutual guaranty of peace on this hemisphere.

Only by this method can we hope to build up the use of arbitration and conciliation for the peaceful settlement of disputes. Only when this is brought about can there be a lasting understanding with the naval powers by which the terrible burden and terrible menace of competitive armament can be forever ended.

There is no use trying even to talk about solving any of these problems so long as there is a standing quarrel between the President and the leaders of his party in the Senate, with the promise that that quarrel will continue.

I pledge an end of that quarrel and an honest, open, fearless, unprejudiced treatment of each problem on the basis of the facts.

I am entirely satisfied that the old order of things can be changed for the better by the adoption of a forward-looking, progressive attitude on the part of the government toward the development of our natural water power resources.

Applying the old order of things, these resources must in time fall into the hands of private persons, to be operated for private gain and private profit. Following the new order of things, they would be developed by the government under government ownership and government control, to the end that the benefits that flow from them may find their way directly to the American people — their rightful owners.

I can only take the record, and, while Mr. Hoover does not come out and say it in so many words, the record clearly and fairly indicates that he is to be found on the side of the old order of things.

Nothing that I could say about his attitude on this subject would be any stronger or any more convincing than that which comes from United States Senators of his own party. Senator Borah said only a few days ago — and I quote him as he is reported in the daily press — " I disagree with Mr. Hoover on the power question. If that were the only issue in this campaign I could not support him."

Only last Saturday night, Senator Norris, of Nebraska, a Republican, but an uncompromising progressive, a man of clear vision and forceful speech, told the American people in unmistakable language a great many reasons why he was unwilling and unable to support Mr. Hoover in this contest. Prominent among his reasons was Mr. Hoover's attitude toward the development of public power resources.

Let me at this point say that, while I was denied the great privilege of listening to the Senator's broadcast — I had just finished my own speech in Philadelphia — I read his speech in the Sunday papers and I want to take opportunity to assure him publicly that he will never have any cause to regret what he said with respect to my attitude toward these great public questions.

What are the forces behind Mr. Hoover which make it necessary for members of his own party to repudiate his views on water power development? Senator Norris himself spread it out before the American people in his speech of last Saturday night — and it is nothing else than what has become known as the American Power Trust, made up of the individuals who have their eyes upon these valuable water power assets and propose to have the wheels turned for their benefit.

So far as our great natural resources in this country are concerned, that is the old order of things, and with that you may be sure that I am entirely dissatisfied. I am thoroughly convinced that the great rank and file of the American people are with Senator Norris and myself in the endeavor to set up a new order of things, and are unalterably opposed to the order that puts in the front seat of privilege and opportunity the power trust, in whose corner Mr. Hoover is unquestionably standing.

Particularly am I unwilling to accept the old order of things as it applies to the framework and structure of the Federal Government. There is no more crying need in Washington today in the interest of greater governmental efficiency and economy than the reorganization of the governmental machinery itself. Disjointed, disorganized, scattered, producing an overlapping of functions, a duplication of energy, a financial waste and a waste of effort, the old governmental machine is lumbering along.

This was recognized by the Republican Party as far back as 1920, when a definite promise was made to improve it. The promise was repeated in 1924, entirely forgotten in 1928, and here, at this hour and minute, the old order of things obtains. Attempts at progress have met with defeat, and the reason underlying the Republican failure is the desire of the Republican leaders to retain the patronage for political purposes and to continue to saddle upon the American people the burden of maintaining a costly, highpowered, political machine. It has been variously estimated that not millions, but hundreds of millions of dollars could be saved by a thorough-going, businesslike overhauling of the structure of the Federal Government.

As against broken Republican promises and failure and inability to progress. I promise on behalf of the Democratic

Party the rehabilitation and reorganization of the Federal machine, bringing it into harmonious and progressive step with the material development in business methods in the last quarter of a century.

In my Louisville speech I outlined my position on the tariff. This position, taken by me and approved by Democratic members of and candidates for Congress, is so constructive, so forward looking, so well designed to protect the workingman in his wages and his standard of living, to protect business large and small, to give to the farmer his fair return and to increase and improve the prosperity of the country generally, that the Republican Party in a moment of panic is forced — through one of its spokesmen — to the reactionary idea that the tariff cannot be taken out of politics.

This I dispute and, unsatisfied with the old order of things, I definitely make the claim that the Democratic Party under its platform and under the formula put forth by myself in my Louisville speech will take the tariff out of the realm of partisan politics, will do away with the log-rolling, and will remove the uncertainty that comes to business by every general revision of the tariff. This our opponents seem to think cannot be done. They seem to believe it is destined for all time to remain the football of politics, to be the object of compromise and of log-rolling.

That is the old order of things complained about by Presidents Taft and Roosevelt twenty years ago. I am entirely dissatisfied with it. I can and I will improve it. The Republican Party seems to think that this cannot be done. Let the American people decide that for themselves.

Unwilling to accept the old order of things as the best, I am entirely dissatisfied with the conditions prevailing throughout this country as a result of the Eighteenth Amendment and the Volstead Act. I believe that both of them ought to be brought into harmony with the best thought on the subject, to the end that we may restore respect for the law,

promote temperance and wipe out official corruption, bootlegging and offenses against public decency and public morals
that follow in their wake.

Standing by the old order of things, the Republican candidate refers to it as a noble experiment, desires to deal with it
constructively, but makes no mention of what he intends to do
about it beyond the appointment of a commission. The average American citizen knows that this is entirely unnecessary,
in view of the widespread knowledge of the effect of these
statutes on American public life and morals.

Mr. Hughes, as spokesman for the Presidential candidate,
says nothing can be done about prohibition; the Republican
Party must continue in the old course of attempting to carry
water on both shoulders. To bolster up its false claim
for a continuance in power it must pretend to being
avowedly dry when appealing to the drys, attempting to
mislead the wets by insidious propaganda to the effect that
nothing can happen — the old order of things must remain.

With that I entirely disagree. I believe that there is no
question in this country that cannot be definitely settled, no
condition that cannot be made better by the intelligent
thought of the rank and file of the American people.

Eight years ago the Republican Party placarded the country with signs that read: " Let us get away from wiggle and
wobble." In no similar period in the history of the country
has there been as much wiggling and wobbling as there has
been in the last seven and a half years. The chief spokesmen
of the Republican Party are wobbling all over on the prohibition question. Their wires are crossed. Senator Borah holds
prohibition to be the overshadowing issue of the campaign.
Governor Hughes, on the other hand, referred to it as a sham-
battle and dismissed it as being no part of this campaign.
Mr. Hoover finds himself caught between the wiggle and the
wobble and he gets off the hook entirely by referring to it as a
noble experiment.

AT BALTIMORE

Let us see the wiggling and the wobbling between the Republican Party platform and the attitude of the candidate and his spokesmen. The party platform, under the title "The Rights of the States," says:

"There is a real need in the country today to revitalize fundamental principles. There is a real need of restoring the individual and local sense of responsibility and self-reliance. There is a real need for the people once more to grasp the fundamental fact that under our system of government they are expected to solve many problems themselves under their municipal and State governments and to combat the tendency that is all too common to turn to the Federal Government as the easiest and least burdensome method of lightening their own responsibilities."

Following that statement in the platform there should come from the Republican Party a clear-cut, plain declaration in favor of my solution of the prohibition question by the application of the theory and principle of states' rights. Instead of that, when I make such a proposal, the Republican orators are in violent opposition to it, the candidate himself calls it socialistic and Senator Borah says that the perpetuation of the condition, violative of states' rights, diametrically opposed to his party's platform declaration, which I just read, is the paramount issue of the campaign. Talk about wiggle and wobble — where is there any more glaring example of it than this?

No man has performed a greater service in the cause of states' rights in recent years than has the Governor of Maryland — and here, in his own State, let me talk as frankly and as freely to you as he has in the past.

Let me say that the Republican Party wiggles and wobbles on this subject because it is held down to the earth by the forces of intolerance, well organized for the destruction of the fundamental principle of states' rights, in order that their ideas of personal conduct may be imposed upon the American people. They are made up of several groups. I can think of nothing that would go further to weaken the structure of our government than to have such organized groups use their money, their political power and their influence to browbeat the elected representatives of the people into submission to their theories. It is a form of political blackmail that the American people can not and — I am satisfied — will not tolerate.

In his book on "American Individualism," friendly with the wets and friendly with the drys, closing its eyes to the evil consequences that grow out of accepting the old order of things, professing one belief and entertaining another, Mr. Hoover, referring to propaganda associations, said:

" If they develop into warring interests, if they dominate legislators and intimidate public officials, if they are to be a new setting of tyranny, then they will destroy the foundation of individualism."

Will Mr. Hoover deny that the Anti-Saloon League is a propaganda association? Will he state that it has never attempted to dominate legislators, or that it has never attempted to intimidate public officials? Just read the warning that was sent to Senator Norris when knowledge of the fact got around the country that he intended to speak for me in this campaign because of my progressive ideas on many subjects that he has been fighting for in Washington. Coincident with the flashing of that news around the country he received the following warning from the Anti-Saloon League:

" The Anti-Saloon League has always supported Norris in the past, but if he makes this speech for Smith the league is through with him. The Anti-Saloon League will oppose Norris in future campaigns if he does this thing."

That is a threat. That is a cold-blooded threat.

All Senator Norris's great work, all of his great influence in favor of progressive legislation for the benefit of the men, women and children of this country, falls to the ground and is lost sight of the minute that he goes counter to the narrow, prejudiced and bigoted ideas of the Anti-Saloon League. I can think of no greater force for evil in this country than an organization which, through any of its spokesmen, threatens disaster to the public statesman who does not submit to its dictation.

Throughout the length and breadth of this land the Anti-Saloon League has been engaged in the propaganda intended to make God-fearing men and women believe that the Eighteenth Amendment and the Volstead Act are dogmas of religion. I know of no church in this country that makes Volsteadism or the Eighteenth Amendment an article of religious faith. It is nothing more or less than legislation ratified during the excitement of war and lobbied through Congress by means of coercion and threat and has no religious sanctity about it.

In fact, every religion worthy of the name teaches the value of temperance, of sobriety and of the danger of self-indulgence; and, to say the least about it, it should shock the American idea of right to attempt to use the great moral authority of the churches to make sincere men and women believe that, if they attempt to deal reasonably and open-mindedly with a great social problem, they are unfaithful to their religion, or that they have offended against God.

You cannot make a new sin by law. If it was not inscribed on the tablets of stone that were handed down to Moses on the Mount, it is not a sin. The Volstead Act was not passed until 1919 — and then over the veto of President Wilson.

In talking about the influences behind the Republican candidate, while in the State of Maryland and mindful of her devotion to American principles and to religious freedom, we cannot overlook the Ku Klux Klan. How must the American people feel, in view of the countless billions of dollars that have been poured into the couse of public education, to have organized in this country a group, referring to themselves as 100 per cent. American, who stand in opposition to any American citizen because of his or her religion? They are entirely, to my mind, without any understanding of the fundamentals of American thought and American ideals. That they are actively engaged in promoting the cause of the Republican Party nobody would have the hardihood to deny, and there is abundant testimony that their activity is encouraged by some of the leaders of the Republican Party.

I hold in my hand a notice of a public meeting under the auspices of the Ku Klux Klan, and it is stated that the meeting is to be in conjunction with the National Republican Committee.

Ordinarily, I would probably pay little or no attention to this card, in that I have nothing to back it up, but its appearance in one of the leading newspapers published in the State of New Jersey, lends color to its truthfulness. It is true that the local Republican leaders disclaim knowledge of it, but one of them makes a significant statement that I would like to call to your attention. When asked whether or not the plans of the national committee were submitted to him for approval, in so far as they concerned New Jersey, he said:

"They are supposed to be, but they have gotten us in trouble before. Once or twice they have gone over our heads on that religious question. I know absolutely nothing about this meeting."

What did the Republican leader in New Jersey mean when he said that the national committee got the local leaders in trouble by going over their heads on the religious question? If that means anything to me, it means that some of the plans formulated in the national committee, without the consent of the local leaders, have had to do with the question of religion.

A newspaper published in Washington, known as the *Fellowship Forum*, is the official publication of the Klan, and its every issue contains the most contemptible and the most outrageous abuse directed against millions of American citizens because of their religion. One of the known owners of this scurrilous publication, the chairman of the Republican State Committee of Virginia, the public prints tell us, was in the party of Mr. Hoover on his trip to Elizabethton, in Tennessee.

I was born in the United States and my father and mother were born in the United States. From the time that I was old enough to understand anything my mother told me that the great crowning glory of this country was the noble expression found in the Declaration of Independence that all men are created equal. I have served the largest State in the Union for a quarter of a century, and for eight years during that period I have been its Chief Executive. That I have given to it the very best that is in me has been, times without number, publicly attested by members of another political faith than my own.

On my recent visit to Indiana, my attention was called to a blazing cross alongside the railroad track, where the car in which I was had to pass, and I was informed that this was intended as a defiance by the Klan of my presence in the State, although I came there, not only as the candidate of a great party for the highest office in the nation, but as the chief executive of another State. What a hollow mockery — men professing a belief in Christianity and in Americanism to find it necessary to raise between heaven and earth the emblem of the Christian faith as a defiance to me because of my religious belief!

Nothing could be so out of line with American tradition and American history. Nothing could be so far removed from the thoughts, the aspirations and the ideals of America. I would rather go down to ignominious defeat than to be raised to the greatest position in the gift of the people by any influence that may be exerted by any organization with such perverted ideas of Americanism. While I think of them as a small group of misled, if not ignorant people, nevertheless, this campaign brings home to the electors, and, in my opinion, they cannot disregard it — that the Klan is one of the forces behind the Republican Party.

That I have had, during all of my public career as Governor, their open enmity and hostility there can be no question. That they are supporting the Republican Party in this campaign there can be no question. As I said in Oklahoma, I seek support in this campaign only upon the record and upon the pledge and promise of what I am able to do for the benefit of all the people of the United States. I want no support because of my religious belief. I repeat my firm adherence to the American doctrine of the absolute separation of Church and State. Political activity of the church is the negation of that separation.

I believe that I have made out a case in Baltimore that the Democratic Party, under my leadership, will not be satisfied with things as they find them, will not accept the old order of things as best, but will strive to make the government constructive and not destructive, progressive and not reactionary. No hope of this kind can come either from the Republican platform, from the Republican candidate or from the Republican record. In the time allowed I have pointed out some of the forces behind the Republican Party in this campaign. I come before the American people as a free agent. I was nominated on the first ballot, not as the result of any compromises, and I made no promises to any individual or any group of individuals.

I will take the oath of office as President of the United States with absolutely no obligation except to devote myself to the best interests of this country and to promote the prosperity, the welfare and happiness of all the people.

XVI

ADDRESS AT NEWARK

Newark, New Jersey, October 31, 1928

I SHALL take for my text this evening a statement by the immortal Lincoln which since its utterance has been heard around the world:

" You can fool some of the people all of the time, all of the people some of the time, but you cannot fool all of the people all of the time."

Before I take up the text, however, let me make answer to some of the things said by Governor Hughes in his Massachusetts speech.

Why didn't Governor Hughes take this nomination? He is the only one who is making any fight. What are we up against? The same old thing that we have been suffering from for eight years; a candidate for the office of the Presidency of the United States who is unable to talk for himself? Who has become the official spokesman? It looks to me like it is Governor Hughes. And it further looks to me as though he is trying to becloud the issues in a vain attempt to set his own candidate right before the people and to question my position.

In the city of Denver I clearly outlined my position on water power. It is as follows:

" I regard water power as the last great, God-given resource that has not been wrested from the people of this country for private profit or for private gain, and I have declared for the nation the policy which I declared for the State of New York: That these water powers ought to remain in the control of the nation if they belong to the nation, of the State if they belong to the State, or jointly where the ownership is in more than one State. And I believe the agency, whether it be State or government, should not only own the site, but should own and build and operate the power house. It is the only way that you can guarantee equitable distribution of the power and fair and reasonable prices to the ultimate consumer, and this is because of the government's power to contract. The whole thing is contained in the sentence: The government must keep its hands on the switch that turns on or off the power."

I have made myself perfectly clear. The man who has not made himself clear is Mr. Hoover. And I now ask Mr. Hughes to ask Mr. Hoover the question that he asked me.

On the prohibition question, which Mr. Hughes refers to as a sham battle, I have also made myself perfectly clear. Here again he is trying to becloud the issue. I know very well that the President of the United States cannot amend the Constitution. And Governor Hughes knows that I know that. What I said I would do was that I would accept the position of leadership of the American people on this question by coming out and telling them the truth about it, laying it before them, and let them decide it themselves — the only way it ever can be decided.

During the whole campaign Mr. Hoover has not made a single suggestion about it except to refer to it as a noble experiment.

Mr. Hughes himself said that he was not satisfied with it. Let him ask the candidate for whom he is working so hard whether or not he is satisfied with it; and if not, what he proposes to do about it.

I also want to serve notice on Mr. Hughes that, so far as I am concerned, I am running my own campaign. He has all he can do to run Mr. Hoover's. And it is entirely unnecessary for him to comment on my attitude to the tariff by speaking about what happened in the past. He himself has publicly said that I know something about politics. He has also said that we cannot take the tariff out of politics. If he is right in both statements, I am the man who ought to handle it in the interest of the workingmen and the business men of this country.

As long as Mr. Hoover seems to be unable to do it and is compelled to rely upon Mr. Hughes to make his campaign for him, he owes it to Mr. Hoover and to the Republican Party to make the campaign constructively and tell us, so long as Mr. Hoover is unable to do it, where his candidate stands on the issues.

Now let us devote our attention to the text I just read.

The Republican record of the last seven and a half years and the Republican conduct of this campaign suggest this text to me as most appropriate. At each approaching election the Republican Party professes its great love and devotion to the workingman and holds itself out to be his great friend.

Let us see how far the record of the last seven and a half years and the record of this campaign disclose an attempt to fool the workingman.

In the city of Newark a short time ago the Republican candidate made a special bid for the support of labor when, in the very opening of his address, he said the following:

"Real wages and standards of living of our labor have improved more during the past seven and a half years of Republican rule than during any similar period in the history of this or of any other country."

I challenge that statement and I submit in fairness to the workingmen of this country that the present comparatively high scale of wages and standards of living were set during the war under the administration of Woodrow Wilson. It is entirely beside the point to argue what brought this condition about; it is sufficient to say that that is when it happened. Mr. Hoover knows this just as well as I know it and just as well as you know it.

He further made the statement that when the Republican Party came into power in 1921, there were five or six million unemployed upon our streets. He uses figures carelessly. There is a big difference between five and six million. There is a difference of one million, but that seems to be of small consequence to Mr. Hoover. The fact is that Mr. Hoover was Chairman of the President's Conference on Unemployment in 1921, and in his report to the President of the United States, dealing with this same period, he said that the decline in industrial employment was less than three million, and expressed his confidence that 2,750,000 was the maximum figure. He raises the figure of unemployed in 1921 from around 2,750,000 to six million for the purpose of campaign argument.

In the course of his speech Mr. Hoover said that unemployment was in part cured by means of immediate institution of public works.

This statement I deny, and I do so because the Republican administration in an effort to secure credit for economy in the administration of the government seriously neglected all public works.

In my speech in Missouri only a few weeks ago I showed that in almost every large city in this country land purchased as far back as fifteen years ago upon which to erect public buildings is still standing idle, and up to this day that statement has not been contradicted.

Further on in his speech Mr. Hoover said that last winter there were approximately 1,800,000 men idle and claims that this is an accurate survey made by the Department of Labor.

What are the facts? A statement was made upon the floor of the United States Senate by Senator Wagner of New York, based upon that very report, that over four million men were out of work and that statement up to this time has not been successfully challenged. It has in substance been accepted by everyone who has made a study of the problem and has been confirmed by reports of charity and relief organizations in various parts of the country.

Let us bear in mind that the Republican candidate was Chairman of the President's Conference on Unemployment during the term of President Harding, and from that Conference came three distinct recommendations requiring legislation, not a single one of which was enacted into law. Indeed, the Republican candidate in his Newark speech again recommends one of the proposals set forth in the original report of his commission, but what he failed to do was to tell the workingman that as far back as 1921 this same recommendation was put forth by him, but he never did anything about it since then.

Last winter a Democratic member of the Senate offered bills to carry into effect the recommendations on unemployment made by Mr. Hoover's commission, but the Republican administration ignored them.

Further on in his speech he speaks about building projects and recommends that these be carried on in such a way as to take up the slack in occasional unemployment. The Republican Party had a chance to do this in the period when he admits that 1,800,000 were out of employment and, instead of doing it, they preferred to make a false showing of economy and allow important and necessary building projects, to which they were committed, but for which they had made no appropriation, to go over to succeeding administrations.

I favor the adoption of a government program to prevent the suffering and enormous losses of unemployment. To that end the Department of Labor should be given the necessary appropriations and charged with the duty of collecting accurate and comprehensive information on employment in important industries.

I favor the adoption after study of a scientific plan whereby during periods of unemployment appropriations shall be made available for the construction of necessary public work.

I also favor an immediate and thorough study of the modern methods of industry, to the end that a constructive solution may be arrived at to absorb and utilize the surplus human labor released by the increasing use of machinery.

The difference between 1,800,000 and 4,000,000 men out of work may mean but little to Mr. Hoover, but it means a great deal to the army of the unemployed and their dependents. Mr. Hoover is most generous in his use of statistics, but no amount of statistics will support the family of a man who is out of work. Take statistics into a butcher or grocer shop and see how far you will get with them.

In the course of the speeches so far made by the Republican candidate he has claimed credit for the Republican Party for everything of betterment that has occurred in this country in the last seven and a half years, even to the increase in the number of children in our public schools, to the number of additional miles of electric wire laid through the country, the number of miles of highways, although they are built by the states, and the improvements in our educational system, although the Federal Government has nothing to do with it.

I do not know just why he referred to education in his speech, or how he believes that is calculated to help his candidacy.

My record as Governor of New York shows that there has been no greater friend of the cause of public education than I have been. During my administration the appropriations from State funds for public education rose from $9,000,000 in 1918 to $86,000,000 in 1928.

Public, elementary and high school facilities were extended, generous appropriations made for agricultural colleges, and salaries to teachers increased to meet the higher cost of living.

I went further than the Republican Party was willing to go when I made a strenuous effort to improve conditions in the rural schools, only to be met by Republican opposition sufficiently strong in a hostile Legislature to defeat the proposal.

The Republican National Committee, to my way of thinking, goes the very limit when they spend large amounts of money in newspaper advertising in an attempt to lead the American laborer to believe that everybody owns an automobile and that everybody lives on chicken dinners and that everybody is wearing silk socks.

The Bureau of Labor Statistics is on record as declaring that it requires a sum of well over $2,000 a year to provide a fair standard of living for a family of five people. The National Industrial Conference Board made up of employers presents to us the following data with regard to the average wages in the United States:

In the printing and publishing business it runs from $1,873 a year in New York down to $1,115 in Ohio.

In food products the wage runs from $1,700 a year in New York to $933 a year in Michigan.

In lumber and its products it runs from $1,630 a year in New York to $1,241 in Massachusetts.

In metal industries it runs from $1,615 in Ohio down to $1,357 a year in New Jersey.

In December of last year both Mr. Hoover and President Coolidge declared that the average wage in all manufacturing industries of the country was $1,280 a year or approximately $4.00 a day. At the same time they made that statement, they failed to point out that the Bureau of Labor Statistics fixed $2,000 a year as the cost of a fair standard of living for a family of five people.

The purpose of the advertisement, put out at great cost to the Republican National Committee, is nothing more nor less than an attempt to fool the American workingman.

CAMPAIGN ADDRESS

My attention was recently called to a circular put in the pay envelopes of workingmen here in New Jersey, which to my way of thinking is the most despicable kind of political propaganda so far devised. It shows a picture of an American workingman's home with a huge wall built around it described as the tariff wall. Figures depicting foreign countries are seen prying loose the great stones of the tariff walls and they are crushing through the roof of the American workingman's home. His wife is fleeing from danger with her children and he is lying prostrate on the ground. In the printed matter the workingman is told that the envelope contains from two to ten times as much as he would receive for doing the same work in Europe, and while it bears no imprint to indicate where it comes from, I am reliably informed that large quantities of these circulars were paid for and sent out by the Republican National Committee to be put in the pay envelopes of American workingmen.

I can think of no more ridiculous performance. It is an insult to the intelligence of the great army of workers of our country. It is a foolish attempt to make them believe that the object and purpose of the Democratic Party, under my leadership, is to destroy their homes, drive their wives and children into the streets and leave them helpless.

I have been the Governor of the State of New York for eight years. During this time I have not only had the united support of labor but a generous support of business men. If that had not been so it would have been impossible for me to have been elected Governor of New York in the year that the Republican candidate for President carried that State by nearly 700,000 plurality.

The Republican Party goes so far in its effort to fool the American workingmen as to try to lead them to believe that my elevation to the most exalted position in the world means that I am to turn my back upon them, that I am to forget their support in the past, that I am to be untrue in the presidency to every tradition that has characterized my public life for a quarter of a century.

Any American workingman who will analyze that circular, study my public record, read the plank in the Democratic platform, or look over my speech on the tariff delivered in Kentucky, will be compelled to come to the conclusion that that circular is put out by the Republican Party, using the employer as its agent, only for the purpose of fooling him.

I hold in my hand another circular signed with the name of a concern soliciting support for Mr. Hoover and threatening disaster to the employees of the company in the event of my election. It makes predictions which, on the face of the record, could never come to pass. It is dishonest, and the merchants or business men responsible for promulgating it are not what could be said, in the strictest sense of the word, good citizens of this country. Our American system of government is not what we suppose it to be if men can ride into public office under false pretenses and in the light of false statements.

In a democracy, above all other things, the truth must prevail. To my way of thinking the time is well past in this country when you can coerce and intimidate the American workingman. The sin of it all is that this coercion and intimidation comes from a party that in the last seven years, under the guise of being the friend of the rank and file of the American people, has been engaged in promoting the welfare and the interests of special privilege, even to the point of alienating the oil reserves of the country destined to protect the home of the workingman by maintaining a great arm of the National Defense in time of trouble.

Just before election Mr. Hoover and the Republican Party behind him profess a great interest in the welfare of labor. Let us see how far they exerted themselves in the interest of labor when they were in a position to do something to help the workers in the coal mines. Mr. Hoover himself was a member of a Commission appointed to investigate the coal problem. That Commission brought in a series of recommendations. The Republican administration did nothing about them. Several of them were afterwards introduced by Democratic Senators, and they all went down to defeat. The sum total of the whole operation was that Mr. Hoover himself attempted to deal with this problem,— we have a report of a Commission of which he was a leading member,— but nothing was ever done about it and, according to the candidate's speech of acceptance, the coal industry today is in a class with the textile and the agricultural industries — it is stagnant, and we have a condition of acute unemployment and distress in the coal regions.

Let me read to you a part of the plank devoted to labor in the Republican platform of this year:

"We believe that injunctions in labor disputes have in some instances been abused and have given rise to a serious question for legislation."

This to my way of thinking is a glaring example of attempting to fool the workingman. This sentence appears in the platform under the title of "Labor" and is followed by the words, "The Republican Party pledges itself to continue its efforts to maintain this present standard of living and high wage scale."

I cannot escape the conclusion that the matter about injunctions was put into the platform without a study of what it really meant or where it really belonged. Somebody must have said, "We have to say something about injunctions. Let us slip in a few words about it." No pledge is made to pass the legislation. It is a matter of record that the Republican Party has had eight years in which to cure the abuses by legislation, and not only did they not cure them but a Republican Attorney-General was one of the worst offenders in this regard and was guilty of as gross an abuse as can be found, when he himself — the attorney of all the people of the United States — applied for and secured from the court certain injunctions which merited and received widespread condemnation.

If the Democratic Party is entrusted with power under my leadership, you have my assurance that a definite remedy by law will be brought forth to end the existing evils and preserve the constitutional guarantees of individual liberty, free assemblage and speech and the rights of peaceful persuasion.

When we speak about workingmen, let us not forget working women. An interesting sidelight on the campaign is the attitude of what is known as the National Woman's Party, an organization of women seeking an amendment to the Federal Constitution that would prevent the states from enacting laws for the protection of women in industry. The effect of this amendment to the Constitution would be to make it impossible for any State to enact laws for the protection of the health and welfare of women in industry not equally applicable to men. Under my leadership the State of New York provided a 48-hour week for women. It prohibited night work of women in industrial establishments. It prohibited the employment of women in dangerous occupations. It required rest rooms in factories and mercantile buildings, and made many contributions by law to the health and comfort of women in industry. All of this progressive and forward-looking legislation applicable to women would be endangered if we attempted to tamper with the Federal Constitution along the lines desired by the National Woman's Party.

When one of the representatives of this organization questioned me over a year ago about my attitude to this proposed amendment to the Constitution, I told her in unmistakable language that I was unalterably opposed to it. I frankly told her that before I would subscribe to any theory of this kind I would see the cornerstone of the Capitol at Albany crumble into dust beneath my feet.

CAMPAIGN ADDRESS

I have always, in my own State, favored legislation that would remove all unjust discrimination against women, so far as property rights or privileges are concerned, and I amended the Civil Service Rules so as to give them absolute equality in examinations for public office.

So far as the nation is concerned, I favor the equality of women with men in all political and governmental matters, and I favor an equal wage for equal service whether rendered by a man or a woman.

The Republican candidate is non-committal on the amendment proposed by the National Woman's Party. The Republican vice-presidential candidate has declared in favor of it. In fact, as a Senator he introduced the resolution for the amendment to the Constitution two years ago.

The Secretary of the National Woman's Party sends out the word that the greatest hope in this election for equal rights lies with the election of Mr. Hoover and Senator Curtis. I make particular mention of this because I regard it as fooling the people. All of the large women's organizations in this country are against this amendment. I admit that the words "equal rights" have a certain catch to them. But bear in mind, when the Women's Equal Rights Association say that I am opposed to their amendment, what they should really say is that I am opposed to women being sweated, underpaid or given work beyond a woman's strength; that I am opposed to a breakdown of the strength and vitality of the future mothers of the race. A strong, healthy, vigorous motherhood is a great national asset, and I am for conserving and not for undermining that asset.

To help accomplish that, I favor adequate appropriations for the Women's and Children's Bureau of the Federal Department of Labor.

At Louisville, Kentucky, speaking on the tariff, I made as clear as the noonday sun the Democratic attitude. I definitely stated that not one single thing under a Democratic administration would happen to the tariff that would take a single five cent piece out of the weekly pay envelope of the American workingman, or would in any way interfere with or injure business, large or small. I made that so clear and definite that the Republican Party managers were thrown into a panic. They were afraid that they had lost their timeworn argument, and one of the Republican spokesmen went so far as to say that the Democratic members of Congress would not sustain my position. That they will is evidenced by the fact that 90 per cent. of the Democratic Senators and candidates for both Houses of Congress have, over their signatures, declared that if elected they will follow the principle and policy set down by me in my Louisville speech.

Unless the American workingman is prepared to challenge my honesty and the honest intent of my party, he will be unable to pay attention to the false alarm raised by the Republican Party for the purpose of fooling him. Nothing, to my way of thinking, is as stupid as trying to convince the American workingman that the Democratic Party, under my leadership, is going to interfere with his prosperity.

He knows that my tariff proposals will increase the prosperity of this country. Not a single Republican has dared to criticise my plan to stop log-rolling, to take the tariff out of politics and to treat it as a business proposition, in the interest of the business man, the workingman and the farmer. The only thing they could do was to raise the cry that my party in Congress would not stand behind me on it; and my party in Congress has rallied behind me almost to a man and left the orators with nothing.

There is no greater cause for prosperity to the workingman than prosperity among the people who buy what the workingman makes. The farmers of this country are 30 per cent. of the population. If the buying power of the farm is destroyed that means, as I have said, fewer trips to the stores on Main street. If the farmer buys less, the merchant buys less from the manufacturer and the manufacturer has to cut down his force of workingmen.

Prosperity, therefore, for the one-third of the American people who live·on the farm, means prosperity for all the people of the country; and distress among the farmers necessarily means distress for business and for workingmen. And the Republican Party concedes that the farmers of this country today are in dire distress.

The desperate plight of agriculture in this country is dealing a heavy blow to the Republican forces. For the first time during my public career the Republican Party is driven to desperation in an attempt to hold the farmer vote of the country. To do it after eight years of broken promises, after eight years of betrayal, after eight years of false promise, they have their chief orator traveling through the agricultural west and northwest and making statements on behalf of the Republican candidate, which they hope will fool the farmer.

Let me take some of them up. First: Senator Borah is busy explaining to the American farmer that Mr. Hoover is his friend, because during the war and immediately thereafter, as Food Administrator, he so conducted his office as to keep up the price of farm products. The fact is that I read a cablegram from Mr. Hoover to one of the farm leaders in which Mr. Hoover claimed that he was keeping the prices down. What is the use of attempting to fool the farmer? Why have a prominent Republican state that he kept prices up when the candidate himself says that he kept them down? Mr. Hoover is to speak at St. Louis on Friday night. I ask him to make the statement definitely to the American farmer that he kept up the price of farm products during the war. I ask him further whether he will deny that such a cablegram ever came from him. Nobody can dispose of the question as quickly as he can himself and, if he fails to make disposition of the question, the American farmer can make up his mind that the Republican spokesmen are fooling him.

In his speech of acceptance, as a means of relief to the farmer from the distress that he finds himself in, he has promised them cheaper transportation by the construction of inland waterways. This in itself is commendable. The Democratic Party is equally committed to the improvement of our inland waterways. But to offer it as a means of relief for the acute and immediate distress of agriculture is in effect to dodge the question, and is, to my way of thinking, an attempt to fool the farmer. It is something which will take years to do and, because of Republican neglect in the last eight years, there has not even been a plan provided for it.

Figures have been used to fool the farmer when he is told that he is being protected by the tariff wall from three billion dollars' worth of imported farm products when, as a matter of fact, the real figure is $500,000,000. To get to the bigger figure they added silk and other things not usually comprehended within the term "agriculture" and not produced in this country, and which the farmer himself in many cases must buy and pay for.

That's trying to fool the farmer. Another measure of relief offered is the creation of stabilization corporations. Everybody who knows anything about the farm problem knows that that is not a cure. If it is, why did not Mr. Hoover suggest it to President Coolidge in the last four years as an alternative for the farm relief bills that he vetoed?

The Republican Party is trying to fool the wife of the farmer by putting forth rosy statements about improved conditions on the farm, the introduction of labor-saving devices and the modernization of the countryside. Alongside of that statement must be read the facts: A million people a year are being driven from the farm; bank failures in the agricultural districts are growing at an alarming rate. The Republican platform itself speaks of the dire distress of the farmer. What is to be gained by trying to lead a man in dire financial distress into the belief that his wife is securing greater comforts at home?

CAMPAIGN ADDRESS

Republican orators throughout the country are busily engaged in an effort to try to make the farmer believe that Mr. Hoover is his great friend; that he is a great statistician; that he is a great engineer, and that he will find some way of relieving them. The Republican Party has been eight years promising relief and has failed to give it. Don't take that from me alone. Take it from one of the great exponents of the farmers' cause, one of the Republicans in the United States Senate who, in season and out of season, has labored ceaselessly and fearlessly in their behalf. I will quote from Senator Norris of Nebraska:

" The Republican national platform, four years ago, promised relief, and four years before that they were going to put the farmer on a profitable basis. We have fed the farmer on promises, but we have never given him a taste of fulfillment. And now, for the third time, the Republican platform presents to the farmer some more promises."

As an indication of the desperation of the Republican Party on the farm question, Governor McMullen of Nebraska hurried to Washington and urged the Republican candidate that he should make a promise to call the Congress in to special session in order to handle the farm question. The story of these conferences is an interesting sidelight on the Republican candidate. They must have begged him to say something, anything to make some appeal to the farmer. They must have pleaded for just a few kind words. Then word came from the headquarters of Mr. Hoover that the extra session was discussed, but no decision was arrived at. Immediately thereafter Senator Borah went into conference with the Republican candidate and, following the conference, Mr. Hoover yielded. He spoke a kind word. He actually got himself to the point of saying " extra session." Aside from the fact that this seems to be a surrender for the purpose of securing votes, what would be accomplished at an extra session of Congress in view of Mr. Hoover's well known opposition to the underlying principle behind the cause of farm depression? He has refused to accept the principle of the control of the exportable surplus, without which control there can be no adequate relief. He and his advisers on farm relief are in effect saying to the farmers of this country, " We have given you nothing in eight years but broken promises. Forget the past; give us a renewal of power on the 6th of November; we will give you prompt action, but no relief."

As Senator Norris said, speaking to the farmers of the country:

" I want to say to them, as I look at it, if you still believe what you have been advocating, you haven't a leg to stand on unless you come out in this great contest and support Governor Smith. I am tired of promises."

I have no doubt that the talk of the extra session will be regarded by the farmers of the country as one more promise that will produce no results.

One of the most vicious and persistent attempts to fool the American people is the constant repetition by the Republican orators of the false and baseless statement that I propose to let down the immigration bars in this country. Tonight I want to nail it finally. The Democratic platform declares:

" Laws which limit immigration must be preserved in full force and effect."

I stand squarely on that declaration. I shall do nothing to impair or weaken those laws.

There's nothing indefinite about that. I said that in my acceptance speech and have never varied from it. Any man who says that I propose to let down the immigration bars is not only trying to fool the people, but is doing it wilfully and dishonestly.

The Republican candidate and all the orators of his party are certainly trying to fool the American public on the question of prohibition. Senator Borah calls it the paramount issue. He believes that there is nothing in the country today that is as important as keeping the Eighteenth Amendment and the Volstead Act just as they are on the statute book. On the other hand, Governor Hughes believes that prohibition is not a part of the campaign at all. He says that it is a sham battle. By that he means that there is nothing to it. The candidate himself refers to it as a noble experiment. He says it must be worked out constructively, but he does not say how.

They are trying to fool, not only the wets and the drys, but also that great American public that does not line up in either group, those millions of God-fearing men and women who believe, as I do, that there should be law enforcement, that there should be an end to official corruption and bootlegging, that real temperance and real respect for law should be restored. I have spoken my mind on this subject to the American people in all parts of this country. The American people will not rest content with the disgraceful conditions that exist in every state in this union today. I have set before them a plan to restore to the people of the several states the right to regulate their own affairs. That rests upon the fundamental Democratic principle of states' rights. I have not hesitated to say how I want to work this prohibition question out constructively, and I am confident that the American people will stand behind me in my effort to cure these evils which today are undermining and sapping that respect for law which must be the foundation of our democracy.

I have so much confidence in the intelligence, the common sense and the good judgment of the rank and file of the American people that I am satisfied all of these attempts to deceive will fall to the ground and the overwhelming majority of the American people will find comfort, relief and satisfaction in the clear-cut, well-defined, honestly spoken words of the Democratic platform. With that belief firmly fixed in my mind I look forward on the 6th of November to an overpowering victory for the Democratic ticket.

XVII

ADDRESS AT BROOKLYN

Brooklyn, New York, November 2, 1928

FOR more than six weeks I have been traveling throughout the United States, and while I live I shall always cherish the welcome I received from millions of my fellow countrymen. The warm and affectionate greeting in every city, village and hamlet will always be a treasured remembrance of the campaign of 1928.

Closing the campaign in my own State, conscious that I am speaking to the nation, I desire to say a word of thanks to Senator Robinson. While I have not met him since last summer I have followed his campaign closely, and I am deeply impressed by the fact that the Democratic National Convention gave me a most worthy running mate, one who has demonstrated his character, his capacity and his ability during his long and distinguished public career.

I know that you have been following my speeches in the national campaign. I propose tonight to devote myself largely to State issues, but I shall relate them to national issues, for, after all, the proper and orderly administration of State affairs rests essentially upon the same basis as the handling of the business of the Federal Government.

No man in the history of the State has had as great reason to be grateful to its people as I have had. They have honored me even beyond my own hopes. Actuated by a spirit of gratitude I naturally feel a keen desire that the State continue to progress and that our people, from Buffalo to Montauk Point, continue to derive the full and complete benefit of a well organized, responsive, intelligent and forward-looking government.

CAMPAIGN ADDRESS

I therefore welcomed with great satisfaction the nomination of Franklin D. Roosevelt. During my governorship I have had his vigorous and hearty support. The measures I have pressed for the betterment of the government of this State are close to his heart. I shall hand over the reins of the State Government on January 1st, and I know of no man to whom I would sooner turn them over than to Franklin D. Roosevelt.

The Democratic Party was wise in its selection of Colonel Herbert H. Lehman for Lieutenant-Governor: A man of broad vision, a capable financier, with a strong human understanding and a keen sense of his responsibility to those less fortunate than himself.

The office of Attorney-General is an important one. His legal advice controls the conduct of the great departments of the government. The Democratic Party has performed a distinct service in nominating for this high office a man of the ability of Albert Conway. He is going to enjoy the unique distinction of being the only "Al" elected on the State ticket.

Our candidate for Comptroller, Morris S. Tremaine of Buffalo, has been my associate in the State administration in the last two years. Democrats and Republicans must agree that he has been one of the best Comptrollers the State has ever had. His broad business knowledge has put the Comptroller's office of the State on a sound footing.

Senator Copeland has given us faithful and progressive representation in the Senate. His re-election will keep the State of New York in line with the other forward-looking commonwealths of the country.

For the Court of Appeals the Democratic Party has nominated Leonard Crouch, an able, fearless and competent jurist who will be a valuable addition to that great court.

The present campaign goes a long way toward making good my argument for a four-year term for the Governor, with the election held in years when there is no presidential contest.

Interest throughout this State during the last six weeks has centered largely around the national campaign. Nevertheless, see how important it is to the State to continue and to progress the constructive, forward-looking policies adopted at Albany.

It is a matter of regret that the Republican leaders, for selfish partisan reasons, refused to separate the elections and allow the people during a gubernatorial contest to devote their attention entirely to State issues.

During this campaign I have been talking to the American people on the subject of water power development. This is a live issue in New York State. Divine Providence blessed the State of New York with great natural water power resources, and in line with progressive thought throughout the nation the Democratic Party has taken the position that these resources are the property of the people themselves and should be developed by the State under State ownership and State control.

The Democratic theory of water power development is in sharp contrast with the Republican theory. The Republican Party believes in the alienation of these resources to private individuals for private profit and private gain. All during my governorship I have battled for the Democratic theory. While I have succeeded in staying the hands of the power trust, I have been unsuccessful in bringing about development under the Democratic theory because of the stubborn opposition of the Republican leaders.

The present Chairman of the Republican State Committee, up to the time of his selection, was the head of the Northeastern Power Company, and while in the Legislature was the most aggressive and outspoken champion the private power interests have ever had.

The Republican Party is definitely on record in this State in favor of private development. It is definitely on record for private development in the nation. The Republican candidate for President himself has taken that position. That the Republican candidate for Governor believes in it there can be no question. As a member ex-officio of the Water Power Commission, by virtue of his office as Attorney-General, in December, 1926, he was ready to lease for fifty years the valuable water power on the St. Lawrence river to a subsidiary of the Aluminum Company of America. I stopped that lease by directing public opinion against it, and he and his brother Republican Commissioners gave in at the eleventh hour. The overwhelming sentiment of the people of this State, expressed in no uncertain terms, stayed the execution of that lease and forced the Republican Commissioners to leave this great resource in the hands of the people themselves.

If you want the benefits of State water power development, you cannot look to the Republican candidate. You will have to look to Franklin Roosevelt to execute the Democratic principle of State ownership and State control in the interest of the rightful owners of these resources, the people of the State of New York.

Let me call your attention to something that was disclosed only a few days ago which fortifies my nation-wide argument against the alienation of these water power resources to private interests.

One hundred years ago the surplus waters of the Erie canal of Lockport were leased by the State to a private company for $200 a year. At that time modern hydraulic machinery was unknown, and power was developed by turning wooden wheels. The lease ran on, and in 1901 the Erie canal was enlarged with State funds made available for that purpose. The Democratic Superintendent of Public Works ascertained that in 1926 the power developed under this $200 a year lease was worth at least $76,000 a year, and after litigation succeeded in getting the favorable report of a referee to that effect. This is a lesson of what you may expect when you make long leases of public property for private gain.

In his speech of acceptance the Republican candidate for Governor says that the State's ownership of the great water power resources should remain inviolate. That means nothing. It does not do much good to retain an empty fee to property if you alienate all the benefit to be derived from it by a long-term lease.

Let us take up the subject of agriculture. This time every year the Republican Party is busily engaged in explaining that it is the great friend of the farmer. Let us analyze the Republican attitude to agriculture in our own State as taken from the record.

The Republican candidate speaks about prompt payment of indemnities to the owners of slaughtered tubercular cattle. What does the record show? It shows that the last Republican administration in the State of New York failed absolutely to make any appropriation for the slaughter of tubercular cattle. When I arrived in Albany for my second administration I was compelled not only to suggest appropriations for the current year but, to meet the deficit left-over as a result of Republican neglect, to make provision for payment of indemnities. We have appropriated for this purpose $20,000,000 in the past five years, the largest sum ever appropriated in this State for this important protection of the public health.

In the last six years under Democratic administration more has been done for the farmer than in any similar period in the history of the State.

Generous appropriations were made to the College of Agriculture of Cornell University.

State subsidies to the county for the repair, the building and the maintenance of county roads designed to bring the produce of the farm closer to the consuming public were inaugurated.

The Cooperative Marketing Bill was introduced in the Senate by Senator Straus, Democratic representative from New York, and signed by me.

The American farmer is awakening to the fact that the Republican Party has been engaged in the political pastime of making promises to him. As Senator Norris of Nebraska said, what the farmer wants today is a little slice of fulfillment; he has been fed to death on broken Republican promises.

Let us take a journey into the field of the State's educational activities. In one of his speeches, the Republican candidate for Governor said:

" The Republican Legislature of New York has in the past ten years made a notable record for itself in this field."

It is a notable record, and we will note it here tonight. It is a record of hostility to improving the educational facilities of the State. It is a matter of record that nothing was done by the Republican Legislature, although I insisted upon it year after year, to improve the rural school system of this State, to give to the children on the farm the same opportunity for education that is given to the children in the great cities. The Republican candidate for Governor will not deny this. Every forward movement in the interest of public education was initiated from the office of the Governor, with the support of prominent and influential citizens of New York who gave of their time, their ability and their energy to a study of the problem.

What happened to the bills that came from the Friedsam Committee, presided over by Colonel Friedsam of New York? The Republican Party smothered them, only to be compelled the next year to accept them under the fire of adverse public criticism.

It was my insistence as Chief Executive that brought about increased appropriations from $9,000,000 in my first year to

$88,000,000 in my last year for State aid to the localities for the payment of teachers' salaries.

It was the same insistence that brought about sufficient appropriation for the construction of Teachers' College at Albany; that gave liberal aid from the State to make possible the increase in the salaries of school teachers, and that effected a definite program for betterment which brought the Education Department of our State up to the high standard it now maintains. The present Commissioner of Education is a Republican. He is clearly on record as stating that as Governor of New York I have been the best friend that the Department of Education ever had.

On the subject of the reorganization of the State Government, let me quote from the speech of acceptance of the Republican candidate for Governor:

" I am in complete accord with the consolidation of State departments which occurred as the result of the enunciation of that principle by Elihu Root and which was constructively developed by the adoption of the recommendation of the Commission headed by Charles E. Hughes."

Did the Republican candidate, when he made that statement, believe that he was talking to the people of the State of New York? Or that he was talking to children under the school age? The whole history of the reorganization of the government constitutes, to my mind, one of the strongest arguments against the return of the Republican Party to power in our State. It is true that reorganization of the government had its birth in the Constitutional Convention presided over by Elihu Root. That was as far back as 1915. Thereafter the matter was entirely forgotten until 1920 when I recommended it to a Republican Legislature. That Legislature approved a constitutional amendment to carry it into effect. But under our Constitution it had to be approved by a second Legislature before submission to the people. In 1921, under a Republican Governor, it went down to defeat in the Republican Assembly presided over by the present Chairman of the Republican State Committee. The effect of that was that I had to begin all over again when I returned to Albany in 1923. I renewed the fight for this great reform to consolidate over one hundred scattered and overlapping bureaus into eighteen responsible departments of the State government and designed to make the government more understandable, to cut out waste and to promote efficiency and economy.

At that very time the same Republican hostility was being exhibited to the subject of similar reorganization of the Federal Government. Promised in the national platform in 1920, promised again in 1924, we come to 1928 with absolutely nothing done about it. It is a matter of record that the Republican Party in this State did every human thing they could to defeat the reorganization of the State Government. However, by the force of public opinion, I succeeded in driving it through the Legislature.

Look at the vote on the constitutional amendment and you will find that it was defeated in every strongly controlled Republican county in the central part of the State. Not only did they try to stop it in the Legislature, but they tried to defeat it on election day.

Now, so far as Mr. Hughes being chairman is concerned, let me give you the real story. The man selected by the Republican organization as Chairman of the Commission was Mr. Machold, the present Republican State Chairman and the known foe of reorganization, the man responsible for ditching it in 1921. When my attention was called to that fact I made a public statement opposing Mr. Machold's selection because of his well known opposition to reorganization, and definitely suggesting Governor Hughes as chairman. I had no desire to play politics. I wanted to get results for the people of this State. Mr. Hughes gave of his time and of his ability to the work of that commission. He deserves full credit for it and nobody in the State will give it to him sooner than I; but I certainly resent the statement of the Republican candidate that the Republican organization is entitled to any of the credit for the passage of the reorganization amendment to the Constitution, when the fact, known even to the page boys in the Legislature, is that they persistently and consistently stood against it with all the vigor they could bring to their command. Nobody knows this better than Governor Hughes himself.

The companion constitutional amendment, providing for an Executive Budget, likewise met with bitter opposition from the Republican leaders. Mr. Machold himself, when Speaker of the Assembly, followed me around the State talking against it. It was finally accepted because of the pressure of public opinion.

I next come to a subject that is very near and dear to my heart, and that is the Department of Labor and Workmen's Compensation. The Republican candidate said that if he is elected there will be a reorganization of the Labor Department. That is exactly what the people of this State do not want. That department has been reorganized and disorganized by each succeeding Republican administration since 1911. The effect of the last reorganization of it under Republican auspices was to cut down appropriations by one million dollars, paralyze the department and leave it helpless. That is the record and nobody can deny it. Just before election, here as throughout the entire country, they talk about their great love and their great devotion to the workingman; but every time they have had an opportunity in the State of New York, they have done every human thing they could to reduce the efficiency of the Labor Department and hamstring the administration of the labor laws.

In 1925 a Republican Senate Committee, presided over by Senator Whitley of Rochester, recommended that in view of the increased business of the Bureau of Workmen's Compensation it was necessary to add two members to the Industrial Board. What became of that recommendation? It was defeated by the Republican Legislature of 1925. Upon what theory? Upon the theory, as one Republican Senator put it, that "It gave Smith two additional appointments." Were they with the workingman at that time? Were they with the injured man or injured woman? Not at all. They were with the Republican machine. Two years later they were forced to yield and, as it turned out, no active member of my party was rewarded with the appointments, because I promoted men inside of the department. Only last year we again find Republican charges against the Labor Department. I appointed Professor Lindsay Rogers of Columbia University as Commissioner to hear the charges; and when the power of subpoena was invoked, and these critics were confronted with the prospect of having to make good under oath the statements made to the newspapers by Republican legislators, they were denied and withdrawn.

No; the people of this State, in the light of history want no reorganization of the Labor Department. They want adequate appropriations to make it effective. They want intelligent, honest, progressive personnel to operate it and neither Mr. Ottinger nor anybody else can say that under my administration these conditions were not fulfilled.

The Republican candidate speaks about extending the benefits by law to men and women in industry suffering from any occupational disease. Why, the Republican Legislature has had four years to do that. I recommended it repeatedly. Bills were introduced to bring it about — one of them by a Brooklyn Senator, Senator Love. Every one of the bills went down to defeat. Nobody can seriously consider that promise. Nobody believes that there is anything behind it. The record of the party is altogether in the opposite direction.

Where did we get the great body of law enacted for the protection of the health and comfort and the well-being of men, women and children engaged in industry? Why, it is a matter of history that it came from the Democratic Party. It is further a matter of history that the Republican Party did everything they could to break down these statutes. I recommended a 48-hour law for women as far back as 1918. It was never enacted until 1927.

I read with a great deal of amusement that Mr. Ottinger claims that we got the Workmen's Compensation Act during the administration of Governor Hughes. He cannot mean that. He could not have looked it up. The Workmen's Compensation Law was enacted and became law in this State in 1913. The act was signed by Martin H. Glynn, one of my Democratic predecessors. What the Republican candidate should have said is that the Republican Party attempted, in the administration of Governor Hughes, to give us some form of workmen's compensation, but made such a poor job of it that it was set aside by the Court of Appeals as being in conflict with the Constitution.

The Republican candidate apparently talks about this 20th of October, made a speech on social welfare and he said a remarkable thing. He urged the establishment of " orphan asylums and other institutions where the mother would be permitted to see her child, to be with her child every day rather than to permit it to rest in an institution away from the home."

What does he mean by that? The whole policy of this State for thirteen years has been to get away from orphan asylums and to leave the children with the widowed mother, and to have the locality wherein she resides make the same provision for her, for the care of her child at home, that would otherwise be made to an institution.

The Republican candidate apparently talks about this matter without even a primary understanding of the State's policy. As far back as 1913, while Speaker of the Assembly, I appointed a commission to study the whole question of pensions for widowed mothers, and I had the satisfaction and the pleasure of leading the fight for it in the Republican Assembly of 1915.

The Republican leader of that body in that year made the same argument against widows' pensions that is now being made by the Republican candidate for President against a great many of the forward-looking proposals that the Democratic Party is urging. He called it Socialism.

I do not think the Republican candidate for Governor means to recommend a change in that policy, but I cannot escape the conclusion that he does not understand it when he speaks about the building of orphan asylums that the mother can go into every day.

While we are on the subject of child welfare, let me say that a great many counties in this State have not established Boards of Child Welfare and have not come into line with the progressive thought with regard to the care of orphan children, because the statute is not compulsory. I had a cure for that and I urged it on each succeeding Legislature for the last ten years. I suggested that the State subsidize the county in an amount equal to that contributed by the county. That would cause the backward counties to come in under the provisions of the law, because if they did not they would be helping to pay the State's contribution to the counties which did, and get nothing in return.

What happened to that legislation, designed to preserve the home of the widowed mother and the orphaned child? The Republican organization in control of the Legislature at Albany smothered it year after year with the regularity of clockwork.

No operation of the government so readily lends itself to misrepresentation as does our financial administration. I assure you that I have no notion in my mind tonight of attempting to make the Republican candidate for Governor look ridiculous in the eyes of his fellow citizens; but it is impossible for me to resist making this observation: In his speech of acceptance he makes promises of further developments in the State variously estimated to cost from fifty to one hundred million dollars and in another part of the same speech says that we must stop spending money.

I can readily understand that the Republican candidate for Governor would feel compelled to poll-parrot what is being said around the nation about the Federal finances and their comparison with the finances of New York. He says that under the wise leadership of President Coolidge the cost in the nation has been reduced from five billions to three billions. Where did I hear that before? It is the old cry of Under-Secretary Mills, repeated by Mr. Hoover himself; although they all know that this reduction represents the difference between the cost of the government in a time of war and in a time of peace.

Mr. Ottinger, in his speech, goes on to make a comparison between 1919 and 1928 in the cost of the government of this State. He well knows that the Governor of New York cannot spend a five cent piece not appropriated by the Legislature. And he further knows that in all of that period the Legislature has never been Democratic, and he knows as well as anybody in this State that year after year I vetoed items of appropriation sent to me by his own party that I deemed to be unnecessary for the proper conduct of the State's business.

If the Republican leaders of the Legislature had their way about it, the government in the last ten years would have cost the people of this State much more than it did.

I am amused at his suggestion that he would wipe from the statute books the personal income tax. And he refers to it as a war measure. That is an astounding example of his lack of understanding of the State's fiscal system. In the first place, it was not a war measure; it was enacted to take the place of the excise tax on the sale of beer and liquor. It brings in approximately $35,000,000 a year. I would like him to answer a simple question. If the Income Tax Act were repealed, where would he get this $35,000,000 which is required to run the government? That, I admit, is a kind of a hard question. There is no answer to it that he can make. He is not in earnest about it, because his speech is intended just as a play for votes.

I cannot restrain a smile when I hear him talk about eliminating the direct property tax. At the last session of the Legislature, on my recommendation, the direct property tax was made the lowest since 1923. I pointed out to the Republican Legislature that the great burden of direct taxation arises from the expenses of the counties and other localities. I suggested that the Hughes Commission be empowered by law to make a study of town and county government to the end that the costs of local government be reduced. I pointed out that in certain sections of the State under old and antiquated statutes supervisors were receiving in fees as high as $43,000 a year. I suggested the possibility of county consolidation to reduce overhead expenses and to relieve the burden on the owners of real estate.

What happened to it? The Republican Party threw it in the waste basket and concededly for patronage purposes, because the Republican Party builds up its organization upon the patronage of the small Republican counties in the interior part of the State.

When the Republican candidate for Governor speaks about taxation bearing heavily upon the owners of real property and particularly upon the farmer, let him read the record and he will be compelled to blame the leaders of his own party in the Legislature for that condition. They can't escape it. They are guilty.

In every campaign we hear this question of State finances always dealt with in general terms. The Republican candidate is not a stranger to Albany. The expenses of his own Department of Law have materially increased under his administration. He came to me when the appropriation bills were pending and he made a reasonable and a fair and a satisfactory explanation of the increases, and I accepted them. He is not a man without experience. If he is sincere in his expression about spending money in connection with the government of the State of New York, let him give the people a little bill of fare. Let him give them a little detailed program. He is familiar with the appropriation bill that came from the leaders of his own party. Let him mention one single item, just one, in the last appropriation bill which, as Governor of the State, he would have rejected. I challenge him to do it, and I do that fearlessly because I know he cannot make good.

Now, as a matter of fact, the largest part of the expense of the State is fixed and definite. The operation of the State Government is a good deal like the operation of your own private home. You have got a fixed amount that you pay for rent. You can approximate the butcher's bill and the grocer's bill and your lighting bill. The State is in exactly the same position. It is just like a household. It pays rent, it pays interest on the money that it borrows, it goes to the grocer and it goes to the butcher and it goes to the clothing store, for the purchase of necessary articles for the great army of wards who are in the hospitals, the prisons and the various institutions that the State maintains. These are all fixed and definite charges and unless and until the people of the State are ready to curtail the service that they give to the wards of the State, no saving can be effected in that department of the government.

There are certain other expenditures, the amount of which is not absolutely fixed, but liquid. We spend a certain amount of money every year for the construction, the maintenance and the repair of State highways. As the State has steadily grown, so have the expenditures for highways. Will Mr. Ottinger state that he intends to save any money in that appropriation? I challenge him to do it because I know he will not.

Another such expenditure is for education. While education in itself is a State function, by policy we have delegated it to the municipalities; but the State makes contributions to the municipalities to help them in their educational work. Those contributions are applied to the salaries of school teachers and referred to as teachers' quotas. When I went to Albany in 1919 the total appropriation by the State for that purpose was $9,000,000. This year it was $88,000,000. Will Mr. Ottinger say to the people of this State that he proposes to cut down the quotas to the educational forces of the State? He won't do it. I challenge him.

Would Mr. Ottinger have the people believe that he is opposed to State aid for public health work in rural counties, to adequate laboratory service, to maternity and infancy aid, to physical examinations of children of pre-school age, and to improved care for crippled children? All these things cost money. I regard money spent for these purposes as the best investment the State can make, because the dividends in the form of better health and increased efficiency are incalculable.

I repeat what I said earlier: Nothing lends itself so readily to misrepresentation as State finances; and I want to call your attention to this fact, that no one who has ever said a word about the State finances in this State has ever been definite enough to point his finger at anything specific. No critic of the fiscal policy of the State under my administration has ever pointed to a wasted dollar. To say that the cost of the government of the State is increasing does not mean anything, because the cost of the government of every State is increasing, the cost of the government of every municipality is increasing and, in fact, the cost of operating the Federal Government has increased under President Coolidge, notwithstanding the false picture that the Republican Party has attempted to paint.

In my speech at Sedalia, in the State of Missouri, I pointed out to the American people that the cost of running the municipality at Washington, operated by the Federal Government, has increased since 1914 100 per cent. The cost of the Federal Government between 1924 and 1928 has increased by two hundred million dollars. And in keeping with the pledge that I made to the American people when I entered upon this campaign of talking out honestly and frankly and fearlessly to them, I make this prediction: No matter who is elected Governor of New York State on the sixth of November, the cost of the government will increase next year.

The attitude of the Republican candidate on the question of prohibition can be summed up in a few words. He is a wet dry. He is carrying water on both shoulders. He has attempted to be all things to all men. On this subject his party platform is as silent as the tomb. He is constantly worrying, day in and day out, as to how he can get over the campaign without being compelled to have anything to say about it.

In one of his speeches he said that he would pass that whole question up until the commission appointed by Mr. Hoover had dealt with it. Well, I will relieve him of all doubt and worry about that by informing him here tonight in Brooklyn that Mr. Hoover will never have any opportunity to appoint any commission on that subject. I will take care of that subject, by and with the advice of the American people.

In one of his speeches in Suffolk county, Mr. Ottinger spoke about the smiling countenances of the little children who were enjoying the State's great system of parks and parkways, and he paid an eloquent tribute to the new Republican leader of Suffolk county, Mr. Kingsland Macy. I cannot attempt this evening to go through the long history of Republican opposition to the park program. Mr. Kingsland

Macy was the head of the organization that opposed State Parks on Long Island, and opposed them on the theory that the rabble from New York would litter up their beautiful countryside with empty cracker boxes and empty sardine cans. Of all men in the State of New York, the Republican candidate is the last one who should speak about the benefit of parks and parkways, because he lined up with the interests against the public parks. He became the attorney for Mr. Macy when he gave unsolicited an opinion as to the value of the property being acquired by the State for park purposes at East Islip. Had his opinion meant anything, had it prevailed, had it had any force or effect under the statutes, the State would have been unable to acquire that beautiful property to make smiling faces and smiling countenances on the children, enjoying the fresh air and the recreation which they are now afforded.

In the time given to me tonight I have done the best I could, in view of the number of subjects to be covered, to leave in the minds of the people of the State of New York the conviction that the return of the government in this State to the Republican Party would be a serious mistake.

For me this is not so much a question of party victory. I make this plea earnestly and sincerely in a spirit of gratitude to the men and women who, regardless of political affiliations, have supported me and stood behind the policies I have advocated. Having in mind the best interests of this State, I strongly urge the people not to take a backward step, but to go forward and to maintain and progress the high standards which now prevail by electing Franklin D. Roosevelt and the entire Democratic ticket.

XVIII

ADDRESS AT NEW YORK CITY

New York City, November 3, 1928

UNDER our American system of politics a campaign should be a debate. There could be no other reason for holding the national conventions as early as the month of June unless it was contemplated that the candidates would use the time between nomination and election day in an effort to make clear to the people of the country their stand on the great problems that are subjects of platform declaration.

No such debate has been held in this campaign, because the Republican candidate has contented himself with six or seven speeches in which he deals with the problems under discussion in the most general way; and instead of debating himself, he has been represented in public discussion by prominent members of his own party who acted as his spokesmen.

That is exactly what the people of this country desire to get away from. They have had all they can stand of the spokesman idea and they want a leader who will talk out plainly and clearly to them, acquainting them with the facts and giving the ordinary man and woman a little more information about the operations of their government at Washington.

Early in the campaign Chairman Work openly made the statement that the Republican candidate would not be drawn into any controversy with me. Obviously that attitude defeats the whole purpose of a campaign. A national campaign, in the very nature of things, is a controversy between political parties as to which policies or methods are best calculated to promote the well-being and prosperity of the United States.

CAMPAIGN ADDRESS

It is hardly fair to the American people for a man who is aspiring to the high office of President to ask them to rely on what somebody else says about the issues. The people of this country, I am sure, would like to have heard directly from Mr. Hoover because, after all, he is the candidate and he is the man who will be charged with the responsibility in the event of his election.

However, I never ran away from a debate in my life, and therefore I have had to take them all on.

Following its old tricks, the Republican Party sought at the outset of the campaign — and is still continuing — to set up a smoke screen behind which they hope to hide the record of the last seven and a half years. To perfect the smoke screen they use the time-worn and broken-down cry of prosperity, as though there were some patented formula by which the Republican Party alone promotes the prosperity of this country.

They were particularly zealous about it this year because they felt the necessity of diverting the public mind from the fact that the present prosperity, high wages and high standards of living came to the country under the administration of President Wilson.

The history of the last fifty years clearly shows that there were more business and financial panics under Republican administrations than under Democratic ones; and the fact is that the Federal Reserve Act, designed to stay financial panics, was passed under the administration of President Wilson and was later referred to by Andrew Mellon, Secretary of the Treasury, as the great stabilizer of business and finance, not only in our own country but abroad.

The difference is that when trouble occurs under a Democratic administration the Republicans call it a panic. When it happens under a Republican administration the Republicans refer to it as a depression. In fact, Mr. Hoover himself in the course of one of his speeches in this campaign referring to the army of men out of work last winter, said it occurred during a depression.

That the country is prosperous in spots at the present time nobody denies. But at the same time we have Mr. Hoover's own word for it that the textile and the coal industries are lagging in the march of prosperity. And the Republican Party in its platform admits that the agricultural industry is in dire distress. I am using their own words.

Of course, it is another Republican trick to attempt to link prosperity with the tariff. After my Louisville speech, in which I clearly outlined the Democratic attitude to the tariff, .the Republican leaders found themselves in a panic. Mr. Hoover weathered the storm by silence. Mr. Hughes said that it was doubtful if members of Smith's party in the Congress of the United States would follow his tariff views.

He was unable to find fault with the views himself; he was compelled to admit that they would stabilize the business of the country, give confidence to business, preserve the standard of living and of wages for the workingman and protect business large and small, as well as the farmer. I made immediate answer to his suggestion that the members of Congress of my party would not follow my views by broadcasting the declaration of 90 per cent. of them that they will follow exactly the policy enunciated by me in my Louisville speech.

I repeat here tonight that under my administration there will be no general revision of the tariff; that the tariff; if amended, will be amended in specific schedules after careful study and investigation of all the facts by a competent, thoroughgoing, able tariff commission. The suggestion by me that the tariff be lifted out of the realm of partisan politics was met with a counter suggestion from Governor Hughes that that was an impossibility.

With that I entirely disagree; and if Mr. Hughes and the Republican Party believe that the people are compelled to countenance log-rolling, political manipulation, favoritism and star chamber proceedings in the making of tariffs, they do not understand the viewpoint of the American people.

Nothing is so ridiculous in this campaign as the attempt on the part of the Republican managers to lead the American workingman to believe that my election and my leadership of the Democratic Party in the nation means that he is to be driven from his home.

I said in Newark that this was an insult to the intelligence of the rank and file of the working people of this country, and I definitely pledge to them that under me nothing will happen to the tariff that will take a five cent piece out of their pay envelopes. If we do anything with it, we shall make those envelopes buy more for them. I say furthermore that in dealing with this problem we will give full protection to the farmer and to the business man, big or small.

The Republican Party has referred to President Coolidge as the great apostle of prosperity. A newspaper report of the press conference with the President at the White House on October 30th reads as follows:

" President Coolidge also permitted it to become current that in his opinion there was no threat of an upset of prosperity by reason of the election. It is hardly a violent assumption that what he meant was that regardless of the result of the election the country would go on prospering."

This opinion from the President does not square with the forebodings of evil coming from the minor leaders of the party in their effort to bolster up a lost cause.

Newspapers supporting the Republican candidate, but desiring at the same time to be fair with their readers, agree with the President and violently disagree with the party spokesmen and the Republican orators generally. Let me quote from an editorial in The *New York Telegram*, one of a chain of newspapers throughout the United States supporting the candidacy of Mr. Hoover:

" But when Hughes goes clear back to the days of Mark Hanna, trots out the battered old full dinner pail and begins howling calamity, he gets down off the high plane where his great public service has placed him and resorts to political bunk and demagogy."

This is the opinion of a newspaper supporter of the Republican candidate. It apparently was unable to give editorial sanction to the false bugaboo of calamity and business distress following Democratic ascendancy that the Republican Party, from the candidate down, has been trying to paint.

For the further promotion of the smoke screen the Republican candidate has made repeated reference to his attitude toward immigration. It is not an issue. I stand squarely upon the Democratic platform, which pledges a continuation of the present restrictive laws, except where they divide families. Mr. Hoover and I are in agreement on this point and it is only brought into the campaign to befog the issues.

Now that I have demolished the smoke screen, let us bring out into the open the real issues of the campaign.

Let us take up the agricultural situation. No man can honestly make the statement that there is widespread prosperity in this country when one-third of the whole population engaged in agricultural pursuits are, according to the Republican platform, in dire distress. And it is that distress that caused the Republican candidate only last night to say, " Agriculture is the most urgent economic problem in the nation today."

Paralyze agriculture and you reduce the purchasing power of one-third of the people. It follows as night follows day that if that buying power is paralyzed the depression must be felt through every line of human endeavor. The farmer purchasing less, the storekeeper sells less. The storekeeper selling less, the manufacturer manufactures less. The manufacturer manufacturing less, the workingman works less.

CAMPAIGN ADDRESS

The Republican Party has had eight years in which to cure the evils besetting agriculture. That they have known of the evils is proven by the speech of Mr. Hoover last night when he said, speaking of agriculture:

"There are ample causes for complaint. The Republican Party has throughout the whole of the last seven and a half years been alive to this situation."

He should have added: "But nothing was done about it. And that is the reason why agriculture is the most urgent economic problem in the nation today."

The trouble with agriculture is basic and fundamental, and it cannot be cured by the application of remedies that do not go to the very root of the disease.

Governor Lowden, Senator Norris and the leaders of agriculture generally throughout the country are of one mind — that the solution lies in a proper control of the exportable surplus with the cost imposed upon the crop benefited, and unless and until a remedy is brought forth based upon that principle you are only administering palliatives and not seeking a cure for the disease itself.

Senator Norris, former Republican chairman of the Senate Committee on Agriculture, in a nationwide address, declared that because of Mr. Hoover's attitude toward great public problems, among which he believed agriculture to be one of the foremost, he was in favor of my election. Governor Lowden of Illinois withdrew his name from the Republican National Convention at Kansas City upon the theory that the Republican Party did not recognize the great underlying principle of cure for the stagnation of agriculture.

Mr. Borah and Mr. Hughes agree with Mr. Hoover. Mr. Hoover rejects the fundamental remedy and seeks to lull the farmer to sleep with talk about developing inland waterways, something about which there is no difference between us, and with talk about stabilization corporations, which will in some mysterious way not explained by him bring a cure for the paralysis of agriculture. The strange thing about it all is that Mr. Hoover was President Coolidge's adviser on this subject during the last four years, and never suggested any of these things at the time Mr. Coolidge twice vetoed the only relief bill that came from the Congress. Even now he is so blind to the fundamental needs of the farmer that he calls the principle advocated not only by me, but by leaders of his own party like Senator Norris, Governor Lowden and Vice-President Dawes, State socialism.

The Democratic platform and the Democratic candidates recognize the fundamental principle and promise a speedy remedy. The hope of the farmer and of those in the country dependent upon his prosperity is in the Democratic Party. The Republican Party, according to the record, is helpless to do anything for them.

There is no more important question in this country today than the one that has to do with the development of our great natural water power resources. Water power has been referred to as white coal, and it is running to waste in sufficient quantities throughout the length and breadth of this land to produce cheap power for industry, the home and the farm.

The division of opinion between the two parties is on the method of development. The Republican Party adheres to the policy of private development by private individuals for private profit and gain. The Democratic Party, aided by progressive Republicans, believes in public development under public ownership and under public control in the interest of the rank and file of the people, the rightful owners of the power.

Senator Borah agrees with me and violently disagrees with the candidate of his party to the point where he said: " If water power were the only issue, I would not support Mr. Hoover."

CAMPAIGN ADDRESS

The Republican candidate stands in the corner of the power trust, and in his Madison Square speech, right in this building, declared the Democratic policy as enunciated by me to be State socialism.

The decision will have to be made on Tuesday by the American people as to the future of their power resources, that will either commit them to the Democratic Party for public development or put the Republican Party in a position to hand them out to the private power companies. I have confidence in the judgment and common sense of the rank and file of the American people, and for that reason I am sure their decision will be right.

There is a crying need today for a reorganization of the structure and framework of the government itself. Duplication of effort, overlapping of functions, waste of time, energy and money grow out of the present complicated, disjointed and disorganized framework of the Federal Government.

This was recognized as far back as 1920, when the Republican Party in its platform promised reorganization. Failing during the administration of President Harding, they promised it again in 1924, but up to and including this day and minute, as a result of the promise, they made just two consolidations or transfers of functions when they took the Patent Office and the Bureau of Mines from the Department of the Interior and transferred them to the Department of Commerce.

This year they have left it out of the platform entirely, evidently regarding it as something impossible under Republican auspices because of the Republican hunger for patronage. The Democratic Party under my leadership brought about a reorganization of the government of this State. Beginning with the fourth of March that party will address itself to the problem in Washington and I predict that its efforts will meet with success.

The Republican Party just before election always professes its love and devotion for the laboring man. The American workingman would be infinitely better off if he could get some of this sympathy after election.

Let us take up some of the problems that have beset labor in the last seven and a half years.

Take the coal strike. By appointment at the hands of President Harding, Mr. Hoover himself was a member of a commission to inquire into the causes of the unrest in the coal industry and to suggest remedies for their cure. What happened to the proposed remedies? It is a matter of history that they went down to defeat although Democratic Senators introduced legislation to carry them into effect.

The whole problem of unemployment has been sidetracked. Again, we have Mr. Hoover as chairman of a commission to inquire into and suggest remedies by law to meet this important problem. What happened to them? The record shows they went down to defeat although these proposals were introduced and urged in the Senate by Democratic members of that body. When the business depression of 1927 again brought to light the question of unemployment the Republican administration was unable to meet it constructively, because they had failed to do anything about the remedies suggested as far back as 1921.

The Republican candidate in his speeches in this campaign spoke about progressing public improvements in times of unemployment. This is exactly what the Republican Party did not do.

The Republican Party in its platform promises an end to the abuses of unjust injunctions restraining labor. How they can make that promise in the face of the history of the last eight years is beyond me, in view of the fact that a Republican Attorney-General himself sued out some of the injunctions most bitterly complained of. A constructive program for the trouble in the mining sections, a forward-looking policy with regard to unemployment and legislation against unjust injunctions can only come from the constructive solutions suggested by the Democratic Party.

There is no public question that the people are facing today that is of greater importance to the future welfare of this country than a sensible, reasonable, proper handling of the prohibition amendment to the Constitution and the legislation sustaining it. There can be no question that ten years ago a great many well-intentioned and proper-thinking people in this country believed that true temperance and the eradication of the evil of over-indulgence in intoxicating liquors could be brought about by amendment to the Constitution.

After eight and a half years of experience it is time that the American people took stock, looked around them and consulted the record to find out if these desirable objects are actually being attained by the operation of these laws.

I hold that the Eighteenth Amendment has not promoted temperance. It has not cured over-indulgence in alcoholic beverages. I hold, on the other hand, that there is more hard liquor being consumed in this country today than there was prior to the adoption of the Eighteenth Amendment. I am satisfied that the prohibition laws have brought about a disregard and a disrespect for law on the part of otherwise law-abiding citizens to a greater extent than was ever created by any attempt to regulate the personal habits and customs of the people.

The illegal manufacture, sale and transportation of liquor is going on in every State of the Union. To help bring it about public officials charged with law enforcement have been corrupted. Bootlegging has become an industry followed by countless thousands. All that I have stated is a matter of public record and can be found in the files of the United States Senate as part of the sworn testimony of public officials charged with the enforcement of prohibition.

The term "bootlegger," its meaning and significance are known to the children in our public schools. It is impossible for the American people to escape the question of what should be done about it. I have frankly met this issue. I have suggested that it be solved by the application of the Democratic and Jeffersonian theory of states' rights. I strongly believe that the right of a State to be dry should be respected. I believe in continuing the protection of the Eighte⁻ h Amendment for the State that desires to be dry; but, at the same time, I believe the State that desires a change should be permitted to have it after a majority vote of all its citizens under the restrictions and safeguards laid down by me in my speech of acceptance.

As to the Volstead Act, I am convinced that the present definition of what constitutes an intoxicant is not based upon study or upon scientific research. Unquestionably the present drastic definition of what constitutes an intoxicant has driven millions of citizens from the use of harmless beverages to the use of hard liquors, which are more easily obtained, more easily transported and which are legally manufactured in so many countries in constant trade and commerce with the United States.

As I said in my speech of acceptance, two duties devolve upon the President of the United States with respect to these laws. The first is to enforce them. That I promise to do to the best of my ability. The second duty is to recommend the changes he deems advisable. I will recommend to Congress the changes I have indicated in accordance with my speech of acceptance. Further than that, I believe it to be my duty to carry this matter to the American people and lay the facts before them, and let them make the decision.

As against this clear-cut and straightforward attitude, let us take a look into the Republican household. We start with the candidate himself, who refers to prohibition as a noble experiment but who makes no suggestion for any change or improvement in existing conditions. In his speech of acceptance he said he would appoint a commission to look into it. That is an entirely unnecessary performance. It has been investigated by the Senate and the record is all in Washington.

Senator Borah, speaking for the Republican candidate, said that the maintenance of the Eighteenth Amendment and the Volstead Act in their present form is the paramount issue of this campaign and proclaims the Republican Party to be unalterably committed to that course. Former Governor Hughes made light of the whole question. He treated it facetiously and said that " so far as prohibition is concerned, Smith and Hoover are engaged in a sham battle and there is nothing that can be done about it." When Mr. Hughes made that statement he was following up the whispering campaign that has been going on in the eastern part of this country to the effect that Smith can do nothing; that there is not any use voting for Smith because of his ideas with regard to prohibition, because he will be helpless.

With this I vigorously disagree. Something can be done about it; something must be done about it, and, if I am elected, something will be done about it.

The Republican Party would be unable to sustain its opposition to my program of states' rights, if they were true to their own platform. It makes a very glowing declaration in favor of the principle of states' rights when it says:

" There is a real need in the country today to revitalize fundamental principles. There is a real need of restoring the individual and local sense of responsibility and self-reliance. There is a real need for the people once more to grasp the fundamental fact that under our system of government they are expected to solve many problems themselves under their municipal and State governments."

Senator Borah, however, wedded to the Eighteenth Amendment and the Volstead Act, would rip this declaration from his own party platform. Mr. Hughes admits the helplessness of his own party to make good that declaration of political faith, and Mr. Hoover refers to its application to prohibition as State socialism.

What is the trouble? The powerful and dominating influence of the Anti-Saloon League, that sets at naught all great declarations of political faith, sweeps aside all men and all measures not in sympathy and in step with their narrow, bigoted ideas and their desire to control the conduct of people who do not believe with them. That is the whole thing summed up in a few words.

The Republican Party welcomes and in this campaign has accepted that support. Mr. Hughes frankly said that he was not satisfied with the present conditions, but at the same time said that nothing could be done about it.

I desire to ask the American people are they satisfied with it and do they share Mr. Hughes's belief that nothing can be done about it? The day will never come when the American people will be prepared to confess their inability to deal with any problem of government as far-reaching and as important as this one.

It would be difficult for me to speak about the Anti-Saloon League without having something to say about its twin brother for the destruction of American principles and American ideals, the Ku-Klux Klan. The Republican Party has made feeble attempts to disclaim responsibility for some of the activities of the Klan. But a campaign based upon religious bigotry and religious intolerance is so out of line and so out of step with the American idea of government that it was impossible for them to conceal it. It was destined to come out in the open before the campaign finished. And we had it laid bare before the eyes of the American people when Senator Moses, the eastern manager of the Hoover campaign, mailed scurrilous literature to be published in the State of Kentucky making an attack upon me because of my religious faith and incidentally upon 20,000,000 American citizens who share that belief with me.

That these practices are arousing the ire and stimulating the anger and disgusting the fine sensibilities of many Republicans is evidenced by an editorial within the week in *The Chicago Tribune*, one of the leading Republican newspapers in the western part of the country, which said:

"Governor Smith's denunciation of certain influences working in or for the Republican Party was a true statement of facts. It is accepted as such by many Republicans. The Klan and the Anti-Saloon League are twin calamities working for the election of the Republican national ticket. Their practices are intolerable. Their intolerance is disgraceful. They have exhibited some of the meanest motives which ever had a place in American politics. What they offer as patriotism and public morality has protected or promoted some of the worst corruption.

"The Republican Party has these two allies, and its connection with them is sufficiently apparent to expose it to the properly indignant language of Governor Smith. *The Tribune* feels precisely as he does in this matter."

That this view is shared by all right-thinking Americans there can be no question.

The American people will never be prepared to accept the doctrine that there is to be no party responsibility for faithlessness and corruption in public office. In this day of enlightenment and education it would seem almost unnecessary for a political party to be compelled to make the statement that it will honestly and straightforwardly conduct the business of the government. It has been made necessary, however, by the Republican record of the last seven and a half years. Men charged with the solemn duty of protecting and conserving the resources of the country were found bargaining them away in a corrupt manner. Men charged with the custody of public funds found their way to penitentiaries for criminal violation of their public trust. The Republican platform is careful to refer to the Coolidge administration, unwilling apparently to take any of the responsibility for what happened in the administration of the President's predecessor.

They have taken a cold and callous attitude toward the whole corrupt performance. Why, in this very year 1928 the sale of the oil royalties in the Salt Creek district, originally made by Secretary Fall to a Sinclair company, was renewed by the present chairman of the Republican National Committee when he was Secretary of the Interior, although the original sale was illegal and void and he had been put on his guard with regard to it. His own action was likewise declared by the Attorney-General to be illegal and void, and yet he coolly dismisses the whole matter as meaning nothing and not worthy of comment. And when questioned about it the Republican candidate himself declines to discuss it.

While the Republican Party was careful to avoid all reference to the record between 1921 and 1924, the Republican candidate is entirely willing to put the stamp of approval upon both Republican administrations when he says:

" The record of these seven and a half years constitutes a period of rare courage in leadership and constructive action. Never has a political party been able to look back upon a similar period with more satisfaction."

And Dr. Work adds that the people are tired of oil. I deny that the American people are indifferent to this outrageous conduct on the part of its public officials. The American people are disgusted, humiliated and ashamed of it.

In his speech at Worcester Mr. Hughes said:

" Qualifications for our highest office are not produced overnight. They are the slow growth of years of observation, of study, of reflection, of contact with practical affairs."

If Mr. Hughes really means that, he should vote for me. But the trouble is that Mr. Hughes and Senator Borah are

Republicans first. They are for the Republican candidate, no matter who he is, no matter what he is. That is true as to Mr. Hughes; it is doubly true as to Senator Borah. When I first read in the "Congressional Record" what I am about to read to you, I could not believe Senator Borah said it of Mr. Hoover. Before I would apply it to Mr. Hoover, I asked the Senator the direct question and he said he referred to Mr. Hoover. In the debate in the Senate on the appropriation of $100,000,000 for the relief of European sufferers to be expended under the direction of Mr. Hoover, this is what Senator Borah said about Mr. Hoover:

"No man who has such perverted views of decency ought to be entrusted with unlimited power to deal with $100,000,000."

The Republican Party, relying upon its numerical strength, expected to walk away with the election by force of numbers. This came very clearly from Senator Moses, when he said:

"Because there are 5,000,000 more Republicans than there are Democrats we are defiant. Bring on your candidate and we will bury him."

The Republican Party was mistaken. The force of numbers is not with them in this campaign. That has been made clear to me in my journey through this country during the last six weeks. Throughout the length and breadth of the land the people are alive to the situation and enthusiastic for a change. They are looking to the Democratic Party, and I am satisfied that the overwhelming, reawakened sentiment of the American people will be reflected next Tuesday in a great Democratic victory.

XIX

RADIO ADDRESS

Studio of National Broadcasting Company, November 5, 1928

I WELCOME this opportunity in closing the campaign to speak briefly to the men and women in the great farming sections of the country.

Both parties are agreed that the farmer and the stock raiser have not shared in the country's prosperity and are in dire distress today. Both parties have agreed that the solution of the agricultural problem is one of the most important duties and responsibilities of the next administration. But Mr. Hoover and I have been in sharp disagreement as to the way in which the farmer's problem should be solved and as to the party which should be entrusted with its solution.

I believe that I can fairly say to the farmers of this country and their families that this campaign has shown that the salvation of agriculture in this country today depends upon Democratic success, and I am going to summarize my reasons for this belief.

First, I want you to judge the future by the past.

The Republicans have been in power for seven and a half years. As Mr. Hoover said last Friday night, they have been alive to the situation of agriculture. I know you will agree with me that they did nothing effective about it; that the promises made in 1920 and in 1924 have never been kept, and that the agricultural situation is worse today than when the Republicans came into office in 1921. So when Mr. Hoover said last Friday night he would esteem it an honor to have the privilege of solving the agricultural problem, I can fairly say that he has had an opportunity to achieve that honor for the last four years as the agricultural adviser to the administration, but he took no advantage of it.

He referred to the farmers' failure to agree as to what they want. I need hardly remind you that there was sufficient agreement in this country to pass two relief measures by a vote of just two-thirds of the members of both Houses of Congress, only to have those measures vetoed by the President, under the candidate's advice, with no solution offered in place of them. Now, that is the record of the past.

There is no farmer and no farmer's wife in this country today who does not know that they are not helping themselves by continuing in power the party which for seven and a half years has had an opportunity to grapple with this problem and has done nothing whatever about it.

I next remind you what Mr. Hoover's real views on this farm question were before he became a candidate.

In 1924, as I pointed out in my Omaha speech, he definitely said that overproduction on the farm " can only be corrected by prices low enough to make production unprofitable." I asked then and I ask you now to reflect whether you want to entrust the solution of the farm problem to a man who definitely said that his notion of farm relief was to make prices low enough to drive more farmers and more farmers' families from their homes.

The next reason why the desire for self preservation should lead the farmer and the farmer's wife to vote for me on next Tuesday is the utter hopelessness of anything that the Republican Party or Mr. Hoover has had to say in this campaign with respect to farm relief in contrast with the definite, specific program which I have offered.

Let us begin with the Republican platform itself. I am sure that there is no one listening to my voice who will not agree that Governor Lowden of Illinois is one of the greatest authorities on the farm problem and one of the best friends

of the farmer in this country today. He has been a lifelong
and a loyal Republican. When the Republican platform
was adopted at Kansas City, I remind you that Governor
Lowden said of it:

" I have urged that it is the duty of the Republican
Party to find some way to restore agriculture from the
ruins that threaten it. That in my judgment the Convention, by the platform just adopted has failed to do, and I
therefore authorize the withdrawal of my name from this
convention."

Can you think of any reason why a farmer or a farmer's
wife should vote for a candidate who stands upon a platform
repudiated by a member of the party itself, who is a leader
in the fight for agricultural relief? And I remind you of
Senator Norris's brave and courageous stand for the principles of farm relief, which have led him, as a leader in the
battle in your behalf, to leave his own party and enlist himself and his great talents in behalf of my election, because he
regards the policies for which I stand as the surest guarantee
of relief to you; and I ask you to recall all the State and
local farm leaders who have studied this problem in your
behalf, who agree with Governor Lowden and Senator Norris as to the utter hopelessness of any expectation of relief
from the Republican Party.

Let me spend just a few minutes in reviewing what has
been said about agricultural relief during this campaign; and
I will take first the things we agree on.

First, inland waterways: There is no disagreement on
that, but I think you will all agree with me that if the farm
population of this country has to wait for relief until a system of inland waterways is developed, there will be very
little farm population to be relieved.

Second, tariff on import crops: We are all agreed on that.
The Democratic Party has promised the farmer, and I have
promised the farmer, full protective duties on all import

crops on an absolute equality with industry upon all agricultural products that are imported.

I do pause, however, to ask why, if higher duties are necessary, the Republicans have not given them during the last seven and a half years.

No, I am for giving the farmer who raises the import crops full tariff protection, but you know and I know that that, standing alone, has never solved the problem, will never solve the problem, and that when the Republicans have argued about it they have simply been trying to get your minds away from the real principle of farm relief, about which I shall presently speak and upon which they are directly opposed to me and directly opposed to your interest and your economic salvation.

Then Mr. Hoover talks about stabilization corporations.

One word about these stabilization corporations to which Mr. Hoover is willing to lend money. Our commodity prices are not made in America. In this very St. Louis speech Mr. Hoover says that they are made abroad. You can no more control or stabilize them by a corporation that has no power to lift the surplus clear out of the domestic market than you can fight a fist fight with a man ten miles away. World conditions, and not seasonal gluts, control domestic price. For the past ten years the seasonal high price of each year has occurred exactly as frequently at harvest time as in growing time. Who will share the profits and who will bear the losses?

And now we come to the great fundamental, underlying principle for farm relief upon which Mr. Hoover and I differ absolutely.

I agree with Governor Lowden and Senator Norris that there can never be any satisfactory solution of the farm problem unless that solution is based upon the principle of an effective control of the sale of the exportable surplus with the cost imposed upon the commodity benefited. For that principle the Democratic platform squarely stands, and for that principle I squarely stand and for that principle you and your leaders and those who have been struggling in your behalf for the last eight years stand and have always stood.

You know full well by this time what that principle means. You understand fully that as to the great cash crops of which we produce an exportable surplus, the tariff simply does not function, because the exportable surplus is offered for sale in this country before it finally finds its way into a foreign market. It is the presence of this exportable surplus in the domestic market that has driven down your prices far below the cost of production, reduced by billions the value of your farms, driven millions of people from the farms to other occupations and brought about the dire distress in which agriculture finds itself today.

And what has Mr. Hoover had to say about this principle of farm relief for which I stand, for which my party stands, and which I am glad to admit I learned to approve from a study of the speeches and writings of Governor Lowden and Senator Norris and those other great leaders who had given their attention to this problem before it became my duty to study it? In his speech at Madison Square Garden in New York Mr. Hoover branded this whole principle as State socialism. You and I and your leaders and all who have been struggling in your behalf — all of us together — are transferred to the Socialist Party because we wish the government in your behalf to follow the same principle adopted in the Federal Reserve System for the protection of money and credit.

Only if you think that you and your family are Socialists because you believe in this principle of the control of the exportable surplus, only if you are willing to entrust the rebuilding of farm prosperity to one who thus denounces the only principle upon which it can be based, only then can you give your support to my opponent in this election.

And at the last minute in his St. Louis speech Mr. Hoover talks about calling an extra session of Congress. An extra session for what? Under his advice the President of the

CAMPAIGN ADDRESS

United States vetoed farm relief measures which were twice passed by a Republican Congress. He had nothing to offer in place of it. What has Mr. Hoover got to offer in place of it today? If he is true to what he has always said, he would certainly veto any bill passed upon the principle of the control of the exportable surplus. You certainly do not think he is going to sign a bill, whether it is passed at a special session or a regular session, based upon that principle which he calls State socialism. If Mr. Hoover were President, what good, then, would it do you to have him call a special session? Ask yourselves this question. There is but one answer you can possibly give, and that answer requires you, if you are true to your own convictions, if you are loyal to your own interests and the interests of your family, to follow the lead of Senator Norris and vote the Democratic ticket tomorrow.

The duty to vote the Democratic ticket rests, not only on your own self-interest, but on your loyalty to your homes and your families. Restoration of prosperity to the farm is not a mere material thing. It involves the continuance and the betterment of the home and the family life of the farm, a lightening of the burden upon the women in the agricultural community, the extension of the comforts of a prosperous and happy family life to the children; in short, the continuance of the traditional American country life: Happy, prosperous, fruitful, and the foundation of American prosperity.

And in closing let me give you this word of cheer and confidence. From every section of this country today I have had reports forecasting a great Democratic victory. The industrial east joins with the agricultural west in its desire for a restoration of Democratic government. I believe that tomorrow will bring a great Democratic victory and I assure you that that victory in turn will bring a solution of the agricultural problem that will restore prosperity to the farm and promote the welfare of the entire country.

Governor Smith tells the nation his conception of Democratic responsibility

XX

RADIO ADDRESS

Studio of Carnegie Hall, New York City, November 5, 1928

UNDER our form of government the citizens of this country must assume an individual obligation to do their full share to keep democratic government the success that it has been. And their share on election day is to be sure to vote.

The declaration of the equality of man is never better exemplified than it is on election day, when the humblest man in the community is the equal of the President of the United States as he stands before the ballot box. A man or woman who is not sufficiently interested in the welfare of the country to take the trouble to cast a ballot cannot be said to be a very good citizen. It is almost as though they say in effect that they do not care what happens. The whole theory of democratic representative government is predicated on the belief that the citizens of the country are sufficiently interested in their government to determine for themselves who is to run it.

Likewise, it is the duty of every American citizen, man or woman, to vote according to the dictates of conscience, solely upon the basis of what he or she believes to be for the best interest of the country itself and not upon the basis of any passion or any prejudice. Any man or woman or any group casting a ballot for any other reason except the welfare of the country is doing what they possibly can to negative the whole theory of democratic government.

For six or seven weeks, as the Democratic candidate for the presidency of the United States, I have been traveling throughout this country. I have spoken to the American people on every important question that is pressing the country for solution. Within the limit of my ability I have endeavored to state my position and the position of my party on the issues presented in this campaign clearly and concisely.

Tonight I am not surrounded by thousands of people in a great hall and I am going to take this opportunity to talk intimately to my radio audience alone, as though I were sitting with you in your own home and personally discussing with you the decision that you are to make tomorrow. If I were physically present with you I know you would ask me to give you the facts to convince you which of the two candidates, by training and by experience, is the better fitted to head your government and lead the American people to a solution of the problems that will confront the next administration. A frank answer to your question makes it necessary for me to speak of my own record.

I am no stranger, as you all know, to public office. Prior to this year I have been a candidate for elective public office twenty times, and have been elected nineteen times. I have served as Governor of New York for a longer period than any man in its history since the days of DeWitt Clinton, one hundred years ago.

Politically, the State of New York is a strong Republican State. Only three men have been elected on the Democratic ticket since 1892, a period of thirty-six years, although we elect our Governors every second year. I am the only Democrat in forty years who has been honored by the people of my State with more than one term as Governor.

In 1924, while the Republican candidate for the presidency carried the State of New York by upward of 700,000 plurality, I was elected Governor by 150,000.

At no time during my governorship was the Legislature of the State in the control of the Democratic Party. I vetoed more legislative proposals than any two Governors in the history of the State. Not a single one of these vetoes was overridden by the Legislature.

In this intimate talk you are entitled to know what actuated me in the appointments I have made to my own cabinet. I appointed to public office more men and women requiring confirmation by the Senate than any two governors in our history. While during my administrations the Senate was Democratic for two years it was Republican for six years; and in all of that period not a single appointment was withdrawn by me or rejected by the Senate.

The test of administrative capacity lies largely in the ability of the executive to surround himself with officials who are competent to transact the business of the government. No living man could do it all himself. If he is to be successful he must have the ability and the will to make the right kind of selections.

For the first time in the history of our State I set up a cabinet. Let us take a look at that cabinet for a minute. Probably the most important appointment made by the Governor is the Superintendent of Public Works. He is charged by law with the operation of the Erie canal. In his department are found the Bureaus of Highways, Public Buildings, Water Control and Architecture.

On highways alone in the year 1928 the Superintendent of Public Works expended $45,000,000. In the Bureau of Architecture and under the supervision of the Engineering Bureau there are in course of completion contracts for public buildings approximating $60,000,000.

At no time in the history of this department has there been as much public money expended as during the last six years. All the skill, the ingenuity and the political sagacity which the Republican Party can bring to bear have been directed to an effort to find something in the expenditure of all this money and in the development of all these projects that might be used against me politically. What they found was that the Superintendent of Public Works is an engineer of unquestioned ability and of sterling integrity; and that this great department, expending these enormous sums annually, is operating like a thoroughly well organized business institution.

Let us take a look into the Department of Mental Hygiene. In the New York State hospitals for the care of the insane and in the institutions for the care of the mentally deficient, there is a population of approximately 50,000 people who have to be fed, clothed and cared for by the State. The annual expenditures for this purpose run into more than $26,000,000. To this cabinet position I promoted from the superintendency of one of the State hospitals one of the most competent physicians in the State service, with twenty-five years of experience; and not a member of my political party.

To head the Department of Correction, expending more than $5,000,000 a year for the care and custody of the people committed to our penal institutions, I selected a doctor formerly superintendent of one of our institutions for the criminal insane, and who had twenty years' experience in the service of the State and who likewise was not a member of my political party.

To the Department of Conservation I reappointed the Republican incumbent of the office because of his ability and his capacity to do the job.

To the Department of State I appointed a man who in a spirit of civic duty worked for years for the State without salary and was primarily responsible for building up the State's great system of parks and parkways.

To the head of the Department of Health I promoted a physician of many years' experience in the health service of the State. He belongs to no political party.

To the Department of Labor and to the Industrial Board I appointed men and women of unquestioned ability, without reference to party allegiance.

As my own Secretary I selected a man who for thirty years was connected with the Executive Department in Albany and not of my own political faith.

To the Department of Taxation and Finance I appointed a New York business man and two tax experts whose judgment and opinion on matters of taxation have been sought to advise the national Congress where they have frequently appeared upon request before the committee of both houses.

Two important positions are held by men not appointed by me, but I have been pleased to welcome them into my cabinet. The Commissioner of Education is selected by the Regents of the University of the State of New York, who in turn are elected by the Legislature. The Commissioner of Agriculture and Markets is selected by the Council of Farms and Markets, which in turn is likewise elected by the Legislature. Both these men, not members of my political party, have times out of number certified that I have cooperated with them to the very last degree in building up the efficiency of their departments.

It has been said time and time again by prominent citizens of my own State, members of all political parties, that the government of the State of New York today is in the best condition that it has ever been in all its history.

During my term as Governor, constructive reforms in the government of the State of New York and bond issues for the replacement of its plant and structures and for the protection of human life have been accomplished, notwithstanding the open opposition of the Republican legislative leaders. You would naturally ask how this was brought about, because you would want to know how I would deal with similar situations in the National Government. They were accomplished by direct appeal to the people. I did not confine my public speaking in the State of New York to election periods. During sessions of the Legislature and in years when I was not a candidate for public office I have talked directly and intimately to the people themselves in practically every city and large village in the State of New York. The success of this method was apparent on election day in 1927 when there were no candidates for State-wide public office. Notwithstanding that, hundreds of thousands of people were watching the bulletin boards in front of newspaper offices on election night for the results on eight amendments to the State Constitution.

In previous years the result of the vote on constitutional amendments was not known until weeks after election. There was not sufficient interest in them for the Secretary of State to make a tabulation of the figures.

Last election day I favored seven amendments to the Constitution and opposed one. The seven were adopted by the people of the State and the one overwhelmingly defeated. Men, women and even children in our public schools knew exactly what was in every proposed amendment to the Constitution, why it was opposed and what was sought to be done about it. That is my idea of Executive leadership.

For years and years the people of my State knew nothing about government, except what they got from government statistics, which at best are involved and not understandable to the ordinary man and woman.

I awakened a great interest in the State of New York by my treatment of the government itself. I divided it into two branches: The business side and the human side, for government must have a human side as well as a business side.

Nearly every constructive reform in government under our American system must be accomplished by law. That means that the man in an executive position must possess the traits and qualities of leadership that make it possible for him to get along with people. The American people will never stand for a dictator any more than they are today satisfied and contented with a policy of silence. What they want is constructive leadership, a leadership based upon the ascertained will of the majority, and the ability to make the governmental problems of different groups in our community the concern of all.

During my governorship it is a matter of record that I have had my strongest and most vigorous support from the women of my State. They have a deep interest in the human side of government. They fought side by side with me, without regard to party, in the struggle to obtain factory laws for safeguarding the lives, health and welfare of men, women and children in industry; to secure social legislation like widowed mothers' pensions, designed to keep the orphaned child in its mother's home; to protect society against the evils of child labor and the overwork and exploitation of women and children in industry; to improve the care of afflicted veterans, of tubercular patients, of the mentally deficient, and to restore to usefulness the lives of crippled children.

With the national campaign about to close I desire to express the regret that I was unable to visit every state in the union. Time, as you can readily understand, would not permit it. This regret is intensified by the memory I will cherish for the rest of my life of the hearty, enthusiastic, affectionate welcome I received from millions of my fellow American citizens during the course of this campaign. It made a deep impression also upon the members of my family and the friends who accompanied me. Particularly am I grateful to the women of the country for their cordial and affectionate greeting to Mrs. Smith and my daughters.

To all who had a hand in the campaign, including the party workers, the members of the City, County, State and National Democratic Committees, independent citizens and Republicans, I express tonight at the close of this campaign my heartfelt gratitude. I thank also the newspaper publishers, writers and editors for their kind and generous treatment of me. I appreciate likewise the courteous cooperation of the radio officials, motion picture and other photographers. I thank the police forces of the various cities I visited. The enormous outpouring of people taxed the mat times to their utmost.

I take advantage of this opportunity also to extend my thanks to the thousands of people who, in the course of the last six weeks have either written or telegraphed me words of encouragement and counsel.

I am about to utter my last spoken word before the American people start in the morning to make their decision, and it is this: At no time during my long public career in elective office did I ever trade a promise for a vote. I have made no promises to any man or to any group of men. Nobody was authorized to make any promises for me and, in fact, none has been made. I can enter upon the duties of the greatest office in the world without commitment to anybody except the American people. I can enter upon the duties of that great office with a mind single to the best interests of this country, and I promise you that in return for your vote of confidence tomorrow, I shall give to this country the best that is in me to bring about a constructive, progressive and forward-looking administration.

XXI

POST-ELECTION RADIO ADDRESS

New York City, November 13, 1928

NOW that the dust and smoke of battle have cleared away, I am grateful for the privilege extended to me by the Democratic National Committee of speaking to millions of my fellow citizens and of presenting to them some reflections on the campaign just ended.

The Democratic Party is the oldest political organization in the United States. So well defined are the doctrines and the principles upon which it is founded that it has survived defeat after defeat. In the sixty-five years that have passed since the Civil War only two Presidents were elected on the Democratic ticket. No political organization otherwise founded would have been able, during all these years, to maintain an appeal to the people that brought to the polls on last election day 14,500,000 voters, subscribing once more to its platform and renewing their allegiance to the principles which it has upheld throughout its long history.

The verdict of the American people last Tuesday was not the crushing defeat of the Democratic Party that some of the headlines in the public press would have us believe. On the contrary, let us see what the facts are: Take the popular vote — a change of 10 per cent. of the total number of votes cast would have changed the popular result. Considering it from the viewpoint of our Electoral College system, a change of less than 500,000 votes, spread around the country, would have altered the result.

RADIO ADDRESS

We have, therefore, the assurance from the election returns that the Democratic Party is a live, a vigorous and a forceful major minority party.

The existence of such a party is necessary under our system of government. The people rule negatively as well as affirmatively, and a vigorous and intelligent minority is a necessary check upon the tyranny of the majority.

Experience has always shown, even in our smaller political subdivisions, that when the minority party is weak and helpless, grave abuses creep into the structure of government and the administration of its affairs. When the majority party believes that it has everything its own way, it loses its fear of reprisal at the polls for mismanagement or misconduct of the government.

A political party is organized to help the country, and not merely to achieve victory. It survives, not on the basis of the rewards it secures for its followers, but on the strength and on the soundness of the principles for which it stands. A political party can only justify its existence in so far as it operates for the purpose of promoting the welfare, the well-being and the best interests of the people.

The principles for which the Democratic Party stands are as sacred in defeat as they would have been in victory. If the cause of democracy was right before the election, it is still right, and it is our duty to carry on and vindicate the principles for which we fought. The Democratic Party today is the great liberal party of the nation. It leads the progressive, forward-looking thought of the country. It holds out the only hope of return to the fundamental principles upon which this country was built and as a result of which it has grown and prospered.

To the young men and women of the country the Democratic Party, with its fine traditions, its high idealism and its breadth of vision, offers the only inspiration.

The Democratic Party certainly would not be in a position

four years from now to solicit the confidence and support of the American people if during that period it neglected to build up a constructive program and relied entirely upon the failure of the opposition party. That cannot be done by the minority party permitting itself to become a party of obstruction and opposition for political purposes only. We have seen too much of that in this country and in many of its civil divisions.

It has been particularly noticeable in the State of New York, where great forward-looking, constructive measures were delayed for years by partisan opposition seeking to withhold from the Democratic Party credit for their accomplishment. The party responsible for such obstructive tactics has been rebuked by the people at the polls no later than last Tuesday. Too often a minority has attempted to ride into power by taking advantage of the failure of the majority to translate into an actuality the campaign promises and pledges upon which it sought the suffrage of the people.

While it is true that every party must adhere to its fundamental principles, obstruction and blockade for the sole purpose of embarrassing the party in power are not calculated to promote the best interests of the country. It would be regarded as a constructive achievement if the Democratic Party at Washington were to formulate a program, adopt it, offer it to the Congress of the United States and there defend it. A refusal on the part of the party in power to accept it, or their inability to bring about party unity for the solution of these problems, would then fix the responsibility and make a record upon which a successful campaign can be waged four years from now.

In other words, the Democratic Party would not be acting in good faith with the people of the country nor in good faith with the millions of those who rallied to its support if it were to sit by and adopt a policy of inaction with the hope of profiting solely by the mistakes or failures of the opposition. What this country demands is constructive and not destructive criticism. A constructive program, embodying the declarations of the Democratic platform, should be promptly developed.

Above all things, the function of a minority party is educational in character. It will not do for the great rank and file of the American people to be intensely interested in the issues and party programs for a couple of months before election and then permit that interest to die out when the result is announced. Political platforms and political promises are not self-enacting. The political history of the United States clearly indicates that every progressive step, every great governmental reform has been won only after a period of persistent effort and by the slow process of educating the electorate.

The first and indispensable element of education is information. A full and complete presentation of the facts. That is easier to do today than it was years ago, with the use of the radio and the increasing interest of our young people in public affairs. It must be remembered that while political parties may seriously divide public opinion throughout the country during the progress of a campaign, after the American people have made their decision the man selected is not the President of the Republican Party, but is the President of the United States. He is the President of all the people and as such he is entitled to the cooperation of every citizen in the development of a program calculated to promote the welfare and best interests of this country. He is entitled to a fair opportunity to develop such a program. Only when he fails to accomplish it does the administration become the subject of proper criticism by the opposition party.

Premature criticism not only fails of its purpose, but often results to the disadvantage of the critic himself. Party responsibility is not confined to its handling of governmental affairs. A political party must also be accountable to the people of the United States for the management of its internal affairs, and no political party can afford to accept the support of forces for which it refuses to accept responsibility. It will not do to let bitterness, rancor or indignation over the result blind us to the one outstanding fact, that above everything else we are Americans.

No matter with what party we align ourselves on election day, our concern should be for the future welfare, happiness, content and prosperity of the American people.

At this point I desire to express my gratitude from the bottom of my heart to the millions who voted for me, to the millions who worked for me, to the party leaders throughout the United States who rendered loyal and devoted service to the Democratic Party and to our country.

I want this to include also the men and women throughout the country, not members of the Democratic Party, who took inspiration from the progressive platform adopted at the Democratic Convention and supported my declarations of purpose with respect to those principles. Thousands of letters and telegrams have come to me since election day, asking that I not lose interest in the future welfare of the Democratic Party. Let me take this modern means of making reply to them by making the definite statement that I do not regard the defeat of the Democratic Party at this election as impairing in the slightest degree the soundness of the principles for which it stands. I am just as anxious to see them succeed as I was when the party honored me with the nomination, and with all the vigor that I can command I will not only stand for them, but I will battle for them.

It would be unnatural for me not to be disappointed at the result. Tonight, however, as I address these few remarks to my friends all over the country, I look back on my twenty-five years of public service. I recall them from the first time the Democratic Party selected me, a struggling youth, for elective office as member of the Legislature. I recall my first official visit to the Capitol at Albany, and never shall I forget the thoughts that ran through my mind at that time.

Many years later I felt that I had achieved my greatest ambition when the Democratic Party made me its standard bearer in the State. To that party and to the people of this State, who have four times elected me as their Chief Executive, I shall always be profoundly grateful. I have in a measure attempted to express that gratitude in the form of devotion to public service. In return for the confidence reposed in me by the people of my State, I endeavored to administer the affairs of the State with an eye single to the welfare and the happiness of her people.

The Democratic Party this year conferred upon me the greatest honor that it can offer to any of its members, the nomination for the presidency of the United States. Regardless of the outcome, in a spirit of the deepest appreciation of the opportunities afforded me and of the loyal support given to me by upward of 15,000,000 of my fellow citizens, I pledge my unceasing interest and concern with public affairs and the well-being of the American people.